THE
ENDLESS
KNOT

THE ENDLESS KNOT

K2, Mountain of
Dreams and Destiny

KURT DIEMBERGER

Translated from the German
by Audrey Salkeld

Winner of the PREMIO ITAS literary award

THE MOUNTAINEERS

SEATTLE

front endpaper: K2 from the foot of Paiju Peak,
rising above the granite spires of the Lower Baltoro
(Leica-Telyt 400 mm, from the South West)
(*photo* Kurt Diemberger)

back endpaper: Kurt and Julie with Arriflex and
Nagra at 6,000 metres on the Abruzzi ridge … 'to
bring the Himalayas down, for others'
(*photo* Highest Film Team archive)

German edition published 1989 by F. Bruckmann KG, Munich
This edition first published in the UK in 1991
by GraftonBooks
A Division of HarperCollins*Publishers*
77–85 Fulham Palace Road, Hammersmith, London W6 8JB

Published in the United States by
The Mountaineers
306 Second Avenue West, Seattle. WA 98119 USA

ISBN 0-89886-300-7

Copyright German edition © F. Bruckmann KG, 1989
Copyright English translation © GraftonBooks, 1990

Printed in Hong Kong

CONTENTS

INTRODUCTION AND ACKNOWLEDGEMENTS

A real book needs more than just a good writer. It needs a deep conviction, a promise to yourself, to others. I could never have finished this book without thinking all the time of Julie and her wish, to pass on to others what we were living for, to have them participate – and writing down our experiences made it real. It was a way of continuing our team, a conviction that grew during my lonely descent on the Abruzzi after the fatal blizzard. It was a promise. Thus, the mountain and our thoughts will be within these pages.

'Anything is possible', Julie used to say. She had a very strong will, was positive, determined and active. However, at times she would just sit still, listen to the sounds of nature, let her mind glide away into the space between the leaves of a tree, between the shimmering walls of ice towers, or up to the clouds beyond them. It was not only Julie herself who made our great days, those years – and with them, this book – possible. You almost never find that your achievements, your dreams, become real without the actions, influence or help of others. Besides herself, it was Julie's understanding husband Terry, her early climbing partner Dennis and – perhaps in the most significant way – her martial arts teacher David who opened up the world for her very special, uncommon personality. Julie has dedicated several chapters of her beautiful *Clouds From Both Sides* to them.

When I wrote this book I considered also how much it might mean to her friends. Our time in the Himalayas were her last years, bringing her the greatest fulfilment as a creative person, not only with the summit of K2, our dream mountain. It was a way of ascent to yet another realization. Then it all ended abruptly in the blizzard at 8,000 metres.

To write about the events up there was hard, sometimes a real struggle, but it had to be. I'll never be able to accept what happened, but at least it should never be repeated. It took me almost two years to complete the book, and I want to thank Teresa, my wife, for her incredible patience, as well as Audrey Salkeld, who translated the book, for hers. Many people helped: Choi Chang Deok, a priest, was sent to me, perhaps by providence, to clear up the mystery of this tragedy, hidden in illegible Korean 'hieroglyphs'; Charlie Clarke and Franz Berghold, high altitude illness specialists; Xavier Eguskitza, the indefatigable chronicler, John Boothe, Peter Gillman, Judith Kendra, and Dee Molenaar … even my daughters Hildegard and Karen have contributed to this work!

And I must not forget those who made it possible for me to start writing at all: Gerhard Flora in Innsbruck and Hildegunde Piza in Vienna, who treated my frostbite; the Pembury Hospital in Sussex which saved me from a sudden lung-embolism in the aftermath of K2; Enzo Raise in Bologna, who recognized at the last minute my totally unexpected malaria, probably caught on my way home in the aeroplane – I almost died from it. While I slowly recovered, Mrs Susi Kermauner in Salzburg took me to her rusty typewriter in that two-hundred-year-old house … and I started the first chapter. Several months later, in Bologna, my little son Ceci interfered with tradition: he taught me how to use the computer! 'Oh, finally, Dad …' he said.

Even if their names are not given, I want to thank many more people that Julie's book now has a companion, *The Endless Knot* – here it is.

Kurt Diemberger
March 1990

THE BEGINNING

K2 from both sides, *that was to have been the title of this book. Julie and I wanted to write it together. On my own, now, I find myself fighting shy of getting started.*

Come on, Kurt!

Well then: testing, testing … This typewriter seems all right, the ribbon is new and all the keys are functioning. The only thing that's needed is for the builders on the roof outside to stop their bloody noise. A neighbour on the other side was mowing his lawn all morning – that, at least, has finally stopped – unless he is simply taking a rest. Perhaps a nip of whisky will help me face all these distractions. I must type with my thumb because the fingers of my right hand are still too painful to use. Fingers, I say – I mean what's left of them after the frostbite.

Perhaps I can at least set my 'new' index finger to work – that's not too bad. I wonder if Susie has a finger-stall? Using only the thumb makes it hard to concentrate on what I want to say. I should try dictating into a tape recorder, I suppose, and then type it up – that way it would just be a mechanical action, and it wouldn't matter whether it was comfortable or not. But you do need peace and quiet to write on tape – not for the writing, exactly, I mean for the recordddddddddddddddddddddddddddddddddddddd ddddddddddddddddddddddddddddddding.

The 'd' got stuck. C'est la vie! Difficulties are there to be overcome. I fiddle the typewriter key backwards and forwards, until at last it moves freely again (the arm of the letter key, I mean.) Now … where were we? Ah, yes … I mean for the recording. The one person you could have in the room would be the person to whom you're telling the story – that's the only possibility. Otherwise, you have to be totally on your own, and with no interruptions, so that you can 'find the centre' – as Julie so often used to say – and which she explained best, perhaps, in connection with meditation – or with the martial arts like Aikido or Budo. There the 'centre' has its importance not only for your mind, but also your body. Oh, those damned builders! The noise of sawing boards chases all thoughts out of your head. Today, I can see, is going to be a battle against innocent opponents. But perhaps it will also reinforce my resolve, since this book is something I really want to write – for Julie, for me, for all those who understand. It seems senseless to have lived through all this only to have it disappear without trace.

Even then, it would not have been meaningless. It made sense for both of us at the time, representing the fulfilment of a lifetime … It is about realization I want to tell, a realization that took place over only a few years, years during which K2 stood over us, remote and chill, yet more beautiful than any other mountain. A symbol, it seemed, of all that is unattainable.

An eternal temptation.

'Will we ever come back to K2? Of course we will.'
(Julie Tullis, 1984, in Urdokas on the Baltoro glacier)

For Julie,
and for all those who come to
touch these great mountains.

'... THE PEAK WE MOST DESIRED' – K2

A strange, filmy mist has settled over everything – a grey silk shroud cloaking the entire pyramid of the summit, fascinating and menacing at the same time. There is tension in the air: it runs through us, through this steep, snowy landscape with its undulations and ice cliffs. The weather is slowly worsening.

All the same, we keep climbing. It can't be much further now. If we're caught in a storm up here, up at almost 8,600 metres, we haven't a hope of surviving whatever we do. Whether we turn back or not. This way, at least, we shall have stood on the summit – 'our' summit – first.

A vertical wall of ice rears out of the silky light. With my ice-axe I turn a titanium screw into its hard surface. It creaks and grinds. Then I cut a couple of holds – no time to waste on artistic effect at this height. Will there be more obstacles above this? Or will we see the summit in a few minutes?

Julie belays me as I move up cautiously. Just a few metres and I am over the ice barrier. And there it is! In the soft, grey light, the highest billow of snow on this high mountain – the summit of K2. It looks so gentle – easy even – this final curve, after the terrible precipices below. A wave of happiness washes over me. 'Up you come, Julie! Come on, we're almost there!'

She appears over the edge, craning to see over its icy rim. Elbows in the snow, she stops to gaze upwards. 'Be still!' she whispers, and I see surprise and wonder in her eyes, those dark, familiar eyes under the frosted strands of hair. She seems to be in silent communion with the last smooth curve of snow.

What goes through her mind? I wonder. What is she telling those summit snows?

For three years we have lived with the dream of coming back to this, our mountain of mountains … Now the elusive summit is within grasp. Nothing can take it away from us.

But it's late. And the weather is about to break. In a strange way, it seems to be holding its breath, granting us a few moments' grace. Yet, even though it looks a little brighter, the magic light cannot deceive us.

'Julie, let's go!' Suddenly I feel uncomfortable.

She looks up with a smile, as if returning from a distant world. 'Yes, let's get a move on! Let's get up there!'

Within minutes, our three-year dream will be fulfilled.

THE LONELY MOUNTAIN

30 years ago – on the Baltoro with Hermann Buhl

Shshsht! Shshsht! Shshsht! Shshsht! Our snowshoes glide over glistening, sunlit powder, across ribs of ice and the gently rolling curves of the glacier.

Ahead of me, still pushing strongly despite fatigue and moving with short, precise steps, is the small, almost delicate figure of Hermann Buhl, his energy clearly visible as he covers the irregular ground of the Godwin-Austen glacier. I can see his grey, wide-brimmed felt hat above his rucksack, his fine-boned hands resting on the ski-sticks for balance each time he raises one of the oval, wooden snowshoes to take another, sliding step; but the expression in Hermann's ever-alert eyes as he scans the way ahead, I can only guess at. Thus, we make our way forward, past long rows of jagged ice-shapes, as if in an enchanted forest where everything has been frozen into immobility. Corridors between the towers lead us along the spine of the moraine, through freshly fallen snow.

We are alone – alone in the heart of the Karakoram, surrounded by mighty glaciers, in a savage world of contrasts, of ice and rock, of pointed mountains, granite towers, fantasy shapes rising a thousand metres or more into the sky, some very much more.

This spring (May 1957), besides Hermann and me and our three companions back in Base Camp, there are no other human beings on the whole of the Baltoro glacier.

Marcus Schmuck and Fritz Wintersteller from Salzburg and Captain Quader Saeed, our liaison officer (who, having no one to liaise with, has been homesick for the more colourful life of Lahore for several weeks now), are fellow members of the only expedition this season within a radius of several hundred kilometres. We are alone on this giant river of ice, fifty-eight kilometres long, which with its fabulous mountains constitutes one of the remotest and

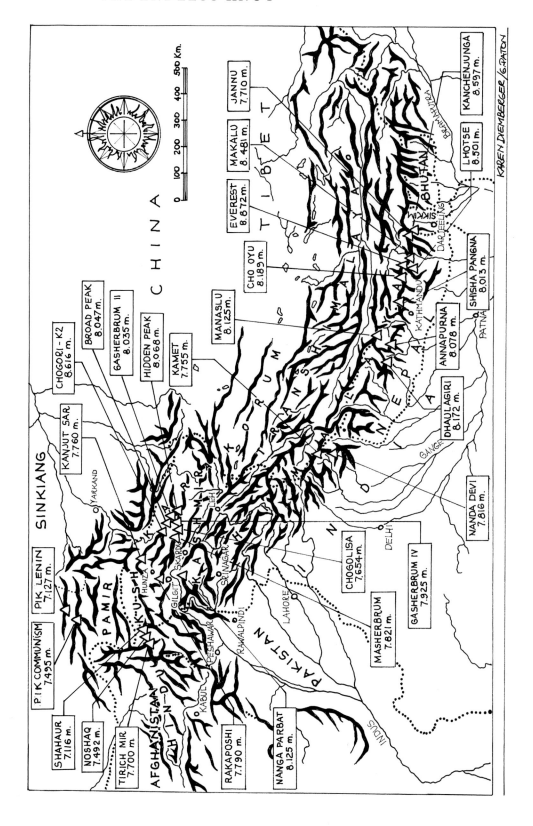

4

5

most beautiful places on earth. Uncounted lateral glaciers fan out to peaks of breathtaking size and steepness – forming compositions of such harmony that they seem to emanate magic – to places where no one questions 'Why?' because the answer stands so plain to see. My great ambition, to go once in my life to the Himalayas and climb the highest peaks in the world, has been realized – at the age of twenty-five. Hermann Buhl invited me to join his team on the strength of my *direttissima* climb of the 'Giant meringue' on the Gran Zebru (Königsspitze), a sort of natural whipped-cream roll widely considered to be the boldest ice route in the Alps to date. I'm ecstatic. Everything I have, I will put into this one big chance.

Now, as we make tracks in the snow at almost 5,000 metres along one of the lateral glaciers (having set off from close to Concordia, the Baltoro's kilometre-wide glacier junction), my thoughts turn to the early explorers. The glacier we are on is named after the cartographer Godwin-Austen, one of the first to set eyes on the Baltoro in the middle of the last century; but Adolf Schlagintweit was probably the first non-local to get close to the Baltoro area and to reach one – the western – of the Mustagh Passes (Panmah Pass). He has not been commemorated by any name on the map. On the other hand, the beautiful, striated glacier across Concordia from us is dedicated to the traveller G. T. Vigne, who never set foot on it. Martin Conway, leader of an expedition in 1892, was the first to come to the Karakoram to mountaineer; he was later knighted and a snow-saddle he discovered was named after him.

We are not explorers in the same sense as those men, yet on a personal level that is exactly what we are. Going into an empty landscape like this, among giant mountains, your heart quickens and the prospect around the next corner is no less seductive to you than it was to the first people who were here. The same silence dominates the peaks, the same high tension arcs from mountain to mountain; days can still seem like a true gift from heaven. So it is with us on this morning ...

Above us soars Broad Peak. No man has ever climbed its triple-headed summit, which rises into the sky like the scaled back of a gigantic dragon. For me, the very rocks breathe mystery: nobody has touched them. I am happy that this mountain, one of the eight-thousanders, is the target of our expedition. But today, Hermann and I are heading off towards K2 ...

The tallest pyramid on earth seems to grow steadily before our eyes in its unbelievable symmetry. Many years ago, British

1. Hermann Buhl at Camp 1 on Broad Peak (June 1957); he was already contemplating a complete traverse of K2 and planned an attempt on the Trango Tower on our return from 'the first eight-thousander in *Westalpenstil*'.

2. A cave in the fairyland of ice towers, facing (3) Julie's and my dream mountain – K2 (Sinkiang, 1983).

4. Climbing the giant North spur (at *c.* 7,600 metres towards the hanging glacier below the summit) and (5) filming at 6,700 metres high above the K2 glacier ... We were both content to combine the two.

cartographers* computed the height as 8,611 metres: 237 metres lower than Everest. The second highest mountain in the world is, however, considerably the more difficult of the two to climb and is without doubt one of the most beautiful mountains in the world.

The international expedition of Oscar Eckenstein, which included the Austrians Pfannl and Wessely, made the first attempt in 1902 and managed to reach 6,525 metres on the North-East Ridge. But in 1909, a large-scale expedition led by the Duke of the Abruzzi opened up the South-East Spur (the Abruzzi Ridge or Rib), revealing that as the most favourable line of ascent. They only got to 6,250 metres, but on nearby Chogolisa (Bride Peak), the Duke and his mountain guides clambered to 7,500 metres, which stood as a world altitude record for many years. They were only 156 metres from the summit.

Hermann Buhl has stopped to look across towards Chogolisa, that shimmering trapeze of snow and ice, maybe thirty kilometres away. 'A lovely mountain,' he says.

To me, it looks like an enormous roof in the sky, but Hermann's attention is already back with K2. 'Such a pity that's been climbed already! But wouldn't a traverse be great; up the ridge on the left, then down to the right, by the Abruzzi?' And he tells me all he knows of the Abruzzi route, how the mountain was first climbed this way by a huge Italian expedition three years ago. They put in no fewer than nine high-altitude camps. And, it's said, fixed 5,000 metres of rope on the ridge itself. Ardito Desio, a professor of geology, was leader and the two summiteers among the eleven-man team were Lino Lacedelli and Achille Compagnoni. It was a national triumph, which threw the whole of Italy into a whirl of rejoicing. It is true that they used bottled oxygen, but it ran out towards the end. And they didn't give up! Hermann is laughing, 'So you see, it does work! You can do it without!' Then he tells of George Mallory and Sandy Irvine, who never came back from a summit attempt on Everest in 1924, despite taking oxygen. Nine years after their disappearance an ice-axe was found at 8,500 metres which can only have belonged to one of them, yet today we are no nearer knowing whether they made it to the top of the world or not. And he tells of Colonel Norton, who went very high on

* T. G. Montgomerie in 1856 (see Appendix 1). More recently, Professor Ardito Desio's 1987 expedition – which I accompanied as cameraman – remeasured the heights of several peaks in the Himalayas by GPS (Global Positioning System, using Navstar Satellite Signals), and found K2 to be 8,616 metres, and Everest 8,872 metres.

Everest without oxygen, and of Fritz Wiessner, who got within almost 200 metres of the top of K2 in 1939, also without using it.

I can see from his animation, from his eyes and gestures, that Hermann can hardly wait to have a go at K2, without oxygen or the help of high-altitude porters. 'In West Alpine style' is the phrase he coined for it. 'Mmm! K2 *is* a beautiful mountain and no mistake,' he concludes, adding pensively, 'and the way to do it is definitely up that left ridge, down the right.'

But the mountain looks so high, like nothing else in the world. We are only tiny dots before this huge mass of rock, which shines like crystal from the snow and ice on its faces. It arouses no desire in me. I am happy with our choice: Broad Peak is still virgin, and almost 600 metres lower than K2. Better for our 'West Alpine' enterprise – already considered crazy by a lot of people – better than the second highest mountain on earth!

With that, my thoughts turn to 'our' eight-thousander: the only time it was ever attempted was in 1954 by a German expedition under Dr Karl Herrligkoffer. They found it pretty hairy: following a line that was under constant threat from avalanches, the climbers one day discovered that huge blocks of ice had stopped only inches short of their tent; and the Austrian Ernst Senn fell down a sheer 500-metre ice wall, whistling along like a bobsleigh to land (by incredible good fortune) safely in the soft snow of a high plateau. At 7,000 metres, icy autumn storms drained the men's last reserves of energy, forcing them at length to abandon the attempt.

A few days ago, buried in the steep ice of the 'Wall', we discovered a food dump belonging to the Germans: advocaat, angostura bitters, some equipment … and a three-year-old salami, which still tasted all right. There was even a tin of tender, rolled, Italian ham, which well-travelled delicacy quickly found its way into our stomachs. I have to confess that this side trip we're making to K2 is purely out of curiosity to see what delicious titbits might still be lying around at the site of the Italian Base Camp!

A delusion: all our efforts to find the camp fail. The wide glacier is white and pristine, and there is no trace on the moraine either. Finally, we turn around and waddle on our snowshoes back the way we came.

It was curiosity, too, that led us to penetrate the avalanche cirque of Broad Peak. Hermann wanted to take a look at the route Herrligkoffer had chosen. The doctor had been his leader on Nanga Parbat and there was no love lost between the two men. Hermann himself had opted for a more direct line on the West Spur of Broad Peak, a line of greater difficulty, it's true, but very much safer, and one that had been recommended by the well-known 'Himalayan Professor', G. O. Dyhrenfurth. A straightforward and direct ascent like this is much more in Hermann's style.

As we approach Base Camp, tired now from dragging these legs with their wooden appendages, kaleidoscopic memories dance through my mind. I remember how, amid a swirl of dust, we touched down in the old Dakota on that sandy patch of ground near Skardu which serves as an airfield; remember crossing the Indus river in a big, square boat; the three-week-long walk-in, following first the wide Shigar valley with its blossoming apricot trees, then through the Braldu gorge, and finally trekking up the Baltoro glacier with our sixty-eight porters … remember being slowed down by snowstorms, so that our loads were dumped twelve kilometres short of Base Camp. The subsequent load-ferrying, backwards and forwards with 25–30 kilograms on our backs, went on day after day until Base Camp was at last established at 4,900 metres – that is higher than the summit of Mont Blanc. And Hermann's words of consolation, 'It's all good training for later on … for the first eight-thousander to be climbed in West Alpine style.' Then the West Spur itself: up and down, up and down, plagued at first by headaches … Later it went more easily. Whenever we set down our loads at Camp 1, we would squat on our haunches in the snow for a fast slide down into the depths again …

After a while, even taking every precaution, we could manage the 800–900 metres of descent on the seat of our pants in just half an hour – including rest stops!

Seen from Concordia, Broad Peak – this three-humped dragon – has the appearance of a mighty castle. From wherever you see it, it always looks different. You can never 'know' a mountain precisely … When we finish here, Hermann hopes to have a go at Trango Tower, or one of the other fantastic granite spires in the lower Baltoro …

We are a modern expedition. Hermann has seen to it that we lack nothing progress has to offer. We have gas cylinders – huge ones like those for domestic use, each a full porter-load – and small ones of about 7 kilos for higher on the mountain. We have simple ridge tents, extremely stable. And advanced, misshapen-looking altitude boots of heavy, solid leather. They have been made especially roomy to accommodate socks or felt slippers or whatever else we feel like using for insulation … we've found newspaper works quite well! Of course, walking on moraine in these Mickey Mouse boots is awkward – you feel like deep-sea divers. No doubt one day someone will come up with a custom-made boot-within-a-boot that is a lot better. But we are not ill-satisfied. Except for one thing: progress dogs us even on the West Spur in the form of a walkie-talkie apparatus weighing 11 kilos. We decide to dump it at Camp 1 (5,800 metres) and from there on use the time-honoured method of a piece of paper: write down what you want to say and leave it in the tent for the others to read when they get there.

Camp 2 is a natural snow hole, which we have enlarged, under the rim of a high plateau at 6,400 metres. We have even set up a kitchen there: Hermann has this weakness for potato dumplings, ox-tongue salad, mayonnaise, and buckthorn juice – in other words, for all things sour – and for beer. But the latter is only available at Base Camp. He calls it Nature's Own Sleeping Draught. His first 'dose' turned into a foaming fountain, a metre high, which only stopped gushing when the blue Bavarian tin was empty. Barometric pressure is quite different at 4,900 metres, and we soon learned to make only a tiny puncture and to keep a thumb over the hole so that the pressure could be released slowly and our nice sleeping draught not sprayed to the four winds.

The days pass. On 29 May, we push up from Camp 3 (just below 7,000 metres) towards the summit ridge. We make it as far as the northern end of the 'roof', that is to a height of about 8,030 metres. Only then do we discover that isn't the top; the opposite end of this enormous ridge is just a bit higher. But it's too late in the day. We descend. Back in Base Camp, we know we have to retrace our steps all the way up the mountain again – just for those extra twenty metres of height at the other end of the ridge. There's no way round it: that is the summit!

Marcus and Hermann both have frostbite on their toes, and Hermann calls for the 'doctor'. That's me! Uncomfortable in the role, but using the calming words of a real doctor, I give him an injection. Then another one. Success! I was appointed expedition 'doctor' only a month before our departure. Hermann justified it by saying, 'Well, you've *studied*, haven't you?' My protestation, 'Yes – but commerce,' was not considered sufficiently valid an excuse for refusal. He must have great trust in me.

With 27 kilos of pills and potions (assembled by a real medic) and a universal tool for pulling out teeth (which by great fortune I have not been called upon to use), I'm the Medicine Man. And during the long walk-in have been approached by many of the locals for treatment. I did what I could, relying when in doubt on my bag of painkillers. Nobody should come to any harm, at least. (After all, we do have to go back the same way!)

The big day – 9 June. One after the other, all four of us reach the summit of Broad Peak. Even Hermann, in the end, despite his frostbite. He had given up at 7,900 metres, but afterwards changed his mind. On my way down from the top, I came across him still plodding upwards and turned to accompany him. As the day faded, this unique day, we stepped together onto the highest point ...

> It was about 7 P.M., the sun low in the sky, as we stood there: ... Moment of truth. The silence of space surrounds and holds us. It is fulfilment. The trembling sun balances on the horizon. Down below, it is already night, over all the outstretched world. Here, only, and for us, is there still light. The Gasherbrum summits shine close by, and further away comes the shimmer off Chogolisa's heavenly roof. Straight ahead, against the last of the light, soars the dark profile of K2. The snow around us is tinged a deep orange, the sky a pure, clear azure. When I look behind me, an enormous pyramid of darkness is thrown across the endless space of Tibet, fading with the haze into the far distance. It is the shadow of Broad Peak! A beam of light reaches out above and across the darkness towards us, striking the summit. Amazed, we look at the snow at our feet: it seems aglow. Then the light disappears ...
>
> (from *Summits and Secrets*, Kurt Diemberger)

It was the great sunset for Hermann Buhl, his last on any summit.

In all truth I admired K2 from up there, that massive wedge of deep blue, like a cut-out against the flood of light. But still I felt no desire. The mountain was too big, unapproachable, easy to leave alone. No thought crossed my mind then that it was to play such a decisive role in my life. Only much later did Eric Shipton's words draw me under its spell.

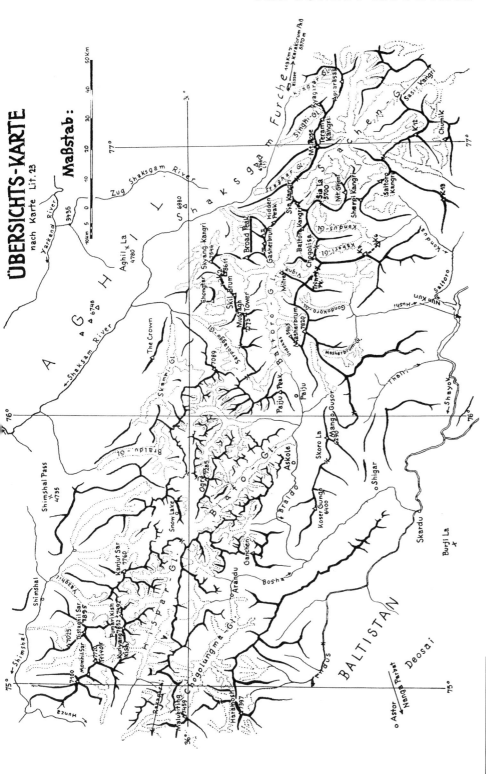

Orientative map by
Eduard Sternbach
after a map of the
Karakoram by Marcel
Kurz (from
*Österreichische
Alpenzeitung*,
March/June 1961).

THE BOAT

Can that be Sirius, that bright star?

No, not in summer. It must be one of the larger planets.

The way it twinkles, it seems almost to be dancing in the darkness behind the mainstay, mimicking the movements of the boat.

When the star moves too far from the dark line of the stay, I gently press the tiller until the catamaran is once more on the right course – for England. From time to time, after glancing at the illuminated compass, I look for a new star ... because everything turns endlessly, even the sky above the North Sea. I prefer taking my bearings from the stars, rather than referring constantly to the compass. With the voices of the sea, the rushing and gurgling of the water under the keel and the singing of the breeze in the rigging, the stars make up the world in which the boat moves, and my thoughts wander.

My sister Alfrun, who is supposed to be sharing the nightwatch with me, has dropped off to sleep. I sent her to lie down on a bunk that groans with each movement of the catamaran. This endless creaking is a reminder to me that the boat is rather old. Herbert bought it secondhand in Denmark recently. Herbert is Alfrun's husband, a successful cameraman, passionately fond of the sea. He has lured the whole family, and a friend too, into this adventure, because he is firmly convinced that the boat must be overhauled in the yard where it was built, close to the mouth of the Thames.

Herbert is a born optimist, and with his radiant smile and contagious enthusiasm managed in two days – back home in Salzburg – to involve me completely in this latest venture of his ... me a landlubber, who has always been suspicious of anything new.

However, I am happy now. I feel like a real sea-dog, and have completely got over the shock of the Limfjord – where we suddenly found the keel scraping the bottom and had to pull up the centreboards to free ourselves – counting the trip now as one of my 'happy-ending' adventures. There is something fascinating about steering a boat – 12 metres long, 8 metres wide, with two masts and two fibreglass hulls, providing living space for four people altogether. You can even sleep on it – if the waves aren't too big!

As I said, my brother-in-law is very proud of his boat, and yesterday, with the air of an expert, he calculated the meridian using sun and sextant, and with it our course. To us, it seemed like magic, even though we weren't convinced he'd got it right. After all we were in the middle of the sea. He became a little nervous when we came across some oil-rigs that weren't on the map, and I suppose I should not have remarked that navigation didn't usually depend on the location of oil-wells.

Now the cap'n is sleeping, having left instructions to be woken only if we see lights. But there haven't been any. The masts sway among stars slowly following their courses, hour after hour – just as they do when you sit in a bivouac on a clear night, keenly observing their steady circular progress. And, in the same way as the voices of the mountain bring overwhelming tranquillity, so here, the sea speaks to you.

Last year, I found a place where the two came together: rocks and the sea. Foamy crested waves rushed at vertical cliffs like wild stallions. Dream of White Horses *is the name given by climbers to a route in Wales where you balance on delicate handholds directly above the crashing sea. Looking down, the frothy water beckons, and not until you have overcome your fear of it can you feel happy.*

One English climber there clearly had no qualms. Slim and dark-haired, Julie moved up the rock smoothly, each movement expressing strength and a joy of living, just as an animal in its element expresses itself in movement. Her partner, Dennis, exhibited a similar harmony, white hair and beard, which framed sharp features, blowing wildly in the strong breeze. You could hear the roar of the sea, and the air was bitter with salt.

The two climbed so well together, it was easy to see they were in their element.

I learned later that Dennis was a photographer, specializing in quite stupendous nature pictures. Julie came from East Sussex, where she lived with her husband Terry, a ranger, a man of great strength and serenity. Julie and Terry, besides the forest, looked after their local sandstone rocks and ran climbing courses; they also had a coffee shop for climbers, where the relaxed and friendly Tullis atmosphere reigned supreme. Everybody loved Julie and Terry. It had come to them one day that learning to move on rocks could benefit handicapped children and the blind, and they began organizing special courses for them. They never climbed together, perhaps because it made Julie nervous or because it led them to be over-critical of each other's style on rock.

I met them for the first time when I was on a lecture tour in England many years ago, and again in 1975 when another trip took me to Wales, where Dennis lived. That was when I had seen him and Julie climbing together. The wild sea at the foot of the rocks made a very strong impression on me. Perhaps, by taking part in this boat trip, I wanted to overcome a fear that the unknown element, the fury of the sea, had generated in me. Perhaps I wanted to demonstrate that I was capable of 'dominating' something that had dominated me. But demonstrate to whom?

To myself certainly, but perhaps subconsciously also to Julie, whose own fearlessness I found so fascinating. It must have been that, or how else am I to explain to myself all that then followed?

After seeing Julie and Dennis so immersed in their element, I must have had a tentative desire to take part, to add to the experience something of my own world.

Now, while I hold the helm and glide over the waves, up and down, up and down, I have the same feeling of strength I encountered there. And I even seem to know why I am approaching this coast.

I begin to dream: in the sky, among the stars, between the silhouettes of the sails, I imagine Lohengrin and his swan, and the legend blends into the sounds of the night. To be honest, I don't remember the story very well, but that doesn't stop me from elaborating a version of my own, tailored to the circumstances.

I want to go and find her, bring her onto this sea that surrounds her island, if only for a day.

'The one thing you must never do,' Herbert had said, 'is to leave the boat. You never give up!' The tone of his voice left no doubt how seriously he meant us to take this. Even though we have a canary-yellow dinghy on board, Herbert (who used to be a mountain guide) has fixed a belay line the whole length of the boat, to which he insists we attach ourselves if the sea is rough. We have to do this whenever we are 'outside' – that is, outside the two floating hulls. It makes sense, but will we really need it?

Herbert has dreams of a larger boat with all the necessary – and unnecessary – extras for ocean-going. (He will spend years building it – it still isn't finished yet.)

The storm! Here it is – hissing and whistling, and the boat groaning and squealing …

' … It's not falling apart!' I cling to the captain's words, and to the helm.

The storm! In front of me, all I see is a huge wall of grey-green water … It hoists up the little boat, but no sooner are we on top than the next wall appears, and down we plunge towards it … Here comes the wall again … It is never ending … The sea is constantly renewing itself …

The sails vibrate in the whistling air. Everything trembles. Foam flies all around. The old catamaran moans. Each time we ride a wave it seems that the hull must break into a thousand pieces. 'Just the wood working,' Herbert declares airily in response to my worried expression. If he says so! We are sharing the helm now. Another wall of water … a valley … a wall … on and on. Not a moment's rest. Before long we are as stiff as these never-ending, never-yielding walls. 'Not one of you is to stick his nose outside without first clipping onto the rope with the karabiner,' Herbert had shouted the minute the storm started. And he explained how impossible it is to find anyone who has fallen overboard in a rough sea. Nobody allowed out without a harness – you can see he was once a mountain guide.

'Wind force 6!' he shouts amid the uproar, his blue eyes dancing with excitement. 'Hey, Kurt … ' I make no comment. All I hope is it doesn't go up to 7.

I hold a diagonal course, as instructed, riding the mountains of water, up and down, just like an intrepid skier taking the humps of a rough slope in a straight line. Nobody can keep it up for long, however, and soon we change over. Having completed my stint, I stagger down into one of the hulls to try and find some rest despite the rolling and rocking. Even down there, everything creaks and squeaks, gurgles and snorts … What on earth brings the Walker Spur into my mind all of a sudden, the Grandes Jorasses? Now of all times? It's a mystery. 1,200 metres of vertical granite, one of the most difficult climbing routes in the western Alps. 'Well, it's not as tiring as this,' I conclude. 'At least the Spur doesn't keep moving about.'

I am amazed how well my sister is coping with this turbulent environment. Having a husband like Herbert obviously toughens you up. Gerard, Herbert's friend, is looking green. 'It's the short North Sea waves,' Herbert comments. 'You can't do anything about it.' It was meant as reassurance.

A day has passed and the storm is over. We feel a lot better, but where on earth are we? The last to be at the helm were Alfrun and I, and together we did our best to slice the waves at the right angle. Our poor captain, Herbert, despite himself, is doing battle with seasickness. Gerard, safely over his bout, now that the boat is once more moving peacefully, finds time for a nervous crisis. He has had enough! But you can't get off a boat in the middle of the ocean, not like on a mountain, where you can simply return to Base Camp. (That's not true, Kurt – sometimes you have to stick it out even up there!)

All three of us try to calm poor Gerard until finally he smiles weakly. It is almost three days since we left the Danish coast. To tell the truth, I feel as if I have made three bivouacs. Nobody has managed to sleep, the best we have *had are a few dozing rests. At this point I am convinced that ocean sailing is every bit as hard as a long mountain ascent. At the same time, however, I feel closer to the sea. The sea has become something special for me.*

When you are on it, far from land like this, it takes on a different character; you feel in close contact with the water, not a bit like being on the deck of a large ship. It is as if you were absorbed by the essence of the water – the land, the coast, is only a distant, imaginary limit. You cannot appreciate what the sea is until you have experienced it like this.

We catch sight of a few large ships … and feel reassured. At the same time, we worry over the danger of a collision. The automatically piloted giants might never notice a tiny sailing boat. The onus is on us to get ourselves out of the way. And soon we are alone again …

'Land-ho!' A coastline has appeared.

Everybody is excited. But where are we?

'Switch on the Sonar!' I yell, remembering how we ran aground in the Limfjord.

'You and your Sonar! I'm amazed you didn't switch it on in the middle of the North Sea.' Herbert is sarcastic. He doesn't like to be reminded of the incident, but how can I help it if I like to know how much sea there is underneath me? 'The big ships have already shown us where the channel is.' With conviction, he declares, 'That's England ahead.'

'Oh, really?' I think to myself, and hazard, 'Couldn't it be the Dutch coast?'

'For heaven's sake, Kurt!' Herbert shuts me up with a ferocious glance and I mutter something about the unpredictability of marine currents. But he's right. It must be the English coast. Only where?

'We must wait until night,' says Herbert when we are a few kilometres off shore. We can just make out houses and trees; we drop anchor.

But why? Why wait until night-time? In the darkness you can see lighthouses and lightships: each has its own special signal. If we count the seconds between one impulse and the next, and look up the frequency on a chart we have on board, we can work out our location exactly.

Simple! However, when darkness falls, the colour of the signals from the first lighthouse does not correspond with the chart, only the intervals do.

'Perhaps the lighthouse-keeper screwed in a red bulb when the last one burned out. Maybe he didn't have another white one.' That's my simplistic explanation. One thing is sure – and another of the lighthouses confirms it – we are lying off the English coast, to the east of the Thames estuary.

*   *   *

London, Saint Katharine's Dock, Tower Bridge. We have sailed up the Thames.

Alfrun and Gerard go home – overland. Herbert and I stay a few days until everything is ready for the Swan's *refit. Lohengrin Mark II – that's me – goes to make a phone call to Terry and Julie …*

Will she say 'yes'? She hardly knows me, after all, and she doesn't know Herbert at all. Two Austrian mountain guides and film-makers. Are these trustworthy professions in the eyes of an Englishwoman? Or will we seem more like buccaneers to her? The only thing I want to do is to repay her for those wonderful days climbing in Wales by inviting her to come sailing with us, so that she can see how marvellous it is to dance on the waves in a catamaran. Maybe we'll even go as far as the French coast. For the weekend. It's all right with Herbert – but what about Julie?

Kurt, I tell myself, stop all this Swan *nonsense. Who knows how the story of Lohengrin really turned out? On the phone, my nerve fails me. I pose the question finally when we meet – in the middle of Terry's birthday celebrations – and Julie turns down the proposition. But I'm not convinced. Next day we go climbing on a sandstone outcrop in the Sussex woods and I make another attempt, 'Why don't we sail across to France?'*

You can sense whether or not a person possesses an adventurous spirit: there is some kind of special emanation – and Julie had this. I could feel very strongly that she was a born explorer. I believe she had the courage and the desire to try almost anything. Often, she felt obliged to stay quietly at home because of her family, but not always. Suddenly, she'd be off! She would run through the woods, climb her rocks, or dash up to Wales to climb with Dennis, or be on her way to some other place. Terry was understanding. He'd long got used to it, he said. So it didn't seem strange to me to be making a suggestion like this. But I was nervous. Shouldn't I have been? Sail in a catamaran to the French coast? Could I still convince her?

She looked at me thoughtfully. The air seemed to be vibrating, in small waves, dissolving into thousands of tiny dancing points, and I was sure that she wanted to come. In that moment she was on the boat and – I don't know why – I was held spellbound by her dark eyes. For several seconds I was incapable of thought, overcome by an emotion I could not recognize. Our gaze almost froze, and I felt sure that her voice could only say 'yes'. When she slowly opened her lips there was consent in her eyes, along with a shyness and reserve, as well as something else I did not recognize, something foreign …

'It's not possible,' I heard her say. 'I have to go to see Dennis. He's ill.' She looked up at the gently swaying trees. Her climbing partner had angina, she explained, and she had promised to visit him. I knew from

when we were in Wales how close they were to one another.

Timidly at first, then with increasing insistence, I pointed out that it would not take long to sail across to France. It was an opportunity that would not come again. Herbert was about to take the boat to the Mediterranean. I so much wanted to show her my 'ocean', the ocean I had just lived with. I could still feel the blue-green waves within me ... and I sensed how much Julie longed for this adventure. It had to be! But she said 'no', and that was that. Even Terry's encouragement served no purpose.

Much later she told me that her loyalty to Dennis was not the sole reason for refusing. She had a deep feeling – call it intuition – that this was not the right moment for us to get to know each other better.

I left, upset and disappointed. We didn't see each other again for three years.

Then, quite by chance, we bumped into one another in a restaurant at the Trento film festival. Julie was with Terry, and I with Teresa and our small son Ceci. We were even staying in the same hotel, we discovered, in adjacent rooms! Even now I find that hard to believe. Neither of us had been to a festival for years, and we had heard nothing of each other ...

Yet there we were, as if the stars had cast the dice.

And nothing had changed; we realized it right away. It was as if I had left England only the day before.

Yet, there was something different.

'I would go on the boat now!' Julie ventured.

'Let's go and climb the Alps,' I said.

The Alps turned into the Himalayas. It was the beginning of our adventures.

... Even the Himalayas were born of the ocean.

DREAM MOUNTAIN – K2 FROM THE NORTH

FLOODWATERS – SINKIANG ON CAMELBACK

No mountain scene has impressed me more deeply.

Eric Shipton

Floodwaters in the high Shaksgam valley: the sky is filled with tumult, a continuous agitation that dominates everything … the very air seems to tremble. My camel leans his full weight against the rushing current. Spume flies everywhere, and the deafening roar of the swollen Kaladjin river drowns out all other sound. I can feel the animal testing the sandy bottom with its feet, looking for hidden holes gouged by the power of the swirling floods.

Floodwaters – elemental, like an avalanche. You are impotent, completely at their mercy if the waters rise further. It's not like a storm on a mountain – then you can grasp what's happening. Here there is just fear … you listen to the roar and ask yourself all the time whether it's getting louder. It is as if somewhere above you, out of sight, tons of snow have broken off and begun rolling towards you – you hear it coming without knowing if or when it will engulf you.

Do Sinkiang camels have a sixth sense, I wonder? My animal seems totally calm as it leans into the water methodically prodding the river bed, moving, stopping, moving on. Just trust the camel, Kurt …

The Shaksgam Valley. Here, in its lower section, we are at 4,000 metres: the deep furrow cuts across uninhabited country, some of the most inaccessible on earth, a region of glaciers and high mountain desert. From one end to the other, the valley is about 200 kilometres, and nobody has ever covered its entire distance. Higher up, immense rivers of ice block it from side to side like giant dams. We have to leave it before we reach these, but now it offers the only possible route. For almost two months practically the whole summer, any passage has been impossible because of the rushing meltwater coming down from the mountains and glaciers. Even now, at the end of August, the kilometre-wide valley floor is a close network of streams and islands, contained within the pale faces of the Kun Lun and the wild Karakoram mountains. For days we have been zigzagging our way through this huge, sinister valley ...

How often will we have to re-cross the waters, fight this current? Twenty times? Thirty times? In my memory I see the clear, shallow stream – marvellously pure spring water ... good to drink – that appeared so unexpectedly out of the interminable, barren gravels of the valley floor during the dry season last May when we were on our way in to K2. Now it is a tangle of glittering, tightly entwined loops, a confusion of meanders and bursting banks, one overlaying another, changing pattern from hour to hour in response to the sun's radiation or the clouds in the sky – and who knows what is happening fifty kilometres upstream? These braided serpents have control of the whole valley floor and hemmed in by the prohibitively steep walls on either side, their brittle rocks torn by heat, we are allowed no escape. There is only one way out: the Shaksgam.

My animal moves forward slowly, up to its belly in the foaming, brown water, the prow wave from its throat carried away by the current so that for some moments it seems we are speeding rapidly upriver, faster than the wind – an optical illusion that has already caused several of us to lose our equilibrium when trying to 'counter-balance' it. I cling to the ropes in the camel's thick fur, arched, tense, ready if the animal should suddenly stumble to throw my weight in whatever direction might be required. A half-strangled cry makes me look round and I'm horrified to see Rodolfo and Giorgio disappearing into the silty waters. Between them, their camel's head rides the surface. The beast was pulled off its legs by the force of the torrent. With frightening speed, my friends are carried downstream towards a vertical rock wall. Nobody can help them. I see them appear and disappear, paddling desperately with their arms. Just before the river smashes into the wall they manage to catch hold of some rocks on the bank. The camel, with its longer legs, had got out earlier. Certainly, without these incredibly resilient, near-indestructible beasts, we would have no hope of making it out of this mountain desert on the Chinese side of K2. Even so, yesterday four loads were lost in the river, and today three. We must be thankful nobody has drowned – there have been plenty of opportunities. The wild torrents of the Himalayas and Karakoram have claimed the lives of so many climbers over the years.

Right now, none of us wants to know about mountain summits – we are a worn out, dissolute crew, scorched in our minds after four months in the high Sinkiang desert. Our only thoughts are for home. This desperate longing drives us to plunge again and again into the muddy waters of the river which stands between us and our return – from stream to stream we go, island to island, day to day … One of us has special cause to be afraid, little Agostino, our first summiteer on K2: he doesn't know how to swim! But without exception, all twenty-two members of this international (but mainly Italian) expedition have had their fill of the Shaksgam waters. Our bodies bear witness to the rigours of the past months on the mountain – rugged faces and baggy clothes flapping wraithlike around spindly limbs. One person has lost 15 kilos, another 20, and I am a full 23 kilos lighter. Julie, our British member who helped me with the filming up to 8,000 metres, has only shed 10 kilos, but however much she might have longed to be slim, she wouldn't win any beauty contests now, any more than would Christina, our doctor. Still, when you have been together on a mountain for so long, gone through so much, coped with all the disappointments, fears and joys, things like appearance matter very little. Helpfulness is so much more important.

Regardless of what she looks like, Julie has lost none of her energy and strength, nor the resilience that I so much admire. It's true her skin is a collection of wrinkles … but the eyes in the thin, burned face are unchanged; and it's what's in them that counts. Sometimes, a fleeting, quiet smile lights her face, and under her tangled hair the eyes shine like the shimmer of mountain ice.

What we have brought back from one of the loneliest places on earth is happiness.

Our expedition team forged bonds of friendship, even if this was one of the toughest and longest enterprises I have ever been engaged in. Maybe, because of that.

Once or twice, as happens on expeditions, tensions arose but they never lasted long. Perhaps the Italian temperament is one of the best for getting over such things. And because we spent so long together, had to solve a variety of problems with no recourse to the outside world, we finished with a real understanding of one another.

A BOOK SPELLS DESTINY

> The afternoon was fine, and nothing interrupted my view of the great amphitheatre about me. The cliffs and ridges of K2 rose out of the glacier in one stupendous sweep to the summit of the mountain, 12,000 feet above. The sight was beyond my comprehension, and I sat gazing at it, with a kind of timid fascination, watching wreaths of mist creep in and out of corries utterly remote. I saw ice avalanches, weighing perhaps hundreds of tons, break off from a hanging glacier, nearly two miles above my head; the ice was ground to a fine powder and drifted away in the breeze long before it reached the foot of the precipice, nor did any sound reach my ears.

These words were written by Eric Shipton in 1937 in his *Blank on the Map*, a book I discovered in my collection years ago, and which was the start of everything for me. It is still a mystery how I came to have it; it was among things we inherited from an aunt who was fond of travelling but who had no particular interest in mountains and didn't speak a word of English. A note inside the cover revealed that she had bought it in India, a long time ago, even before I could walk. How on earth did she come to choose it? She died before I could ask. It must have been my father who put it into my 'library' (the shelf in the top of my wardrobe). Sometimes I wonder about the strange coincidence that brought this book to me … without it, I would probably never have gone to the north side of K2, and K2 might never have become my mountain of dreams. Shipton's words caught the magic of the secret side of this mountain and I read them over and over again.

'Whatever you do, exploration is always the best part.' (That's an old explorers' saying.) It is definitely a greater adventure to discover unknown valleys and mountains than to climb a mountain by a known route, however high. But there is a link between discovery and climbing: to explore the hidden side of a mountain, to seek out a route, then to try to follow it to the top … This is true also of 8,000-metre peaks – like K2's north side. Eric Shipton only wanted to see what was there, and was caught by its spell. It is as if the spirit of the mountain enters you there when you first gaze upon it. Shipton certainly felt it. And I think I absorbed the same feeling from his words; they aroused in me a deep longing to see this enchanted world for myself, to climb on this lonely mountain.

*　　　*　　　*

At 8,616 metres, K2 is the second highest mountain in the world. But if Everest stands higher (by a mere 256 metres), K2 is the more beautiful, more fascinating and quite the more difficult of the two. The Chinese call it Qogir, a variation of the local name Chogori, which means, simply, 'big mountain'. A perfect pyramid, it dominates the ocean of peaks around but remains somewhat obscured unless viewed from quite high up – as from an aeroplane, when you see its outstanding shape soaring far above anything else. On the Pakistan side, the mountain is generally known as *Kei tu* these days, a name derived directly from the topographical symbol 'K²' employed by Montgomerie in 1856 when he numbered the peaks for identification ('K' signifying Karakoram). From this side I had seen the peak first in 1957 with Hermann Buhl during our expedition to Broad Peak, and then again in 1979 when I stood on Gasherbrum II. The north side, however, Eric Shipton's 'magic' side, where the immense North Spur sweeps almost four kilometres into the sky in a straight line, I only saw with my own eyes in the spring of 1982, when I went with 'Bubu' Enzo de Menech, an Italian friend. We were making a reconnaissance – having a special permit from the Chinese – and were accompanied by four Chinese, six camels, two camel-drivers from an Uigur tribe (locals of Sinkiang and Chinese, too, by definition, but a minority group), and two donkeys.

That same year the north side was climbed for the first time, by a large Japanese expedition. At about 8,000 metres, the mountaineers left the main spur, traversed over a steep hanging glacier and climbed to the summit by way of a lateral ridge. Thus, the final 600 metres of spur were still virgin when Francesco Santon's Italian expedition (to which Julie and I belonged) arrived in the area with 120 camels at the beginning of May 1983.

We had passed through the harsh gorges of the Surukwat and the Aghil Daran, crossed the southern mountains of the Kun Lun ranges, had come over the Aghil Pass (4,780 metres) and descended into the Shaksgam, which, because it was spring, was dry.

Finally, we moved up a wide side valley, the Sarpo Laggo, an immense plain of gravel, where at 3,850 metres we came upon the paradise of Suget Jangal, a green patch of meadows and willow bushes, about a kilometre at its greatest length, a natural wonder in this high desert. Shipton wrote of it with enthusiasm; Francis Younghusband and Ardito Desio visited it on their even earlier expeditions (1887 and 1929, respectively); otherwise this uninhabited place was known only to a few local herdsmen. No European had been there since Shipton. From Lower Base Camp, which we established there (calling it *Campo Casa*, Home Base), we could still take our camels on as far as the mouth of the K2 glacier at 4,000 metres, but after that they were on holiday. Upper Base Camp was to be installed a thousand metres higher, on the glacier and closer to the mountain; but zigzagging through a maze of moraine hills and ice towers is too much even for Sinkiang camels. There was only one solution: if we were to get all the material we needed up to this place we had to ferry it ourselves.

A FAIRYLAND OF ICE TOWERS

Along more than 25 kilometres of gravel beds, over rocks, moraine humps, ice slabs, tacking between towers of ice as big as houses, sometimes hanging over raging torrents, unbalanced by the heavy packs on our shoulders, we toiled up and down this interminable glacier. Hump up 20–30 kilos – come down empty. It went on for several weeks. A thousand metres of height separated the end of the glacier and the side of Upper Base Camp at 5,000 metres – that is the painful reality of being human camels. It took three days to carry a load along the whole length of glacier. And so many loads! Some of us made the journey thirty times. Even with two intermediate camps, it was the hardest work I've ever been called upon to make on any of my expeditions – at least so far as transporting stores goes.

Why didn't we have porters? The answer is simple: there aren't any in Sinkiang. Nepal has its Sherpas, Pakistan its Hunzas and Baltis, Tibet its Tibetans, but in Sinkiang the locals will go only as far as their pack animals. At the beginning we were helped by over twenty Italians, who had been 'invited' along specially just for this, but before they were properly acclimatized (and two were even on their honeymoon), they had to go back, together with the last of the 120 camels, as it was already the middle of June and the floods could come down at any moment. By this time, too, the hay for the camels was exhausted.

Even if Sinkiang camels have no liking for glaciers, we did wonder if donkeys could be persuaded to go on them, and kept our two back with us – not without some anxiety. On a fine morning we tried to coax them from Home Base to the glacier. It was a real disaster. They simply would not grasp what it was we wanted them to do – or perhaps, they understood a bit too well!

But there are some creatures still to be encountered even above 5,000 metres. We saw butterflies happily circling between the ice towers, or visiting the flowers at the side of the glacier; there were spiders running over the moraine debris, there was an eagle, and high up, here and on the ledges of a smaller mountain, sometimes we were lucky enough to catch sight of a herd of *bharal*, mountain sheep.

And then there were the mice. They appeared out of nowhere on the moraine among the rocks in our kitchen. When we were eating, they would scurry between our legs and feet with no fear at all, so that Julie and I didn't dare move for fear of disturbing our droll little guests. They would be having their meal, too: poised on back legs, the better to be able to use their 'arms'; they would hold a long straw of uncooked spaghetti (much longer than themselves), chomping it up in record-quick time with sharp front teeth. There were only three at the beginning, but by the end of the summer we were playing host to seven 'regulars'.

Down at Home Base, plant and animal life was well represented – even to the temporary addition of new species: small gardens with spinach, salad, onion plants, radishes were planted by our Sinkiangese companions, thus enriching the customary expedition diet with unexpected delicacies. There was a flock of fifty sheep as well, placidly grazing between the bushes of the meadow – they too were destined for the cooking pots.

Such abundance could not pass unobserved. A big wolf, curious and hungry, came visiting several times from a nearby valley. His incursions reduced our hooved food reserves by at least seventeen units. All our defence strategy proved in vain – not even the battered old rifle belonging to our liaison officer Liu, one of Mao's weathered old partisans, had any effect against him. The 'wolf' always managed to sneak away. Today I know better: it must have been a snow leopard.

With good old Liu, Julie and I had a special relationship – although he always regarded us suspiciously if we left with a rucksack, heading in an unaccustomed direction. Then he would set us strict time limits, and announce that other glaciers were not allowed. He was great! Quite soon, Julie and I had become real Sinkiang mountain marathoneers … but usually we started, heavily loaded, towards the K2 glacier. That summer we each wore out a pair of boots: between our glacier treks, film excursions and explorations we covered over a thousand kilometres. Every time we came back into the ice towers, it was like entering a new, though familiar world. We felt utter happiness; we loved this ice and its colours, its surprises ...

Rising to sixty feet or more, ice towers develop a strange regularity of shape and positioning on the glacier surface, like a frozen procession of the Ku Klux Klan. A whole army, indeed. Sometimes you find a hollow tower, and if you shout into it, it produces a strange sound. They are constantly worn away by slow surface melting, but as the surrounding glacier for some reason melts faster than they do, they give the appearance of actually growing. The highest towers are usually found in the final section of a 'procession'. Sometimes you can hear the thunder of one of them collapsing and breaking into thousands of pieces and blocks of white, blue and green ice. You should keep a respectful distance from them, but this is not always possible. The K2-glacier is not the only one that has these towers. The mightiest 'processions' that Julie and I discovered were on the Gasherbrum glacier. (We filmed there and reached, for the first time, the base of the unclimbed North Face of Gasherbrum II.) The tallest of these pointed towers I ever saw was in 1988 on the Singhié glacier – some fifty metres in height. To walk in the corridors between the towers is to be in a fairyland. Only fantasy could create such shimmer, such a world of crystal. Yet it is real.

The first tents at the High Base Camp were in place at 5,000 metres by the end of May, but the load-ferrying to this place continued into the beginning of August, when all the high camps were established. One of the most original of these was Camp 1, tucked inside a crevasse at 5,800 metres on the sheer face close to the North Spur. Julie and I spent several days there, getting used to the altitude before going higher and (naturally, and just as importantly) doing some filming.

Julie had never been to 8,000 metres before. Now for the first time we were in direct contact with K2, could sense the great mass of the mountain, the vast sweep of the spur – an unimaginable 3,600 metres of vertical height. (The climbing distance is of course much more.) But these are only figures, after all; they tell you very little about the thinning of the air as you climb higher, the great effort required, the increased hazards of altitude.

How would she fare up there? On Nanga Parbat Pierre Mazeaud, the expedition leader, didn't give her a chance. He is no sympathizer of women on expeditions and forbade her to go above 5,000 metres – a bitter pill for Julie to swallow when four years earlier she had climbed 6,768-metre Huascaran in the Andes. But regardless of any medical tests you take beforehand, you never know for sure – not even these days – how anyone will perform at altitude if they have not been high before. Marco Cortecolo, a first-class mountaineer on our expedition and an extreme-skier, found himself in Camp 2 suddenly fighting for his life. Only oxygen and the combined efforts of the whole team saved him from certain death. Instead of filming a daring ski-descent down the steep face beside the lower third of the spur, Julie and I (from Camp 1) shot his rescue along the fixed ropes. He had no use of his legs, and without the uninterrupted sequence of ropes anchored to the face with rock pitons and ice screws, it is unlikely that any of us could have got him off the mountain in time.

Apart from this unfortunate incident, the atmosphere on the spur was usually happy.

LIVING IN A CREVASSE AT 5,800 METRES

'Watch out for those icicles when you operate the clapper board,' I (as film director) shout at Pierangelo, a bearded bear of a man from Bergamo. But it's just my little joke. He is standing outside the icicle curtain at Camp 1 in his bathing suit; out there the sun is merciless, while here inside the crevasse where we've set up home, the temperature is around zero. That is why we're not short of icicles: they grow faster than mushrooms in the woods (especially given the two hours a day of rain, or heavy dripping, that we get here, one of the drawbacks of this campsite). So you can always 'pick' them for icicle soup, icicle tea, and for mixing with the freeze-dried food; and if you sit long enough inside the cave, you even get icicles in your beard. I have just filmed the red tents inside the crevasse through a curtain of icicles, and Julie has fixed her microphone between two of them.

'Take one!' Pierangelo bellows through his mighty beard, then while the camera and recorder are running, provides the 'Action!' by leaping as fast as he can out of our ice-box cave and into the sunshine.

Altogether we shot 1,000 metres of film of the climb and life on the mountain itself, and we filmed many days on the North Spur; in four months we collected 11,000 metres of celluloid. It certainly needs strong faith to realize what you want to create under the circumstances of a major climb and most mountaineers do not concern themselves much with the mechanics of filming on a climb like this. Julie and I had already learned that the hard way on our Nanga Parbat trip. But here it is much better: tomorrow Luca wants to carry the big Arriflex camera up to Camp 2, which is about 900 metres higher than here. That means a wearisome oblique traverse over ice slabs, steep snowfields and rocks to the right of the ridge. Julie and I will carry our personal gear as well as our lightweight tent, the sound equipment and a summit camera. The unpredictable nature of filming often makes camera teams difficult to accommodate within normal expedition planning and routine. When the two of us reached this crevasse on the first occasion, for example, there was no room for us in the tents. Well, we shovelled out a snow hole and passed the night in our nylon bivouac bag comfortably enough. However, since then, we have preferred always to carry a super lightweight tent in the rucksack: if the weather gives us the chance, we could even dare a summit attempt (it's a secret dream of ours). But will fate grant us the chance?

As the number of loads carried up to Camp 1 grows, and more people visit it, the crevasse becomes increasingly comfortable. Alcoves for cooking have been carved out of the ice, and benches of snow; there are pitons in the walls on which to hang up equipment (but you do have to take care in choosing a good spot, not one where the icicles grow, or you may find all your gear frozen into a compacted lump that you may never get off the wall!).

Only the toilet facilities remain uncomfortable. Holding on to your ice-axe as a self-belay, you half hang, half lean over a vertical drop of fifty metres. We've all scratched our heads for a less exhausting solution, but so far no one has come up with one.

Even in bad weather, there is no shortage of humour on an Italian expedition. However, in Camp 1 when the avalanches sweep over you, you don't hear anyone laughing. There is this sudden sound, like a waterfall racing down the slope, and a mighty hissing across the mouth of the crevasse. Soft snow and powder comes in all over the place. It's certainly frightening. We managed to partially close the opening with a sheet; even so, when the avalanches roll, it is not the best place to be.

Still, who would ever have thought you could get used to living inside a crevasse in the middle of a steep mountainside. But you do …

7,000 METRES – GIVE UP OR GO ON?

'We've filmed enough with the big camera. From now on we'll only use the summit camera – and make our own attempt ...'

On 31 July, exactly twenty-nine years to the day after the first ascent of K2 by Lino Lacedelli and Achille Compagnoni, our lead climbers Agostino Da Polenza and Joska Rakoncaj have reached the summit. Others, Sergio Martini and Fausto de Stefani, as well as Almo Giambisi and 'Gigio' Visentin, are in position for their try. None of them has been on the ideal direct line that we had dreamed of, but they have made the Japanese exit from the spur to the left and crossed the hanging glacier. All the same, the summit is the summit! Especially on K2 ... where you have to be really lucky with the weather and in extraordinarily good shape if you want to do it at all, particularly if you climb without bottled oxygen, as we did. (We had just three bottles of oxygen on the mountain, for medical purposes: they served well for mountain sickness and frostbite.)

What should we do, Julie and I, give up or go on? The question hung in the air for only a few minutes when Francesco Santon, the expedition's leader, came on the radio to ask why we were still filming on the spur. Hadn't we had that big camera up here for some while, long enough to get all we needed? Wouldn't it be a good idea to spend some time back at Home Base?

It sounded like a bad joke to us. Now of all times! No, we had no ideas of that kind. We wanted the summit, too! Or, at least the chance to climb as high as possible. We had already worked hard on this expedition; and we would still take film and sound while we made our attempt.

That's why we have come up even further with our lightweight tent and all the many things we need – climbing gear, food, stove, summit camera, sound-recorder – to an airy pulpit here at 7,000 metres beside the ridge. It juts out like a ski-jump, or rather a 'sky-jump', over an ocean of peaks. Immeasurable distances extend before our eyes, mountain to mountain, valleys filled with blue haze, glittering, shimmering belts of glaciers, like huge drowsy snakes ...

Now that we have seen this, we know: the summit of K2 is not everything. Living way above the ocean of peaks like this is at least as good. Days when infinity belongs to you ...

And also, all that is close, below you: the small saddle above the Skyang glacier, where we were not long ago ... and further out, in the wide gash of the Shaksgam valley, the round head of Tek-Ri, a place we know well.

'Nanga Parbat! Can you recognize it?' Julie wants to know.

'Yes, there on the horizon. All by itself.' That was our first expedition.

'And those high blue mountains, way to the west?'

'Rakaposhi, one of them. Kunyang Kish another. The Batura Wall – all those seven-thousanders above the Hunza valley.' Last year we were there …

Today it is all ours. A day above the world. Far and wide, near and far – ours.

One of the mountains down there, a six-thousander, rising at the edge of K2 glacier, is the one we have named Shipton Peak. It has to have been the one he used as his viewpoint.

During the night comes the storm. It seems impossible after a day like that. 'Never take anything for granted,' I think and say as much to Julie. The wind pulls and rattles at the tent. There is not much space on our little 'sky-jump'. We are exposed to the full power of the storm. In such situations, you can't help thinking about the 2,000-metre drop beneath you, and wondering how strong the fabric of your tent is. Are the seams well stitched, and shouldn't we have piled more rocks on the anchoring pegs? Such a high camp is always a gamble: if you go down because of the storm, you may lose the only possible day for the summit, yet if you stay and snowfall starts, avalanches could cut off all hope of retreat. There is no immediate solution, but at the same time, you know you won't give up: you have come here in full knowledge of the risks. These are the recurrent thoughts on stormy nights high in the Himalayas.

In the morning I have a headache, but it passes. The storm, however, goes on until the afternoon. We make the decision to sit it out. All of a sudden, from above, Agostino and Joska appear on their way back from the summit. And from below, Soro and Giuliano come up. Congratulations and big hugs all round. We are very happy to be together again.

Julie and I record the reunion for our film, but we are heart-and-soul mountaineers, too. Tomorrow we will go on up to Camp 3! Then to Camp 4 – and after that, who knows?

7,600 METRES – ON OUR OWN AND HEADING SKYWARDS

Camp 3 is situated in a horrible place. Two tents in the midst of a terribly steep snowfield, which extends up for at least another hundred metres. A slide of snow from up there could very easily wipe away the whole camp. You wouldn't stop falling for 2,500 metres. There is a fixed rope attached horizontally into the rocks of the spur, to which we can belay when in the tent, but it would still give you a nasty shock to wake up suddenly to find yourself hanging upside-down on it, all rolled up in the tent like a sleeping bat in its folded wings. No, I don't want to sleep in such a place. As soon as I arrive with Julie and Giorgio, who has joined us, obstinately I start looking for a better spot, but in vain. It is too late – I can't find one. But at least we could pitch at the edge of the snowfield, where we can belay more directly to a fixed rope anchored in the rocks above us. Giuliano doesn't spare himself in helping me shovel out a platform in the gathering darkness, and Julie gets the tent up while we're still recovering from the effort. We're all gasping for breath in the thin air.

Not a good night. There doesn't seem to be any end to all the brewing-up. The rule is that you should drink 6 litres of liquid a day at altitude, but whoever could melt that much snow? Even if there is no shortage of the damn stuff. To hell with it! I am very grumpy and completely done in.

Morning light: the weather is fine, but today all of us are late getting up. Julie, too, has spent a miserable night. Up here at 7,600 metres (where even sleeping takes so much energy), you feel life burning away all the time. As a precaution, two days ago I dumped an oxygen bottle a bit further down the ridge against emergency.

Good, friendly sunshine! Giuliano, without a shirt, is standing in the morning light wiring his chest up to an electrocardiograph. Then he and Soro, who is also up here, set off, to be followed a short while later by Julie and me. Giorgio wants to sleep in a bit longer. Only Luca decides to give up and go down. He has our sympathy: we were all impressed that he should even have wanted to give it a try – some weeks ago he was badly injured when a cooking stove blew up in his face, and the wounds have been slow to heal.

Above us the view is grim: the jutting ice cliffs of the hanging glacier, like a huge balcony clinging between the ridges of the summit pyramid. To its right, a fantastic row of towers – unusual for

K2 – shaped from a pale yellow crystalline limestone, which I recognize from the Baltoro; it tends to build inspired formations. The ragged sequence of towers and notches up there, rising one above the other, is incredible, a Jacob's Ladder to heaven. Will anyone ever do the Direttissima?

Julie and I, despite feeling so low this morning, packed up our entire camp and are carrying it with us. We move slowly, one arduous step after another towards the first rock step. Gasping, we struggle over it – moving at slow motion, like robots. Again and again we stop just to be able to breathe. Nevertheless, we are back in condition, both of us feel well again and that encourages us.

Now we are on a steep slope of loose gravel, and there is nowhere to make a belay. We can only move with extreme caution. Then we tackle another steep step in the great rib to the right of the hanging glacier. We are on that yellow, metamorphosed limestone now. If only our packs were not so heavy! On a prominent rock among some broken slabs, ledges and snowpatches, we sit and take a break, have a bite to eat and drink from our bottle of tea. It's great to have everything with you like this, to push on completely on your own. Any time we wanted, we could set up camp and nothing would be missing.

Wherever is Camp 4? We should be close to it by now. Obliquely below us, back towards the hanging glacier, we discovered an oxygen bottle; it must mark an old Japanese campsite, perhaps their Camp 4? Agostino had told us about it, and also spoke of an old bivouac site around here somewhere.

Giorgio has come into view below us, climbing up from Camp 3. He's bringing bad weather with him, by the look of things: dark, heavy clouds are rolling in to the mountains below us from Pakistan, from the South-West. It looks worrying. Not long after, Giorgio shouts up to say he has decided to go back down … and … Julie? Might it not be better if she went with him? As she's never been this high before?

For a moment the question hangs in the air. I glance across at her and catch the silent, imploring look in her dark eyes. No, I can't face the thought that Julie might have to struggle down through a break in the weather, across those icefields, while I am still trying my luck up here.

'It's OK, Giorgio, thanks!' I shout down. 'Julie's all right!' We'll go on together, and if it's not possible, then we'll come down together.

I hear Julie let out a deep breath, and I too feel relieved – despite the fact that below us the clouds are getting darker by the minute, and the huge billows, like weird helmets, roll up towards us. So much we have shared on this expedition: carried so many loads together, made this film together, dreamed (if all went well) of having a go at the Direttissima … or at least to make it possible, the one for the other, to get to the top. Perhaps the weather will get better once more!

We zigzag further up the steep face, with the impressive towers looming over our heads. Then, suddenly, at the end of a ledge in the vertical rock of the spur, I see a natural windbreak of fallen blocks of snow protecting a little niche. A real swallow's nest. The afternoon sun shines right into it, and bathes the surrounding rocks in a golden glow. It's such a lovely, unique spot, we decide to stay. Even the clouds below us seem to have ceased their boiling. It's a good choice. We'll soon have our little tent up. No sooner have we settled down than we hear noises above us. Gigio is feeling his way down over the rocks, with strange jerky movements, and behind him, Almo. They had bivouacked on the hanging glacier, reached 8,200 metres – but no summit. Resignation, disappointment, exhaustion mark their faces.

We offer words of consolation – but what help are they? The pair continue their descent. Who knows how long they were up high …

We sit in front of our tent. 'It was a good day,' says Julie in a low voice. Indeed, it was. Later a beautiful sunset flushes thousands of peaks in a flood of golden light. We are so high above them, we must soon touch the sky.

8,000 METRES – OUR DREAM SHATTERED BY STORM

Places blessed with evening sunshine cannot expect to enjoy the first warming light of morning. We have to wait a long time next day before the sun reaches us. It is 5 August. We haven't far to go up today and the weather is beautiful, so we drape our frost-covered sleeping bags and all our damp clothes along the rim of our rock ledge to dry, and simply pass the time.

The scratching of crampons above us announces the arrival of Fausto and Sergio. And Soro is with them. Soon we know: the two reached the summit, but had a terrible bivouac the night before. The altitude has left its mark: Fausto's fingertips are frostbitten and

Sergio has frozen toes. There is no happiness in their eyes, only utter tension. They will feel differently once they're down safely. Soro, good man, will accompany them.

The night in the open on the hanging glacier must have seemed interminable. Really it's quite remarkable that they went on after that. Sergio wishes us well for our attempt, gives us a friendly smile and they continue their descent.

It is almost 1 P.M. when we set off. The others told us that Giuliano and Adalberto hope to traverse out onto the hanging glacier today – with a tent. Tomorrow they will try for the summit from there … a wise solution. Days ago, when we were much further down and it was uncertain whether Julie could get as far as 8,000 metres – she suffered stomach trouble at Camp 2 – I wondered whether I might go for the top with Giuliano, my old friend from Everest 1980; but then Julie decided to go higher, and now I am convinced – she has proved it – that even great altitude is no barrier to her.

Fast clouds – low down, over there, from the west – advance towards us. Is the weather going to break today? We are climbing now towards an overhang of yellow rock, beside which there is a vertical wall. Disconcertingly close the towers soar above us … the Direttissima.

Please God, give us one more day! No, two! Two days of fine weather. Then we can make our try and get back down again, and perhaps the summit will be ours.

At the very least we want to climb a few hundred metres up there, reconnoitre, touch rock that until now no hand has felt, no eyes seen; we want to know what is there …

Another length of rope, and we reach a small rocky platform. Amid the rubble lies a crumpled tent – blue, shapeless – containing a few bits and pieces of equipment. There's nobody around. Then I spot Giuliano and Adalberto on the steep and exposed Japanese traverse, making their way out towards the hanging glacier. A breathtaking view from up here. *'Buona fortuna!'* I shout. Good luck! They wave back. But the atmosphere is growing more and more threatening. The sun has disappeared and patches of fog are drifting around the towers. It looks like trouble.

Julie is quick to put up our small blue tunnel tent, while I heave over every rock I can find to weight down the guys. Not more than a metre from the entrance there is a sheer drop, first to the hanging glacier (from our airy spot we can look straight onto the edge of the huge 'balcony'), then on down into the depths beyond. Hard to imagine in this grey mist that it is 3,000 metres to the bottom. I can't help thinking about the terrible fall taken by one of the Japanese mountaineers into that abyss, and pile more rocks onto our tent pegs. Please God, give us one more day before the storm breaks! But the air masses are bubbling up.

Would we be fit enough tomorrow to go higher in any case? At present we both feel well, despite having carried up our camp in one go. It doesn't look too difficult from here, even though the exposure is tremendous. The main problem of the direct route will doubtless be getting back down it. But what surprises are hidden by the next rocky upheaval? We've got pitons and rope … We crawl into our sleeping bags and start melting snow – and, alas, tip it over. (I fell

K2 – the North face.

1. K2 (8,616 metres) photographed from the top of Broad Peak (8,060 metres) during the first ascent on 9 June 1957. The British mapmaker's 'number-code-symbol' (K stands for *Karakoram*; followed by 1, 2, 3, etc) in fact results in the most commonly used name for the mountain. But the locals' original 'big mountain', *Chogori*, with its outstanding beauty and impressive regular shape, is often referred to as 'the mountain of mountains'. (Compare this photograph with the one on the jacket, taken from the same spot almost three decades later: the slow, worldwide diminution of ice is apparent on Broad Peak's subsidiary summit, just below K2 – in the more recent photograph it has become a rock tower.)

2. The mighty Baltoro glacier, 58 kilometres long, and the Matterhorn-like Masherbrum (7,821 metres) photographed from Broad Peak.

asleep for a moment while holding the pot.) *Porca miseria!* Chaos, water everywhere … with handfuls of snow we try and mop it up as fast as possible. Julie stays calm, but I'm swearing. We start again, throw the wet chunks of snow in the pot and wait … and wait … minutes of exhausted silence … then, finally, tea!

The first storm squalls hit us. Everything is grey now outside. (The others have taken shelter in a crevasse, higher up on the hanging glacier.) Snowflakes whirl through the air. Gusts of wind strike the tent with full force, and slither along it.

Time has become unimportant: up here at 8,000 metres what counts is the rising tide of snow around us, and the might of the wind. Our tent withstands the fury of the elements, thanks to its streamlined shape and the anchorage of heavy rocks, but we barely close an eye all night. It is pretty certain now that we shall have to abandon our attempt, and knowing that, we talk and talk and think about what we would have done *if* … wonderful thoughts, nearer to the truth perhaps for us being so high, thoughts of the summit, of a push, of a reconnaissance into the last recesses of the mountain, of the Direttissima … of the life we have begun to lead … It is great to be here, to have reached this place – even if the storm will not grant us one step more. We have reached the upper storey of our 'dream mountain'. Having lived with K2 for so many days now has made it 'ours', from its base to its highest ridges. Here we are, two hidden spiders, clinging to the edge of this giant, stormwracked crystal.

Will the summit be ours one day, too? Tomorrow? Another year? 'I wanted so much to know what it's like up there, around that corner,' says Julie.

Not until noon on the next day did the storm calm down sufficiently to allow us outside. We had been trapped in our tent for twenty hours. We looked about anxiously for our friends – and there they were, moving slowly back along the traverse! The weather was just good enough for starting the descent: the summit was out of the question.

It took the four of us two days to get down the 4,000 metres of rope, with strong currents of powder snow dragging at our knees and threatening to tip us down the face. Adalberto had altitude sickness; for half a day I helped him down the ridge until the air was thick enough for him to manage on his own. It was hard: three times the fixed rope anchors pulled out and we fell short distances –

2

3

a year afterwards I still had a pain in my elbow to remind me. But all four of us made it without frostbite.

Was it worth it? A strange question – it doesn't arise until you get back. With his frozen fingers, Fausto needed days before he could find an answer. 'Yes,' he said. 'I wouldn't have missed being up there, standing on top, not for anything.'

To Julie and me, the four months of living in the mountain desert of Sinkiang brought more than reaching the summit of K2 could ever have done – even though we longed for it so much. The desire to return to this landscape would never forsake us. Exploring, discovering this fantasy glacier world and the endless ocean of peaks that faded into the blue of distance, the climb on the wild North Spur of K2 – all these were part now of our lives. We could never turn our back on them. Both of us had heard the siren voice of that empty land.

It also re-emphasized the importance of our film work, not just for us but for what it brought others too. This was a great joy to us – and after our return to Europe, we called ourselves 'the highest film team in the world': filming would be our path from now on.

K2 itself, whose summit we had come so close to, remained our dream mountain, a symbol of everything that the magic world of glaciers and desert mountains had aroused in us.

3 . Kurt finds a piton, which he had hammered into the rock almost 30 years earlier, on his expedition in 1957.

4. Kurt starting out from Salzburg with Hermann Buhl, Marcus Schmuck and Fritz Wintersteller in the spring of 1957 for 'the first ascent of an eight-thousander in *Westalpenstil*'.

5. No high altitude porters, no oxygen – Hermann Buhl's idea is great, but initially gives us headaches. Chogolisa, the pure, white 'Bride Peak' of the British explorers, looms in the back-ground.

6. The Welsh coast at Holyhead, and (7) Julie, in 1975, with her climbing partner, Dennis.

ENGLAND – TUNBRIDGE WELLS
The highest film team in the world

'Look!' With large capable hands, Terry starts folding a letter-sized sheet of cardboard, humming softly to himself as he does so. I see it take the form of a triangle with side flaps. Now it gets a base as well. (I had never realized he had such a talent for origami!) I notice his satisfaction – he's obviously got it all worked out, and as he chews on his beard, engrossed in his creation, the first glimmer comes to me of what it is he's making. The white pyramid on the table can only be …

'There!' declares Terry, surveying his work with the pride of an inventor. 'K2! Here, you write THE HIGHEST FILM TEAM … on this side you put Julie's c.v. … and yours on the other.' He points to the two side flaps, which keep K2 upright. Light dawns: it's a memo to put on the desks of television executives, carrying caricatures of both of us and highlights of our careers, along with our addresses …

'That's fantastic!' Nobody would ever hide such an original piece of advertising in a filing cabinet.

Julie beams, leaping between the living room and the kitchen as she fetches wood for the fire – everything always at top speed. An enormous Newfoundland dog dozes unconcernedly in her path, a woolly mound, a metre high, practically unable to see out of his eyes for hair, a natural buffer of stoic calm.

Terry throws me a quick look. 'Man, how did you put up with her for five months in China?' How? I shrug. Well, the truth is I'm sorry it's over, I think to myself. Terry is in high spirits: Julie's climb on K2's North Spur was the highest a British woman had ever been. Supposing she had made it to the summit, too? That might yet come. He has nothing against this fresh start of hers: their son and daughter are grown up and away from home – Julie is free to travel the world if that is what she wants. But what does Julie feel about it? She told me once that Dennis and I had awakened in her a restlessness to see unknown places.

At the same time she loves her life at home: it has so many facets, between which she flits happily, sometimes turning in on herself, sometimes dedicating herself exclusively to a project, and at other times impatiently on the move. She and Terry have been married for twenty-five years, living in the Sussex woodlands. She climbed once in the Andes (with Norman Croucher, the mountaineer with two artificial legs); once in Yosemite with Dennis; now the Himalayas have captured her imagination – with a vengeance. Yet there is something else – a no lesser, indeed an all-penetrating force – something of which she said to me, 'You find it in the mountains in your own way – and it allows me to approach the big mountains.' She has discovered it, too, through the martial arts, budo and aikido. It is difficult to explain: to an outsider these warrior sports can seem brutal, more or less so according to which of them you are watching and how they are being practised, but from what I have seen, they appear more like a highly disciplined ballade, as an imagined opponent (who is not an enemy) is engaged and reacted to. It is an exercise in the deepest concentration, which in the end leads you to the real you, to it, the centre of your (and all) being, from which you gain force and resistance beyond expectation, as well as something else for which no word exists … I have experienced it in the mountains, have derived it from them and do so still, and it is this shared understanding that links Julie and me together so strongly. In a way I find it strange – but on the other hand, quite natural – I can somehow become part of the process, just sitting quietly and watching the martial artists as they 'fight' – or meditate. The whole space around them seems filled with an energy, as if a single spirit pervades their movements – I too can tap into it. David, the Sensei (or teacher), a man whom above all I admire for his simplicity and depth, not just for his ability, has tried several times to encourage me on to the mat. But I always shake my head. My ice-bear shape and my phlegmatic constitution are not suited to it … and whenever Julie (she wears the black belt of the masters) whirls somebody a dozen times through the air, or tumbles on the mat herself, like a runaway wheel, I say to myself: better just to absorb the essence! David is an extraordinary person. In Julie's life many things have been made possible by him. Several years ago it was discovered that he had cancer. Then, the disease halted by itself, quite suddenly …

Julie is able to find a dojo anywhere, wherever she is, somewhere suitable for practising aikido. It might be a flat, sandy spot between the glacier and a mountain meadow, as on Nanga Parbat, or a great shield of ice at 5,000 metres between the seracs and the foot of K2 … always it is a special place, you can feel it. There she meets and engages an imaginary opponent, fights or simply sits quietly on the sand between the ice towers, sunk in meditation

– for an hour at a time, or even longer. It is not something I find I can explain – you either understand it, intuitively, or it remains totally incomprehensible, like climbing towards a summit. From it, Julie most surely derives her incredible strength and endurance in the Himalayas.

The film team memo card.

ITALY – BOLOGNA

Once more to our dream mountain?

Of course. No question! Somehow we will make it possible. Gasping, I walk up a hill near Bologna – what is it, a hundred, a hundred and fifty metres? Again I am much too fat! In this country people seem to have heard of potatoes (my favourite vegetable) only from legend; instead there is pasta!: tortellini in brodo, tagliatelle, lasagne al forno, spaghetti con le vongole, *et cetera, et cetera. Enough? What do you mean, enough? That was just the first course!*

I puff on. There is of course a perfectly respectable road up this hill, but I chose the steep slope for good reason. The next course will be bocconcini *(small pieces of fried meat swimming in oil),* salsiccia, faraona, pollo, maiale, prosciutto *(ham),* grana *(Parmesan cheese) – a spicy aroma permeates everywhere, it sizzles and drips from all the kitchens in the area. The* vino *made by these farmers is* fantastico *and* genuino *– but you do need to know where to go for it.*

'You know, it's true,' I think to myself, wiping the sweat from my brow, 'The Emilia-Romagna boasts the best kitchens in all Italy. That's why the people here have such nice rounded temperaments ... and not just temperaments ...'

I labour higher towards the round hilltop, where in this whole so-round world of Romagna, my round mother-in-law – a real symbol of the area – will doubtless have spread the (round) table with the latest of her oh-so-tasty culinary inventions, a real Italian 'square meal' for me, my wife Teresa, her two sisters, and for Ceci, my son.

I squint down at myself; it's high time I went on an expedition. I must be 20 kilos overweight again. Or I should move, for a week at least, to my comparatively Spartan home town of Salzburg, where I mostly do my own cooking.

At any rate, there, the mountains rise before the door. Here, the highest things (since we came back from K2) are the phone bills.

Perhaps I should take up jogging? I cannot feel the slightest motivation for anything so uncomfortable. Skiing, then? There is this white bump not far from here which in winter swarms with a hundred thousand people – but either you are a slalom specialist, or you are not …

My son Ceci is great! A real champion skier. But the Alps are a long way away, you only see them on the far horizon on days of exceptional clarity.

Nevertheless, I am glad that we left the terrible plains of Portomaggiore a year ago, with their network of water channels, since when we have been living in the Apennines.

Mostly I am not here anyway, but off on lecture trips or in the Himalayas.

I am glad to have Ceci there to back me up sometimes – living in a house with four women! Not that I should complain: there's Teresa, my wife, who originally wanted to become a judge but has now settled for being a lawyer (it means I have to keep on my toes, too); Angela, an electronics engineer; Alida, a book-keeper (that has certain advantages); and, finally, mother-in-law – who, I really have to admit, is a superb cook.

But the mountains are such a long way away.

In Peking, Julie and I made the acquaintance of an energetic Swiss expedition leader, Stefan Wörner. 'How efficient he is,' she remarked, 'and a really nice guy.' With him was the ever-cheerful Markus Itten. We all hit it off right away and agreed that we simply had to do a trip together. Stefan is really on the ball: last year his Baltoro expedition had the unprecedented success of climbing Hidden Peak, Gasherbrum II and Broad Peak – all three!

Stefan has that dry, irrepressible Swiss humour: 'Three eight-thousanders in a fortnight' was the title he came up with for his lecture programme – not out of swank, but because it was nice and snappy. All the same, there was a discernible twinkle in his eye and he gave a huge wink when he told me of a chat he'd had with Reinhold Messner. Having good-natured digs at one another is all part and parcel of the spirit of mountaineering (and no one else could claim the right to a lecture title like that, however hard he might try to figure it out …)

Stefan had a permit for K2, granted by the Pakistani government. Julie and I could go with him, he said – but how were we to finance it? Money, money! Always money! The telephone wires burned hot between London, Zurich and Bologna. Finally, it looked as if Julie had caught something in the net. But was it really going to come off?

Teresa is a good wife. When I am agitated, she smooths things with her calm. She has an angel's patience. You can't quarrel with her, anyway – try quarrelling with a lawyer! Moreover, Italians are always good-natured, especially towards foreigners (perhaps not so much amongst themselves: avvocato is a way of life in Italy). Teresa is no mountaineer, although she did enjoy coming to Everest Base Camp once. In some way, she is above all that, so balanced that the summits don't draw her. But she understands that I have to go … my life up there, she knows, I can never give up. It will never be any different. Sometimes, when I come back home – like a Greenland polar bear returning from the icecap to the edge of the sea – I find there a quiet contentedness, a different happiness.

But now it has seized me again: K2. I could never have imagined that a mountain could bring so many sleepless nights, just not knowing whether you will get there or not. It has all to do with being there, not with the summit. You know that depends on a lot of things … and there's no point in worrying your head about them in advance.

Zurich: spring 84. At last, it's all settled: we shall go with Stefan Wörner's expedition … In England they want a film about Julie for a series called Assignment Adventure. *David South (originally a geologist) has worked out a treatment as thick as a thesis. We like him, and Julie is already on her way, backwards and forwards to Scotland, getting together the best possible mountaineering gear.*

The air is vibrating again … K2 …

Will we? Won't we?

K2 …

Finding out … that is what makes life worthwhile.

The clever person that he is, Stefan Wörner has acquired permission for a second eight-thousander, one that is not all that high, one well-known to me – Broad Peak.

'RAID' ON BROAD PEAK – 8,047 METRES

An eight-thousander is
only yours once you are
safely down from it –
before that you belong to
the mountain.

(from my diary, 1984)

Twenty-seven years after making the first ascent with the now legendary Hermann Buhl, I, who had been his last rope-mate, stood once more on the topmost point of the three-humped dragon – this time with England's 'highest woman', Julie Tullis.

Hermann Buhl's last summit proved an adventure for Julie and me that nearly cost us our lives. The challenge we had set ourselves was to climb this eight-thousander as a twosome, without a large expedition, without high-altitude porters or oxygen gear, just relying on each other. We were probably the oldest couple climbing in the Himalayas, but after two months on K2, we were at a peak of acclimatization and condition. Time and again the big mountains of the world have proved that being young is not the deciding factor, neither for making the climb, nor for surviving it. One thing, however, is the same for everyone: you cannot say the eight-thousander is yours until you are down from it safely; until then, it is you who belong to the mountain …

When, in the night that followed the 18 July, Julie and I finally crawled into our bivvy tent and sank into a deathlike sleep, we had not the slightest idea what the morning held in store for us.

THE AVALANCHE

From somewhere outside comes a strange hissing sound, like sliding snow. An avalanche?

'Strange,' I think muzzily, through my doze. Last night, when we crawled into this bivvy at 7,600 metres after so many hours of difficult descent from the summit and clinging to the rocks of the sharp ridge with a drop of 3,000 metres beneath our feet, only dimly able to make out the glaciers of China way down below, there had

been stars   r seemed then to have taken
a turn for   had of it, searching among
those clif   eam from our one and only
head-tor   ng which way on earth to go.

I pull   g bag. Yes, it certainly was a
tough d   ight-thousander is always an
escape,   d – even though you have just
given e   uggle to get up there, to where
the su   ade it – for a few unforgettable
mome

The   low the gap at 7,800 metres had
taken   as we belayed down, one rope's
lengt   an invisible bivouac tent – out in
the d   to the face at the lower edge of a
crev   elow the gap, but in our weariness
and   an eternity away. Then we found
it, a   the overall darkness, an island of
san   was ten o'clock at night before our
str   end …

                     outside somewhere, like sliding
sn

                     dawn – 5.30 A.M. Surely there can't
b   e are on a west-facing slope. Except
t   as if from an electric shock, for all at
                     ushing down the tent entrance and on
                     drumming. I cling desperately to the
fabric, press myself into the mountain. 'Julie! Wake up!'

But deep in her sleeping bag, she doesn't hear me. Thank God, we re-anchored the tent last night with the rope and our ice-axes, otherwise we would have been swept away by now. The drumming eases off. I am in such a state of agitation, I can hardly breathe. The tent has withstood the onslaught. With trembling fingers, I open the zip. There's a wall of snow outside – deep snow everywhere, and more falling silently … the weather has obviously broken in the night. And we slept through the whole of it! We are in such a ghastly position here – with the 200-metre slope above us so heavy with snow it could come down at any moment – that for some seconds, I cannot utter a sound. My thoughts seem to have frozen, paralysed with the hopelessness of our plight, with the knowledge that we are sitting on Death's shovel and there's no way out. We may have only minutes left.

I don't know how to break it to Julie, I'm scared to tell her, but she must know the truth: 'Avalanches, Julie, everywhere! We have to leave at once! It might be too late already, but perhaps we can still get away if we move really fast!'

From her eyes I see she understands, but as she sits up, the next surge hits us, like a waterfall. I have jumped to my knees and, gasping, succeed with frantic arm movements in splitting the flow which is piling against the tent, diverting half of it downhill and the rest into the deep crevasse to our side. For a few minutes, this is our salvation, for we are in the direct path of the white flood. Our taut, firmly anchored nylon shelter, the mini-tube tent reinforced by metal hoops and designed, strictly speaking, just for one person, offers so little surface to the pressure that it quickly sloughs the snow into the crevasse before it can squash us flat – so that we make it through even this avalanche.

However, at the front of the tent where there is no crevasse, it is catastrophe. Against all my efforts, snow has come in that end, where Julie is struggling to gather up essentials or put on her boots – I'm not sure which – and it's chaos. Several things have disappeared under the snow. We dig feverishly for the stove, that's vital, and yell a sort of countdown to each other, listing all the things we absolutely have to have if we are to get down this mountain alive – if by any stroke of fortune we don't finish up under an avalanche. Fat chance! Here comes the next torrent! I've only managed to get one boot on but hurl myself in the direction which it's coming, paddling like mad against the invading flood. 'Julie! Watch our boots don't disappear – or we're sunk!' We've got to get away from here, that's obvious, we can't survive much longer if we don't. Over – over – the cascade of snow has passed once more. I'm gasping for breath. Where's that boot? That second boot? We've not lost it down the mountain? The tent is half-filled with snow. Julie struggles free, breathing heavily. She must have her boots on already – how is it that she's so quick? Then panic seizes me: 'Julie! Where's my other boot? I can't find it anywhere!'

'It was just here a moment ago – no there!' She scrabbles in the snow inside the tent while I dig at the entrance. It's curtains for both of us if we don't find it. For a few minutes the horror of the avalanche danger fades …

'Kurt, I've got it!'

Faced with setting out into this almost hopeless chaos of snow at 7,600 metres, finding a simple boot seems a miracle. It brings home to us, as do the ensuing events, that we either manage the descent together or we both perish. We abandon the tent, taking only our sleeping bags, stove, the barest essentials. And, as usual, we're roped together – luckily. Twenty minutes after the first snowslide, we are on our way, carefully probing the steep new snow above the blue serac walls of Broad Peak. We don't get far: at about 6.15 a big avalanche detaches right above us from a couloir between the rocky flutes of the ridge.

Everything is spinning: down is up, up is down; terrible forces against which all resistance is vain; they toss you, carry you, twist you, crush out your breath ... your mouth is stuffed with snow ... you grab another gulp of air, and then you're sucked in again ... moving down Broad Peak ... remorselessly ... That's it ... the end ... I think, but ... no! Not yet ... air. Don't give up! A pause. Then the tug of the rope again, pulling, pulling ... more of this terrible tumbling ... Oh, Julie! You, too ... caught somewhere in this never-ending whirl. Don't give up! We haven't to give up – never – even if this is the end ... air ... horrible twists ... somersaults ... bumps ... air ... there's no stopping this whirling ... until it stops by itself ... I don't want to d ... I have to try and stop ... need air ... a kick! (another impact) ... the rope pulls onwards ... No! I won't give in. Hold on! ... Stop! ... It's stopped!

Stopped. I'm jammed between blocks of ice. The avalanche has moved on.

Sky up there. Blue. I can move, try and get up: blocks of ice near me, the rope goes straight down ... Where *is* Julie?

... There's a figure, immobile on her back, arms widespread, head downhill, sprawled on the slope below me. I cannot see her face.

Julie!

Great God, let her be alive.

I yell: 'Are you hurt?'

Seconds of eternity. Answer, please answer.

'I'm all right, but I can't move. Please help me get up.'

Her voice. Alive.

Soon I have her freed from her awkward position. The avalanche, when I came to a halt, had carried Julie on, catapulting her head over heels into the slope, where she stuck on her back. We can hardly believe we are still here ... and unhurt. When we look up, we see a vertical wall of ice, as high as a house, over which the avalanche has carried us before depositing us onto this steep slope of ice blocks. We've come down more than 150 metres over the seracs and we're incredibly lucky to be still alive. The snowfall has stopped. There's blue sky looking down on us through a hole in the clouds …

In the shelter of a huge ice tower we crouch in the snow, the events of the past minutes still etched in our faces. We are badly shaken, even if we appear to have got away unscathed. As we brew some tea, we slowly calm down. Julie is in some pain from a bruised thigh, and I have a haematoma above my left eye – small matters. I lost my snowgoggles and the avalanche pulled the gloves from Julie's hands (luckily she has spares in her rucksack), but such things do not bother us at present, when we think of what might have happened. We keep looking at each other in disbelief: here we are, both of us! If we hadn't been using the rope, we would each of us be, if not dead, on his own somewhere, without any possibility of help, and unaware whether the other was alive or not. We might never have found each other.

That was how I lost Hermann on Chogolisa in 1957. We had no rope.

'When I was lying on the slope,' I hear Julie say, 'there was only silence all around me. I couldn't see anything – my goggles were choked with snow. Then suddenly your voice asked if I was hurt, and I knew you were alive … '

Reflectively, I sip my tea from the lid of the aluminium pot and my eyes slide up from Julie, who is now also engrossed in drinking, to the ridge of the mountain …

What made me want to climb Broad Peak again – after half a lifetime?

Did I want to recapture the memories of my first summit experience in the Himalayas? Or was it simply that I wanted to see the places again, stand there, where I had been with my companion – the ridge, the face with its seracs, the high gap and the view down into China, the summit with its cornice – to see if they were still the same, or whether Broad Peak had changed over the years? Did I perhaps want to know whether I could tackle an eight-thousander at the age of fifty-two as well as I had at twenty-five …?

Or was it a totally new challenge: for Julie and me as a team of two to make a 'lightning raid' on it – to climb it again in quite a different manner?

Probably it was a combination of all these things.

While we slowly sip our tea below the huge ice tower and gradually recover our composure after our devastating adventure, in my mind images of the first ascent in 1957 dissolve into those of the present. When Julie and I, a fortnight ago, during a first push got to 7,000 metres, I suddenly found something …

A twisted, rusty piton – a piton that I recognized. A heavy piton with a ring, both of solid iron, one of those pegs which long ago in the fifties were equally good for rock and ice but which nobody uses these days. I clearly remember Hermann hammering it into the rocks here – twenty-seven years ago – for anchoring our tent at Camp 3. He was swearing, as the piton did not want to grip in the friable limestone of the rocky island which we called the Eagle's nest. Several pitons had to be used in the end. Finally, in the evening of that day, 28 May 1957, we had two tents up and our assault camp was ready for the first summit bid. Ready for the final stage of what others had so often called 'madness', the 'first eight-thousander in West Alpine style' – without high-altitude porters or oxygen respirators. A hard adventure: a true Buhl enterprise. One giant mountain and just four climbers: Hermann, Marcus Schmuck, Fritz Wintersteller and me, the 'Benjamin' of the expedition. God, what a lot we carried! But it was one of the last unclimbed eight-thousand metre peaks. A dream – my first Himalayan trip. With the great Hermann Buhl … so thin and frail he looked. But he was the idol of a whole climbing generation – not only in Germany and Austria: the whole world had been electrified when he got to the summit of Nanga Parbat on his own. At the time, that icy giant, the 'Naked Mountain', had already claimed nearly forty lives. Coming back down, he'd had to stand the whole night on a narrow ledge leaning against the rocks at 8,000 metres, a 'bivouac' few others could have withstood. Yet he made it. I still remember the famous picture: his face ravaged by sun and wind under the slouch hat, goggles pushed up onto his forehead, that staring gaze. In the forty-one hours of his summit ordeal Buhl's face had aged into that of an old, old man – it was an image that moved the world. And me with it: I worshipped him from that moment. And when, after going to one of his lectures, he wrote '*Bergheil*' on my Austrian Alpine Club membership card, I guarded it like a treasure. I was twenty-one and could never have imagined that in just four years I would be standing with him on the summit of Broad Peak watching the sun go down behind a savage sea of peaks.

When we climbed down the West Spur, I saw that face again –

haggard from the struggle of the long, steep night-time descent and his own iron determination to return to life, just as he had been on Nanga Parbat. The unforgettable face of Hermann Buhl.

Our acquaintance was far too short. We only reached this one summit together. But we had great plans for the future …

Neither of us could imagine that barely three weeks after that sunset on our eight-thousander, Hermann was to die on Chogolisa – when he simply stepped out of this world, over a cornice in a storm …

'We plan to stay on here for a while; make some excursions, perhaps do one of the other six- or seven-thousanders … ' Buhl wrote home. To me, it's as fresh as yesterday: after Broad Peak, the expedition divided – Marcus and Fritz dashed off to grab a light-weight Alpine-style ascent of a seven-thousander in the nearby Savoia group; Hermann and I – moving with just one tent, which we planned to carry with us and set up day after day – had as our target the beautiful 'roof in the sky', 7,654-metre Chogolisa.

It all seemed to work well. Our 'mobile high-altitude camp' was fine. At 6,700 metres we left the tent on the ridge and set off towards the summit. It was 27 June 1957. Hermann was in fine form and really pleased with life: climbing such a high mountain in only three days, rather than three weeks, was like a dream, even for him.

But it was to turn out very differently …

A little cloud came rolling up the slope below us. It grew larger, enveloping us, enveloping the peak. Without any warning, all hell broke loose. Grey veils of mist scurried across the ridge … We fought our way forward through clouds of blown snow, bending double to meet the fury of the gale … Yet such a deterioration in the weather seemed impossible after the glorious morning we had had.

'We must turn back at once. The storm is wiping out our tracks,' Hermann said suddenly. 'We'll end up over the cornices if we're not careful.' And he was right. Those were his last words at 7,300 metres. It was soon after that it happened.

'*Whummm!*' The noise ran through me like a shock. Everything shook and for a moment the surface of the snow seemed to sink. Terrified, I jumped out to the right.

It was the cornice breaking under Hermann Buhl. But I did not suspect that until later when he failed to join me, when I waited for him and he didn't come. I hurried back and discovered footprints, his last steps, leading to a fresh fracture line: at a bend in the ridge, he'd left the track and gone out towards the edge of the cornice …

And supposing we had been roped? Could I have held him, or would he have pulled me with him into the void?

I still do not know, and so often have thought about it. Hermann fell down the north face of Chogolisa, probably 500 metres – there was nothing to see on account of further avalanches. A later search revealed nothing. That I got down from there at all in that storm, I put down to a lucky star. And to myself – never giving up.

Hermann Buhl's face dissolves and the white roof of Chogolisa blurs into the distance: above me soars the huge ice tower, the sheer, vertical serac wall over which we have fallen. There is still a patch of blue sky above the rocky ridge of Broad Peak, but already the clouds are moving together to block it out.

Yes, I am infinitely grateful to the fate that has allowed Julie and me still to be here, sitting in the snow. It is nothing short of a miracle that we have both survived. It was the rope that prevented us from being separated by the torrent of snow …

I clasp the pot of tea in my hands, knowing that Julie and I need another lucky star to get us down to the place where I found that old piton; we have to descend at least another 400 metres across these avalanche slopes …

Julie smiles. The shock has evaporated from her face, and from the expression in her dark eyes, under her helmet I can see that she has regained her concentration. We'll need plenty of that to get down. Julie is another of those who never gives up. Otherwise we would not be here now.

WILL WE MAKE IT DOWN?

Five hundred metres below the serac zone into which the avalanche threw us, Broad Peak's hanging glacier terminates in a vertical drop. Two thousand metres further down lies the Godwin-Austen glacier. It would make no sense at all to climb down in a straight line from where we landed …

We must traverse obliquely down towards the upper end of the West Spur, which offers the only feasible descent to the glacier bed. We came up this way, along the rib of rock and ice, in a day and a half – it was the first stage of our raid on Broad Peak. Two days later we reached the summit. This, now, is the fifth day we have spent on the mountain.

Shortly after 8 A.M. Julie and I leave our spot below the ice tower.

*   *   *

In the milky light, there's a slow-moving fog above us; below, the dull blue snow slopes sometimes change to brilliant white ...

Slowly, carefully, step by step, we feel our way down. Julie says nothing about her sore thigh, but she moves a little awkwardly. Is it giving her trouble? I don't ask. We have to focus all our attention on the slope. Curving away below us, the shimmering slope is cut diagonally across by a matt strip – the trail of an avalanche; we are going to have to cross it somewhere if we want to reach the West Spur. Everything is still, now, unbelievably still – no more snow slides – it is as if Broad Peak had fallen into an enchanted sleep.

But our hearts are far from still: the menace continues to lurk above us on the summit slopes, like a monster that might wake at any moment. And you can feel the tension in those blue slopes – know that one false step can destroy its precarious harmony. For it is all steep, fresh snow.

At first I hug the edge of the serac zone as it seems safer. It is like the bank of an invisible river, which we are going to have to cross sooner or later. Julie is behind me on the rope and, like me, thrusts her axe deeply into the snow with each step. Lucky for us we did not lose our axes during the fall in the avalanche – thanks to the wrist loops. They take some of the strain of descending, and also give us at least a chance of holding one another in the event of a slip. But in these conditions, it's the whole slope that could start moving ...

'We must play it by ear. It's the best way to go in this snow: test each step; sense what is the right line of descent. The risk of the whole lot sliding away with us on it would be less if we went straight down, rather than traversing, but we have no choice – we have to traverse, we dare not lose too much height.' A dilemma. I am going to have to leave the edge of the serac zone and launch into that immense snow slope.

Cast off, then! Leave the safe shore behind.

We cross the nearby avalanche runnel, holding our breaths, and step out onto the silent billows.

I suppose two hours have passed since then. We've slipped into slow motion. Every step needs probing with our feet: deep, soft – fathomless ground it sometimes seems. This is no invisible river; this is a tilted, frozen ocean that goes on for ever ...

Only instinct can pilot you through its waves, tell you the best angle at which to cross the slope. Like mariners in slow motion, we sail the ocean of snow, and the prize to be gained is Life.

Another step.

After a while the sea starts to heave – in your mind, while you fight for balance – and as your thoughts cut free and flow into the waves of snow …

One more step into the waves. And another. Hypnotic – so much regularity in white … another step … and another … and another …

Yes, Julie, we're in our boat now – at 7,400 metres on Broad Peak, and everything is under the law of gravity. The waves … the waves … the waves … Beyond are only dreams – and yourself in the middle. In the middle it's you.

Life … these hundred thousand steps. Yes, life bounded by the law of gravity! As are these waves of snow … steps, waves, steps. Everything living!

… only dreams range free. They are like light, always floating free above. That's why we are here. Steps, waves, light, thoughts … us. The life … light and gravity. And dreams … and you and you and you, in the middle. Love. Everywhere.

Another step. Many hours. The deep yielding snow, into which you sink as if in a dream. Tiredness, exhaustion – they take over the body, penetrate the spirit. The will: pull yourself together. Onwards! Keep going!

And we do keep going – for the sake of all that constitutes life. To save that. Our dreams, as well. It is they that have brought us this far.

Is there such a thing as a sixth sense?

If so, you need it here on the avalanche slopes.

I've succeeded in forging a line across the slope so that now we are back on the route by which we came up – we struck it at the big crevasse. But now my eyes hurt from the strain: the constant concentration and all this deep snow have drained the last of my strength. It becomes increasingly difficult not to slip into apathy, not to give in to a paralysing indifference.

Behind the big crevasse I crouch down in the snow. Julie stops. 'Kurt, why don't you take my goggles? You'll end up being snow-blind otherwise.' We hadn't been able to find the spare pair after the avalanche had ripped mine from me – we must have left them up in the buried tent.

'No, I'm OK. I just want to rest a bit. It can't be much further to Camp 3, and when we get there, I'm sure we can improvise something for my eyes.' I've been breaking trail for seven hours now, maybe more. Julie's sore thigh has improved, thank God. Really, I suppose I should take her goggles, but that would leave her without; besides, a kind of torpor has engulfed me. I just want to sit.

Grey patches of cloud well up from the depths – a fog creeping over the slopes – so that we can't see a thing around us, neither summits nor glaciers, just the cotton of the clouds. The weather's miserable. Is it going to snow again? That makes me sit up: we must find Camp 3 at 7,100 metres before it's too late. 'Julie – *vorwärts!* The fog … ' More to myself, I say it.

Down and down we go. Bloody hell, not there yet? Already snowflakes are beginning to fall again. If only we could find it, the tent. Otherwise, we'll just have to sit it out in the snow in our sleeping bags, or find a crevasse, but it will be a miserable bivouac. Dig a snow hole … but which of us has the strength for that? I'm worn out, and perhaps that's why I'm hurrying so much now to get down. We must find this camp!

Julie is in better shape than I am. Since leaving the avalanche danger behind at the big crevasse, I have let go a bit. 'I want to sit down again, just for a moment … '

Fourteen hours after our narrow escape from the bivvy camp below Broad Peak's summit gap, we clamber down a wall of hard snow in the fog and make out the vague shape of the tent that constitutes Camp 3. Right up to the last moment we've been spared nothing: when, after many rests, we finally reached the right spot on the icy wall above our tent, we found we couldn't get down it for the huge amounts of fresh snow. The necessary detour drained our last reserves. But now, finally, we are safe.

Had we actually been frightened?

Certainly for some of the time, especially taking the first steps on these bottomless slopes, and when we had to cross the avalanche path, where every movement caused the snow to slide under our feet … and again, when the immense danger of our position suddenly struck home to us, and we realized how powerless we were against this mountain. But finally, you reach a state beyond fear, where you simply have to react, like a sailor, to the next wave or to the next squall striking the boat … and you alter to a sort of destiny. You don't recognize it, but still you follow it because it is your path, and because you know that only by doing all you can, will the path not be lost. You must not leave the boat.

SNOWED IN

It's as if this mountain will never let us go. Storm follows storm. Great clouds of ice crystals patter over the firn-wall onto the tent. We are so utterly relieved to have made it this far, where at least we can feel safe. Julie has just put a heaped pot of snow onto the stove and taken off her helmet, and her flattened hair frames her thin, finely cut face with the dark, expressive eyes, elegantly arched eyebrows and straight nose. She radiates strength of personality, and at the same time sensitivity. I watch her through the clouds of breath and steam as she chops up the snow in the pot with a knife, then leans her head back and closes her eyes. A sense of content- ment washes over and warms me. No longer do I feel alone, neither in my thoughts nor in what is happening here – though my companion can often be as enigmatic and changeable as the mountain itself. Familiar, reliable, dependable – yet unpredictable – perhaps that is precisely what I like about her. Against my original belief that she was Anglo-German, she is, more properly, very European: she is Spanish (which one can see from her features), but she also has German and French blood, though she was born and brought up in England. When we have a difference of opinion, which does happen, I find myself dealing with several nationalities at once! Julie opens her eyes and looks at me quizzically. Did I say something? I reach across with a conciliatory smile and a piece of snow for the pot … It took a while for us to come to a common understanding: Julie is as strong-willed as a snow leopard, and certainly has the endurance of a Sinkiang camel. For my own part, I can cope with being called the 'Ice Bear': I am every bit as persistent as she is, have equally strong convictions, can override any resist- ance on sheer obstinacy … in other words, when we do have a clash of ideas, the result is a Gordian knot of some intricacy!

Fortunately, both of us have the same positive view towards life – obstacles and difficulties are there to be overcome … thus, so far, we have always found a solution to the insoluble knot – a mutual comprehension. From the many winds that bore the love of her ancestors, Julie has inherited kindness and understanding; from the cocktail of nationalities a strong sense of justice and the will to fight for it. Not simple …

Yet there has to be somewhere, some common ground where the soluble and insoluble can meet …

One of the eight sacred emblems of Buddhism is the intricately interwoven 'Endless Knot', symbolizing the unity of all things and the illusory nature of time. It could be our sign.

Mostly, Julie and I think in completely the same way: last year the two of us carried our tent and all the gear we needed up to 8,000 metres on K2's North Spur and were poised for a summit bid when a break in the weather crushed our dream. Yet we did not give up. And what we started two years ago on Nanga Parbat, this shared and adventurous life of making films, we continued on the 'big mountain' where we founded 'the highest film team in the world': this year we shot another 9,000 metres of film there, with Julie doing the sound-recording, until eventually we had to retreat for the fifth time in one of K2's notorious storms, down the Abruzzi Ridge.

It takes an eternity to make a pot of tea. From a giant snowball you only get a thimbleful of water … your tongue is glued to the roof of your mouth before it's ready. Julie throws more chunks of snow into the billycan … that might bring it up to a third full … I close my eyes.

Again and again the summit of K2 faded into the clouds like an unattainable *fata morgana* – whenever we drew near, it vanished:

> *Going up and down, up and down. Sometimes you don't even get as far as you did the time before. You come to hate the boring, repetitious, arduous climb up, and hate even more having to come back down. But something draws you back … somehow it's part of the fascination.*

This is how Julie described the two months on the Abruzzi Ridge in our film *K2, the Elusive Summit.*

Was all this yo-yoing a reason for our 'raid' on Broad Peak? Was it becoming inevitable? Like a steel-spring which you have wound and loosened many times, until it leaps, finally, whirring out of its case?

Broad Peak was certainly a liberation for us. More than that: it was an emotional necessity. ' … All is well, we are both very fit – but there is no conclusion. We took the dramatic decision to stay on,' wrote Julie in our film log afterwards. But the film itself was not really the reason.

When it finally became apparent that nobody was going to reach the summit of K2, the international Swiss expedition, of which we were members, went home. Julie and I – a couple of die-hards –

were unwilling to accept such an ending, neither for the film nor for ourselves, and decided to stay behind to try our luck on Broad Peak. That was not even a week ago. And we had every intention, as soon as we were down again, of going back to K2 and climbing as high as possible – and not just because our cameras are still up at Camp 2 … 'Something draws you back,' Julie had said.

Thus Broad Peak gave us fulfilment – our first eight-thousander together; and it was indeed liberating after the Abruzzi Ridge. But the summit of Chogori rises high above it: a mountain on top of a mountain. This year it seems bound to remain no more than a cherished dream. Snowed in as we are, who knows how long we will be here yet …?

'Tea's ready!' Julie's voice breaks into my thoughts and I sit up with a jolt – not really possible in this cramped space. The precious pot topples off the stove. Luckily it falls into a downhill corner. I swallow dry-mouthed. That tea – I had already drunk it ten times in my mind! My tongue passes over sore, cracked lips. It is at times like this that thirst in the high camps reaches almost unbearable limits … 'It could happen to anyone,' Julie commiserates, and using some absorbent fresh snow as a sponge, calmly mops up the mess. 'Anything is possible.' She smiles.

I give her a hand. Now we have to begin all over again.

Anything is possible: that's Julie's catch-phrase. In Nanga Parbat Base Camp, she offered to shorten a pair of blue jeans which I had inherited from a French expedition and, having no needle and thread, did the job with Pakistani Airlines stickers. Very practical, Julie is, resourceful and determined. I always call this example to mind when she puts my own tolerance to the test. (I gave her a sewing kit after that, which she keeps by her like a talisman.)

Needlework is certainly not one of her strong points! On the other hand I admire her organizational skills: singlehandedly she collected together almost all the mountaineering equipment for our film expedition, the best and most lightweight available. Everything the two of us needed on the mountain…

Crystals of snow patter monotonously against the roof of the tent, like the steady rhythm of Salzburg rain; I stretch my tired limbs and listen to the hypnotic sound – it's like lying on the bank of a stream, listening to the water …

'Tea's ready!' Did I drop off? Greedily we slurp the hot liquid – taking care not to spill it this time. My eyes hurt – I hope I'm not really in for a dose of snow-blindness. Julie makes some cold compresses for me out of the used teabags. She looks anxious. It was a hard day, yesterday, no mistake – we don't say much.

Snow fizzles in the pot again; Julie has wasted no time getting a fresh brew going. 'We must drink, drink, drink.' I remind myself of the constant refrain of Urs, our expedition doctor – now on his way home. The teabags bring some relief to my closed eyelids.

Are there such things as castles in the air? For two years K2 has been 'our' mountain, even if we haven't succeeded in reaching its summit. We live with it, dream of it – it is never out of our thoughts. Certainly, we will come back another year. But will we be any luckier? And if we're not, what then? This summit is not everything. Perhaps we never will stand on top. Perhaps, for us, K2 is meant to be an everlasting castle in the air, a vision, simply *there* above the sparkling glaciers – looking down on us while we discover hidden lakes and valleys with no names, while we peer into gorges and climb higher up untouched ridges, struggle through the dust of the northern deserts, and drink from the clear springs at the mountain's foot.

Perhaps that is the way it is meant to be. After all, haven't we just been given back the gift of life? Only yesterday. And we are not down yet.

Yes – we have found a second home in the clouds. It's there, our castle, and it doesn't have to be the summit. We would never want to give up this life.

Dream mountain, K2. You can win or lose everything on a big mountain. Do we have any idea what K2 still holds in store for us? Will we hear the voice?

Anything is possible. Always.

There is no let-up to this storm, and it is still snowing. The pallid light filtering into my eyes through the violent yellow of the fabric dims as the mass of snow outside rises steadily – a dark, narrow strip creeping up the tent. On the side closest to the mountain, the weight of snow threatens to overwhelm us. Quick, out! Shovel it free! For a while it's better. Then the dark line inches its way up the tent again.

During the night, I am suddenly seized with terrible pain in my eyes. Snowblindness. Desperate, I wake up Julie, but when she turns on her torch, just for a couple of seconds, it is such absolute agony that I beg her to put it out. The irony of fate: as we grope in the rucksack, searching for eyedrops in the dark, we come across the spare goggles. We had them with us all the time. Like this, I can't possibly leave here, yet every hour that passes makes it less and less likely that we will be able to get down.

We are both silent, realization slowly dawning that soon we won't have an escape any more. Julie takes care of me, and we wait. The weather has never been so bad; never before has the mountain slammed its door on us with such decisiveness. A whole day passes. And another night. We are at the mercy of the eight-thousander. We belong to it.

I think of the summit day. When we arrived at the gap between the middle and main summits at 7,800 metres, high above us the final ridge of Broad Peak's large roof came and went through racing clouds. It was noon, and we waited for two hours, hoping for an improvement in the weather. But it didn't come. I was on the point of giving up, my feet terribly cold. We decided to go a little higher, just to get out of the wind that was funnelling through the gap.

The night before had been awful. No room and hardly any sleep in the cramped bivvy tent … but perhaps we were simply nervous. Although it is better to start high (7,600 metres), rather than from an assault camp at 7,000 metres – after our night descent in 1957, Hermann Buhl certainly thought so – the clear disadvantage is that if the weather breaks, you are trapped that much higher up. That was why we did not dare go much beyond the gap, which was already 200 metres above the high camp.

Then, suddenly, a miracle: the storm eased. We could hardly believe it; fantastic cumulus towers piled high on the Pakistani side, but over China, it was clear. Julie and I could continue towards the summit! I was full of joy and pleasure at the prospect of seeing that high place again – at least we had hope now. *Hinauf!* Up we go!

How the ridge had changed since I was here with Hermann … where in 1957 we plodded with two ski-sticks, we now had to climb along a sharp and exposed rock ridge. There was less ice every-where – in some places it had disappeared entirely. The ridge was much more difficult than it had been then. Twenty-seven years bring many changes – even to a mountain. Down at Camp 1 by the rock tooth, I had already noticed that the natural platform on which Hermann Buhl and I had pitched our tent was missing. There was another one now, a bit further away. Up here, on this serrated ridge, all the saddles and upthrusts have become more sharply incised over the years.

We approached a rounded top. It was just after five o'clock and we must now have been around 8,030 metres. Julie's face was shining with joy.

'We will be on the subsidiary summit soon … and over there is the top,' I told her. She looked surprised. Did she think we had already made it, or was she shocked at how far we still had to go? My own heart was thumping with pleasure. Over there, the shimmering triangle of Broad Peak's summit had appeared in view, just as I remembered it, just as it was all those years ago.

Another kilometre further on, perhaps … bathed in sunlight and surrounded with fairytale clouds. Julie, too, quickly realized that despite the distance, nothing was now going to stop us getting to the summit that day.

An unexpected feeling of happiness overwhelmed me. The way over the enormous roof-ridge of Broad Peak was revealed as an indescribable walk in the sky. We kept to the upper edge, towers of cloud sailing slowly past us … an ethereal shimmer in the air from millions of twinkling ice crystals, the sunlight … shining veils of fog materializing and dematerializing around us … It was summit magic. Quite different from when I was here with Hermann … but undeniably there. I felt it.

The final cornice appeared. And very close now, just beyond the last rocks on the ridge, the bright snowfield of the summit. I was surprised: from the gap to here had taken little more than three and a half hours. Despite the altitude we both felt well, and merely knowing that filled us with pleasure. That didn't mean we hadn't noticed the thin air! Nearly there at last – with one of us always sitting on a rock, looking out at the shining dance of the crystals, the slow floating of clouds … breathing deeply, while the other went to the end of the rope. It was unspeakably beautiful: to watch and breathe, to go and look … with millions of flashing seconds of ice around you. At 17.45 we reached the highest patch of snow.

Julie – our Broad Peak.

The atmosphere is unreal. Low-angled sunlight. Joy. The summit snows. This is it! Hermann Buhl … whirling crystals. Julie … dark eyes shining with tears … shimmering clouds … wonder! The Gasherbrum peaks …

Then and now. Past and present embracing in a whirl of crystals, beyond time. The magic of this mountain.

'Just the two of us,' Julie says softly. The two of us, up here.

*   *   *

'Let's go out onto the rim of the cornice and look down into China – first you, then me. We can belay with the rope.'

The view is breathtaking. The marvellous sweep of the Gasher-brum glacier, the barren, deep incision of the Shaksgam in the arid mountain wastes beyond, the countless thousand peaks of Sinkiang ... Down there, 3,000 metres below the snow at our feet, we were exploring last year. 'I can see the place the camels came to, there! By those glowing towers that look as if they should be in the Dolomites. And the great bend of the glacier that we couldn't reach because of all the ice towers in the way – that's there, look! Just below us! Goes in a different direction from what we thought, goes up between Broad Peak and the Camel-hump mountain.' Julie, above me at the edge of the cornice, points down, eyes shining ... That nameless, uninhabited land down there – how we love it, long for it. Why couldn't we go down and explore it right away? But the view alone is already a gift.

Looking back to where we have come from, we see, high above the long ridge, high above the slowly welling clouds, the huge pyramid of K2, towering into the sky. Our mountain. But when might that be?

High as the sky, the pyramid stands apart in all its crystalloid regularity, a symbol of all that is unattainable.

Nobody's mountain.

Yet wasn't it already our mountain? All those hours, two whole years ... We knew it to its highest ridges – it was ours, even if we were never to reach its top.

Would we return? It was as if it held us in thrall: Mountain of mountains – yes, we are yours. Mountain of mountains, how beautiful you are. Of course we would come back ...

We returned above the clouds, the sun very low now; we had to hurry, a night descent would not be easy. Now that we'd been to the top, tiredness and thirst invaded our minds. Still on the roof, near the subsidiary summit, I got out the stove and made a cup of Ovaltine for Julie. We sat there for some minutes, while the last light disappeared and twilight began. Then we headed down into the night.

Camp 3 above 7,000 metres. Julie and I were still snowed in, waiting. The pain in my eyes was much better. We would try to break out, down the spur, as soon as the weather gave us the chance. It was hopeless to imagine anybody coming up, there was far too much snow; there was no one on the mountain, even if there were still three expeditions waiting down at its foot.

Julie covered one of the lenses in my goggles with sticking plaster to protect the eye worst affected, but in the morning I noticed it was no longer necessary. We could start the last act of our Broad Peak odyssey, the 2,000-metre descent down the West Spur.

There were still a lot of problems in front of us, but nothing we couldn't handle: in the deep snow it took us another one and a half days to get down. On 24 July, nine days after our start for the summit, we were back among the ice towers of the Godwin-Austen glacier. Before returning to our 'mini base camp' below K2 (the whole place was ours since our expedition had left; we had just kept back two Balti porters), we allowed ourselves some time off at the foot of Broad Peak, wanting to look up friends and companions among the other teams. For two days we feasted our way through all three base camps.

WHY?

Adventure is beyond time and age.

Yet why the same mountain twice?

I remember the summit sunset with Hermann Buhl and the odyssey of the long descent with Julie. But that is not all.

Why? Because a mountain offers so much to discover, dimensions a person might otherwise never dream of.

How many times will we go to K2? Each time new facets of the crystal shine. Each step is a step into boundless possibility.

Julie says it more simply: wherever I go, anything is possible.

I say: where anything is possible, there I go.

That's why we are together.

(Written in autumn 1984)

TASHIGANG – PLACE OF HAPPINESS

In two weeks we will meet again, this time in Vienna. Our life leads us all over the place: London, Paris, Venice, Frankfurt, Munich … and the far Himalayas. It depends upon where an expedition is going, or a film is to be shot or edited – which sometimes takes several months. Last year, after taking part in an attempt on the North-East Ridge of Everest, we made a mad dash back to England via Peking and Hong Kong for a stay in Europe of only ten days – Julie wanted to organize a party for Terry's fiftieth birthday, a really big celebration. Then, with me coming from Bologna, we flew to Islamabad, and a week later were on the Diamir side of Nanga Parbat, ready to film for Lutz Maurer's TV series *Land der Berge*. But to be honest, we live this way because we like it. Neither of us suffers from any shortage of breath: in Lhasa, between us, we blew out 99 candles in one go – our birthdays are on following days in March, so we marked them together.

I used to be known as the 'cameraman of the eight-thousanders' – now we are 'the highest film team in the world' and we're kept pretty busy.

That is one side of the coin – the other is that we must always be alert to every opportunity, ready to jump in order to hang on to this insecure, adventurous existence. It is like leaping from one island to another – and we don't always make it. But perhaps it is in our characters, never to give up, either of us … And so we are content with a life that quite often becomes a dance on a tightrope.

This time the pan of destiny in which our eggs are sizzling is in Vienna – on the Küniglberg, where rises the modernist 'palace' belonging to the all-mighty Austrian Television, ORF. I regularly get lost in the galleries of this colossal building, which seem to have been designed to the harmonic principles of a superior but

'It's a crazy life, but it's a good life!'
Julie writes in a letter.

inscrutable brain. To find a way through the wildest icefall is nothing compared with finding a particular department within ORF. At least for me. Whenever I have to spend four weeks in the cutting room here, the fully air-conditioned atmosphere always fills me with a desperate urge to escape, and I dream longingly of bivouacs ... But the equable Austrian temperament can rise above even places like this – and I know several quite amiable people who work here! So the eggs of our fortunes are sizzling this time in the pan of the ORF – and the handle is held by no less a personage than the financial controller of the science division: Mr Peter 'Panhandle' (Pfannenstiel). His face has the calmness of the full moon, and his appearance is immovability itself – a quality present also in his soul. Julie and I warmed to him immediately (and it wasn't just because he approved our budget) – as we did to his boss, Dr Alfred Payrleitner, who seemed on the one hand to be an exact scientist, and on the other a winged poet, radiating optimism and confidence. As also did the friendly, round woman, with whom we used to have such nice chats over coffee. Julie and I indulged in dreams of how we would suggest lots more villages to this sympathetic trio, villages in which we wouldn't mind living and filming – in Tibet, with the Eskimos, in the jungle ... somewhere at the end of the world.

It was obvious that our first production for them had to be absolutely first class ... We invested it with all our enthusiasm.

With that alone, however, we could never have succeeded in making the film. Hildegard, one of my two daughters from my first marriage to Tona, studied ethnology in Vienna; together with Christian, a friend and colleague, she had immersed herself in the life of a Tibetan village in one of the remotest regions in the Himalayas. Its inhabitants for some unknown reason had emigrated several hundred years before from the province of Tingri and settled in the border area between Tibet, Nepal and India. Hilde and Christian spoke some Tibetan, were adopted by a family and soon learned to speak it fluently. Their life with the Tibetans and their discoveries would certainly fill a whole book on their own.

As I also knew this place – it was close to a holy mountain – we decided, the four of us, to make a documentary, in which the scientific authority came from the two ethnologists and the technical and creative film work from Julie and me. It was a very fertile union: even if the film team were not 'adopted', in the village we did belong 'to the family'. This was of inestimable value to our work, and moreover, living with Tibetans was one of the most beautiful times of our life together.

At the last moment something almost got in between. A holy place in the nearby mountains, where there was a magic rhododen-dron grove, was the site of a fertility cult – it fell also into my daughter's field of study. That must have been a special twist of destiny: I was a bit surprised when we made the first of our two journeys to Tashigang – we intended to cover all the seasons – to see that the blessing of the holy place had not passed without effect on Hildegard: I was going to be a grandfather! Austrian science however closed one eye – having regard to the future – and we rolled the cameras for the first part of the film with Christian alone. For the second part, however, Hildegard was with us very, very actively – while for two months Tona accepted the fate of grandmothers the world over: she babysat. I was in Everest Base Camp when I learned of the birth of my granddaughter Jana: we were sitting on boxes of Scottish whisky and within moments several of the bottles were on the table. With our British mountaineering friends, we raised our glasses to Jana, facing Chomolungma! So easy is it to become a grandfather!

Karen, Hildegard's sister, also studied in Vienna. She's married to a landscape architect. When I remarked to her she should take her time – and I wasn't referring to her studies – she seemed to me to be embarrassed. Moved, I stroked my grandfatherly beard. It was going to happen for the second time, obviously! This grandchild was called Rubi.

The first part of the film about the Tibetan village was in the can. Mr 'Panhandle' 's smile almost split his round face in two; he pumped our hands and sent us off with his blessing – and money – back to Tashigang. Christian had already been there for seven months … he practically lived in the village full time.

Hildegard, Julie and I picked up our luggage in Varese, Bologna, in Tunbridge Wells, in London and Vienna … we met in Munich and on a sunny March day flew to Kathmandu.

Julie and I had with us all our gear for K2. Returning home after Tashigang was going to be out of the question, timewise. We would have to go directly to Karachi, and meet there the mountaineers of Quota 8,000 – to which our enterprise was attached. Most of them we already knew from our trip to the Chinese side of K2. They were our friends from the Italian expedition to the North Spur. While we sat in the aircraft, I thought of how difficult it had been to come up

with an arrangement which made it possible for us to go back to K2
… It seemed jinxed; it simply didn't want to happen: when I heard
of an American expedition, going to the north side of K2, I was very
excited and ready to do anything they wanted! That was the place
Julie and I dreamed of …

I wrote immediately to the leader, Lance Owens. I even received a
call in reply from a mountaineer in Washington, but then it all
fizzled out. Nothing – the connection seemed broken. My letters
remained unanswered. It was a mystery. How often in life people
could spare others so much heartache simply by giving a clear 'No.'
Did they need or want a film team? Was it significant that their team
included an American woman? So far no woman had been to the
top of K2. Julie, who was so firmly against any form of competition,
would never have tried to muscle in on being first … We were just
very sad that our great hope of going back to K2 was withering from
lack of nurture. The next shock was even greater: I got to hear of an
Austrian mountain guides' expedition which had a K2 permit. Only
three of them, as I learned later, had Himalayan experience, and as
a mountain guide myself I saw an almost 100 per cent chance of
attaching myself to them in a purely nominal way. For Pakistan
rules for expeditions say that a team has to have at least four
persons, thus no two-man expedition has any choice but to attach
itself somehow or other to another.

I had made it clear to the Austrians that we would be self-
financing, that we were an independent team and wanted to remain
that way, with our own equipment, own food – everything – yes, we
even offered a free film for their lecture tours. Their answer really
shocked me: 'We don't want any stars.' That was what Hannes
Wieser told me over the telephone after first – as he said – having
discussed it with the 'powers that be'. I could not believe my ears: I
didn't see myself as a star, even after having survived thirty years in
the mountains of the world; I have never behaved like one. My only
concern was to find a way round a bureaucratic formality. It was
totally incomprehensible. But there was something which up to
then I had not appreciated: K2 had not had an Austrian ascent …
unfortunately. Perhaps that was the rabbit in the cabbage patch, as
we Austrians say!

Some friends from Poland also had permission for K2. They
would have loved to take us with them – but they needed dollars and
no film.

We spoke next to Maurice and Liliane Barrard in Paris, and they too would have welcomed us into their mini-expedition – but they were leaving so early that we could never have finished in Tashigang in time. You cannot alter the customs of a village to fit in with a film: it has to be the other way round.

Then at that critical point Renato Casarotto offered to help us out of the hole. He was prepared to let us join his expedition; he had already done the same for Mari Abrego and Josema Casimiro, another two-man team who because of the damned regulations also found themselves in need of an 'umbrella'. We knew them both very well – Basque friends from Everest 1985 – and it would have been an ideal combination. However, again it seemed that the filming of Tashigang was very difficult to fit into the same timetable … At the very last I got to know that Agostino was also going to K2 – our friend Agostino Da Polenza from Bergamo. We had been with him in China; moreover, he was going out later. Agostino absorbed us with no problems at all. Julie and I were delighted with this solution. The thing that did astonish us was that half the world seemed to be gathering on K2 this year!

Kathmandu: bad luck strikes. An apparently harmless insect bite during the airflight seems to have caused a dangerous infection and allergic reaction in Julie and her fingers are swelling. We hurry her to the Canadian hospital for treatment. The swelling goes down, but two of her fingers remain numb. This worries Julie for a while – thinking of K2. Fortunately, it later appears that the numbness is not linked to any increased sensitivity to cold, and will slowly get better. We also learned in Kathmandu that people have been dying of meningitis during the last month in the area to which we want to go, so we get ourselves vaccinated against it. Ten days later we finally reach Tashigang – and all else is forgotten.

The hills are blanketed in a thick mist of trees – black and dark green, and sometimes a shining green-yellow, according to the light that falls in this virgin forest: crimped silhouettes thrusting upwards, billowing storm clouds of twigs and leaves, strangely twisted trunks, moss-covered, often tangled together, writhing bodies with arms uplifted on which delicate lilac orchids spread out the fingers of their leaves; curtains of ropey lianas dangling almost to the ground from these strange giant shapes. Here and there appear some steep, cleared slopes, a projecting shoulder – and there, in the midst of terraced fields, one above the other like a staircase, are a few clusters of low houses, pitched roofs constructed of several layers of bamboo matting, often reaching almost to the ground. They give the impression that a party of fishermen have upturned their boats on the terraces ...

Even if the next big river in this mountain area, the Arun, is a full day's march away, there is water everywhere in Tashigang: the jungle ferns, the lichens and mosses hold it like sponges from rainfall to rainfall, and grey veils hang almost continually above the country ... 'There's water all over my tape!' complained Julie after taking her first sound recordings in the village – but laughing as she said so, because it is too beautiful here to let any worries take root. All around there is rushing water: in green gorges, from dark walls of rock, down which the waterfalls pour their white ribbons, and from the deep, brown-green valley floor. Immediately behind the small corn-store, sturdily constructed of woven bamboo and supported above the ground on long legs, in which Julie and I have made our home and stowed all our film gear, even there you have only to step around the corner between the rocks to reach a wonderfully clear stream of marvellous water. Then there are the shining red dots of sweet wild strawberries in between ...' *Phagpa-lemu*,' grins Drugpa Aba, his dark eyes regarding us benevolently from his tanned-leather Tibetan face under its shock of black hair while the fruit dissolves on our tongues ... Since Hilde and Christian were adopted here, he has been their 'brother' – and they live with him and his extended family in the house directly below our shelter. There, grandmother rules the roost – she is Drongpa Ama, which translates roughly as Mother-of-the-Household. The grandfather, a calm, still man, who – Hilde assures me – is a marvellous story-teller, lives for most of the year up in the high pastures – up at around 5,000 metres. As soon as spring comes this seventy-year-old man moves up with his herd, crossing a snow-topped mountain pass in his bare feet to get there. Sometimes his old wife pays him a visit up in the high valley. She brings 'Schnaps' and checks up whether he has made enough butter!

Drugpa Aba is their son. He has five children – but his name means Father-of-Drugpa ... referring to his firstborn, a son. Pasang-phuti Ama, Mother-of-Pasangphuti, who became his second wife after he divorced the first, is a very resolute person. Her shrill laugh penetrates the bamboo walls and is the reason we dubbed her, not very politely, the Squealer. They are all great characters here. Kaili – who Hilde calls the Merry Widow – was even responsible for Julie getting out the sewing kit and mending my shirt; she feared a

1. Was it worthwhile? Fausto back from the summit of K2.

2. A place of magic: the mighty flow of the Gasherbrum glacier. Exploring in 'Shipton's country' ...

Tibetan *Love Story* would not look so good in the film. For when I was in desperate need of running repairs, strong, good-looking Kaili – she was a real picture when I filmed her ploughing with the bullocks – heard my cry for help from two houses lower down and came running: she nodded, looked carefully at the damage and ran an experienced hand over my chest, back and arms … but then, as I said, Julie in the interest of the film came up with her sewing kit.

Unlike the ethnologists, who as a matter of principle want to live like the locals – and do – I took care to secrete into our lofty home some supplementary food, more appropriate to an Austrian mountain man (and a film-maker who has to wield his heavy Arriflex): a 'yak's' milk cheese from Kathmandu, as big as a wagonwheel, and several sides of good Austrian bacon. They are my consolation after sitting in the family circle around the fire, and out of politeness sharing with them the daily ration of millet gruel, enlivened only slightly with a few vegetables.

My idea of making them a gift of a chicken – in the hope, I have to confess, of maybe catching a wing – was gratefully accepted. For five days our millet was flavoured with chicken juice and included millimetre-long fibres of meat …

That was on the first trip. Now, on the second, like an old bear, I regularly retreat after supper to the privacy of our airy Eldorado where Julie shares my weakness for non-ethnological dishes. One day, when I appeared at the grandmother's with bacon, tuna fish and cheese for the whole family, I earned thanks but also an ethnological reproof – I was not to make a habit of it.

Well, then …

Besides the *gonden* – as the thick, sticky millet porridge is called, and which together with a few potatoes forms the staple diet – grandmother also used millet or maize to make a sour alcoholic brew, *chang*. And from this again, she distils the schnaps-like *rakshi*. It is an adventurous spectacle: a metre-high, three-storeyed still made of pots and an inverted copper cone which is filled with cold water, around which the alcoholic vapours cool and condense.

Because of the *rakshi* I filmed only one sunrise. For at first light Drugpa Aba appears at the door of the airy grain shed with the morning song on his lips. He knocks for me and pushes in the steaming cup, the size of a small soup bowl, filled with hot *rakshi*. Even if you play deaf, there's no help for you, you have to empty it: Drugpa Aba smiles, we exchange some Tibetan words, we sip the hot schnaps, Julie offers me the cup, I offer it to her, she passes it

3. Our caravan crossing the Shaksgam river. (4) Julie interviews an Uigur tribesman. (5) The incredible camels of Sinkiang, chewing calmly in a snowstorm on Aghil La – nearly as high as Mont Blanc.

back to me – and Drugpa Aba waits with the patience of an angel.
After this 'mallet-blow' you sink muzzily into your sleeping bag,
and blink finally and rather late into the sun of the new day …

What shall I tell of our film work? It was interesting and
extensive: two journeys to, and four seasons in, a paradise, which
we could grasp because we were living it, far from the clamour of
our everyday life. The only way it was possible. Here nature rules
time: the people of Sepa – as this area is called – have a hard life
certainly, but they are in perfect harmony with their surroundings.
They are a contented people. We have rarely laughed as much as
with the people of Sepa. When Julie and I were not in Tashigang,
Christian filmed events on his own – such as during the summer
monsoon – because we wanted to cover the whole year. Over the
space of three years Hilde and Christian came repeatedly to this
place for anything up to eight months at a time, either alone or
together, while they worked on their common thesis.

Phagpa-lemu, the local name for the wild strawberry, means 'pigs
– good'; however, as Hilde explained to me, it could just as well
mean 'white man – good'. Whoever has tasted the fruit of Tashigang will understand why both like them so much.

I took Hildegard up the Gran Sasso (the highest peak in the Abruzzi
Mountains) when she was only seven years old, and much later she
came with me to the Base Camp of Mount Everest, where we
climbed Island Peak (more than 6,000 metres); now my sometimes
dreamy, sometimes resolute daughter speaks fluent Tibetan as her
fourth language. The slim, blonde beauty has always had the spirit
of adventure in her blue eyes and will not allow anyone to interfere
with her plans. Tashigang has become a second home for her and
Christian – it goes far beyond work; they study the life of these
villagers and their religion which is one of the oldest of the Tibetan
people. In the village is a bearded *naksong* (one who goes in the
dark) who is in contact with the powers of nature, the spirits which
dwell in the rocks and trees, and in the water; he is also a medicine
man, healing not symptoms but the root of the disorder. There is
also the lama – he belongs to the Red hat sect, followers of the oldest
form of Buddhism in Tibet. The two men collaborate regularly – at
marriages, pilgrimages to holy places. Both are married, have
families, houses and fields. In this region you don't get monasteries
or monks and nuns.

When somebody wants to know what will happen in the future,

he asks one of the 'oracles', three old Tibetan women who live in a neighbouring village. They read your hand; or – if they fall into a trance – the spirit of a mountain or the voice of a long-dead lama may speak through them … *In the dimness of the room, firelight flickers on the face of the* lakama*; her eyes are upraised, scanning the darkness, and a strange, high, rhythmical song comes from her mouth. She starts to tremble; her arms, head, her whole body shake as the trance takes hold of her. The lama poses the questions and she answers in a weird, unearthly voice* … In these moments K2 seemed far away from Julie and me, as we from it. We both knew we would always want to come back to Tashigang. It had become a treasured part of us.

Many years ago I came under the spell of a holy place in one of the nearby high valleys, although I did not know then that it was a site of magical powers. Plagued by high-altitude cough and at the limits of my endurance, I had retreated from the final slopes of an eight-thousander to take refuge in the rhododendron forest below.

When I came to take stock, it was obvious what I should do: I had to come to terms with reality – with myself and the world. I had to give up high-altitude mountaineering. How could I have been so audacious as to tackle the fifth highest mountain in the world at the age of forty-six? And after a break of eighteen years, during which I had come to know many corners of our planet, but never once made another push up to the 8,000-metre mark?

For a week I lived alone with the blossoming rhododendrons and huge Himalayan firs in that very special place I call the Enchanted Forest. There it happened. Not only did everything suddenly become clear, the prospect of renunciation no longer gave me a pain, but I was physically restored to perfect health in a few days. Strangely, once I had surrendered to the inevitable, strength flowed back into me sufficient to tackle anything.

I went back up and climbed Makalu; a little later, that autumn, Mount Everest; and the next summer Gasherbrum II. Dedication to filming cost me some summits, it's true to say, but even so I frequently climbed really high.

Julie and I were prepared now and again to relinquish the thrill of climbing to the highest point in order that others through our films might share the experience of the wild, crystalline, stormswept world of the Himalayas.

Julie was now forty-seven – even if she looked as if she were in her thirties – and I, well … I was fifty-four. But both of us still felt really well at altitude – it was as if the mountains themselves radiated energy to us upon which we drew to spend it with them. We intended to carry on climbing the highest peaks for several years yet. Nanga Parbat still beckoned, and Julie had thoughts of Everest, too. She even tried to talk me into climbing Makalu again with her … but Tashigang gave us pause … There was our future …

To bring home images of how people lived in places like this is totally different from making a film about an expedition; certainly it holds more significance for other people. That was confirmed some time later when *Tashigang, Tibetan Village Between the Worlds of Gods and Men* won first prize at the Trento Film Festival.

But our past was slow to release us. Julie once asked the 'oracle' about Makalu (the old Tibetan was not very clear in her answer: Julie would climb very, very high, she told us), and meanwhile in the far distance K2 was waiting for us. When I spoke with Hilde again about my mystical experience under Makalu, she smiled and said that perhaps it had something to do with the *jinlab*. And then she told me what she had learned about the bountiful magic of the mountains from a Tibetan nun who lived at Rongbuk at the foot of Mount Everest.

Pelbe, the endless knot, one of the eight auspicious symbols of Buddhism. It signifies the infinite cycle of rebirth and the illusory nature of time. It is also sometimes called the life knot or love knot.

JINLAB – THE MAGIC OF THE MOUNTAINS

An extract by Hildegard Diemberger

The mountains, those bridges between heaven and earth, are the abode of the forces of fertility. To the people of Tashigang, Everest and Makalu are the Goddess Mother and the Great Father of the World. Mountains are believed to be the homes of giants and fairies – as is Nanga Parbat in Pakistan – or, as the bold granite spire of Shivling in the Garhwal in India symbolizes the lingam of Shiva. Those who live among or at the foot of mountains have always seen them as a border zone between the human world and the domain of gods. Mountains may even 'speak' to humans through the mouths of oracles.

Today they have become the target of mountaineering ventures, which often result in the defilement of sacred and secret sites – and are doubtless responsible, too, for changes in social and economic conditions, and probably for other things as well.

In the same way that each mountain has its own personality, its own emanation, so the way you perceive it depends upon who you are – be that Drugpa Aba, a farmer in Tashigang; or Sheraman Khan, a shepherd from Chanchal in Pakistan, driving his flock across flower-starred meadows at the foot of Nanga Parbat; or Sundra Nanda, spending his days as a yogi at the source of the Ganges river; or Kurt Diemberger or Benoît Chamoux, mountaineers from Europe ... you experience the mountains within your cultural horizons, and your relationship with them depends deeply upon your relationship with yourself and with the world.

Perhaps climbing a mountain is the western way of experiencing transcendence, of relating to the border zone, whether consciously by total confrontation with yourself and with what the mountain offers in the way of beauty and drama, or by unconditional surrender without asking why.

Once, in a remote Himalayan valley, we spoke of this: Anila, a cheerful and learned Tibetan nun, and me, the young ethnologist adrift between too many questions and experiences and too few answers.

It was evening … in a wooden hut: two simple plank-beds, two bowls of Tibetan butter-tea, into which we stirred a handful of tsampa *– the roasted barley flour was a present from Anila's former art master, whom we had met on our way.*

We were tired, as always when we had done a lot of walking, but the impressions of the long day would not let us sleep. Would the light plane for Kathmandu be able to take off tomorrow? Would the clouds lift? Anila took off her dark red cowl and stretching out on the planks of the bed began to tell her story.

Twenty years had passed since she was last here, in this nunnery. She had met people she had not seen for a long time, and had recognized familiar objects which whisked her thoughts back to the old days … to the years she spent in Dza Rong Phug (Rongbuk), north of Everest, when she was a young girl … and to those later years, after the Chinese occupation of Tibet, when she came to this new monastery in Nepal, Tubten Chöling.

She spoke of her studies and experiences …

After instruction from the lama in the Rong Phug monastery, she was often sent alone to one of the mountain caves that are found around 5,000 metres, where she would then spend several days practising chö *and* tsai lung.

Up there at the foot of Everest, she experienced chö *– the ritual confrontation of all that frightens you – and* tsai lung, *the control of your energy through what is known as 'the channels of wind', a form of breathing which relates to the pulse of the universe.*

Such consciousness and control over yourself and your own body allows you to develop warmth, energy, endurance, and resistance to an incredible degree – way beyond what is normally held to be possible. The aim is to dissolve all barriers between yourself and the cosmos, between one's own individual energy and the energies of the universe, to join the eternal flow … cosmos into cosmos, one into the whole, emptiness, to tap the naked power of the creative forces … lung *is the breath of life;* lung *is the wind. The numerous prayer flags flapping in the wind at monasteries and on mountain passes, at all the sacred places, are the* lung ta *– the wind horses, but also the* pneuma *of the universe, the energy of life.*

Anila was at last ready for the final test – which she passed. The one thing she particularly remembered was having to stay in an icy cave with snow all around, and a thick, wet, cloth wrapped about her naked body: she was required to dry it by using sheer body energy, produced in deep meditation and by the recitation of mantras.

Anila said: 'In Dza Rong Phug it is cold, so cold that if you don't drink your tea right away, it turns to ice. It is different from here, but oh, so beautiful! In the beginning, I found life hard – I was only twelve years old when I was accepted into the nunnery – and was very embarrassed to stand there in front of the lama with the other girls, naked but for our red meditation ribbons for holding our yoga positions. As time passed, you learned that in mystical experience, there is no place for shame. You go beyond that … '

For many generations, in remote caves, mystics have confronted the forces of life, death, and being. Around Everest and Makalu, in all the 'power places', all the be yul *(sacred hidden valleys of the Himalayas which radiate power; 'navels of the earth' … sai lhe), they have passed time in meditation.*

These mystics are the ones who exceed the limits of the normal, the conventional; they withdraw from society in order to understand the energies, to control them, in order to transcend fear and cut free from ego, to capture the deepest essence of being. It is said that they were able to cover enormous distances on foot without resting, to levitate during deep meditation – to float – and to produce incredible energy with their bodies while standing immobile for days in front of a mountain. Extraordinary accomplishments, yet only the means, side effects even, on the road to enlightenment, for all living beings.

The barleymeal in my bowl did not mix well with the butter tea; I was not too adept at preparing it, and as usual spilt most of it down the dark red skirt I was wearing. Flour-dust everywhere! Anila looked at me and laughed, then taking the bowl from my hand, with quick, deft finger movements, had it mixed in moments. 'This is the food we always take with us in Tibet,' she said, 'when we go to the mountains. It does not weigh much and provides plenty of energy … It's delicious with fresh cheese, but good without, too …' That's true – maybe being so hungry had something to do with it, but I found the mixture fantastic.

Now it was my turn to tell a story … How many adventures danced together in my mind, like a kaleidoscope: the mountains – I have never learned to know them like a dedicated mountaineer, being always more interested in the ordinary people who live here, up in the Himalayas. I have climbed sometimes, taken part in expeditions. So I have some experience of most perspectives that come together there – and sometimes clash with one another: the shepherd, the yogi, the mountaineer. They all cling to the mountain, all experience its power, its magic, can all learn fear from it. It's not by chance that the ne *– those sacred places which radiate power – are mostly to be found in hidden valleys below the magic giants. To my surprise, I found myself telling Anila all about Nanga Parbat – and my adventures with a small enthusiastic group of mountaineers enjoying a sympathetic relationship with those who lived there, the porters and high-pasture shepherds.*

Base Camp was almost part of the mountain … avalanches of powder snow silently swept the slopes above, then reared up with an enormous roar, before hissing to rest around the tents, plastering them in snow dust despite the protection of the moraine. Clouds and more clouds boiled and billowed in eternal movement as ice towers and seracs thundered one after the other over the rocky buttress at the end of the glacier – the voices of Nanga Parbat, the voices of Diamir. The 'Naked Mountain' in front of us, around us, was like a sleeping goddess – a massive and wilful deity, forcing her everlasting presence upon us. Higher up, you could catch the shimmer of her loosened icy tresses – the wide, finely fluted slopes of the Bazhin. At her feet glowed a few small red dots – our tents – one on a little rocky bank. In that one sat Benoît, a young man of singular originality, a 'child', and above him his 'beloved', Nanga Parbat – smooth of flank, naked-white, bewitched …

At the critical moment, Benoît withdrew into himself for three or four days of the hardest concentration; he was learning to know and grow intimate with the mountain and its personality, to develop the deepest possible awareness of all his actions, to control the energies of his whole body. His strict vegetarian diet was regulated to produce the highest energy at the moment when his climb demanded the greatest physical exertion. And still he remained light-hearted …

Then there was the question of selflessness, to be with and not against Nanga Parbat, to love and not seek to conquer or violate it. At eight o'clock in the evening Benoît started out – by himself, with a tiny rucksack, a flashlight, some chocolate and six pistachio nuts in his pocket. At about 8,000 metres, he met his friends on their way down; at seven o'clock in the evening, he reached the summit himself, twenty-three hours after setting off from Base Camp. It grew dark almost immediately … the flashlight failed to work, and all night long Benoît wandered around the Bazhin, lost, only finding the right way down when dawn came up. Later that same morning he was back in Base Camp – totally exhausted, but possessed with the magic of the mountain …

Anila interrupted: 'This is the jinlab *of the mountain!' she said, eagerly. 'This light, this warmth, which the mountain gives you – if you love it, offer yourself to it totally, if you "live" it deeply. Tibetans do not have a tradition of going to the tops of Himalayan mountains – except for Milarepa, he did –*

even though they seek ultimate inner enlightenment through meditation in the special power places below the mountains ...'

Yet whoever climbs high on the mountain for the merit of his soul (sem ky don), *seems to me to have some experience of the* tsai lung, *to be perhaps also akin to the person who practises* chö, *who pits himself against himself, confronts his fears and with the released energy tries to overcome the gap between 'I' and 'it', between subject and object: it is unification, becoming one with the world, with the lover, with the mountain.*

Once more I hear Anila's voice: 'If you are in harmony with yourself and with everything that you do, then you are light – your whole body is light and you can do incredible things. No doubt the reason why you actually climb mountains comes into it, too. People often go to the mountains to make a name for themselves, or to earn money out of it – but that alters everything – then you become ''heavy'' ...'

(from her diary)

RETURN TO K2

Karachi Airport, 2 A.M. on 15 May 1986: 'Agostino gave me a big hug ... and the warm greeting I got from the rest of the group made me feel I was in a big happy family.' Julie is clearly moved to be meeting our friends from the North Spur again. Three years have passed since we saw one another, but we still feel very close. We embrace. It will be great, all being together again on K2. But there are new faces, too: altogether the Quota 8,000 expedition has sixteen members – they fill a whole bus. (Quota 8,000 is a club which intends to climb all 8,000-metre peaks within the space of five years.) The atmosphere is happy and, as one would expect, noisily Italian!

A few days later we are batting along the notorious Karakoram Highway to Skardu – a 23-hour journey. And what a journey: 'The Pakistani driver disregarded potholes and corners, relying on his grip of the steering wheel to keep his seat. His unfortunate passengers were all bruised and battered by the time the journey was over, and poor Kurt had also contracted a virulent form of flu,' Julie records in her notebook of our latest film trip, as usual keeping the log for both of us. It was a bad beginning. I could hardly move my right arm and my shoulders were wracked with pain. Finally, I had to stay in bed in Skardu with a high fever. Karl Herrligkoffer, the German expedition leader and doctor, was in Skardu with a large group of mountaineers and looked after me before setting off on his walk-in. He got me more or less back on my feet, but I found the march through the Braldu Gorge, with its relentless ups and downs, such a painful struggle that Julie and I with a group of five porters dropped back to follow at our own pace, two days behind the rest of the expedition. This gave me time to recover and had the advantage of detaching us from the frantic rush to reach Base Camp.

'Part of Kurt's cure,' Julie wrote in the log, 'was to rest for an extra day at the natural hot springs just before Askole. We spent hours lying in the round rock bath tubs, with the smell of sulphur in our nostrils, gazing up at snow-covered peaks all around. This would be our last soak for at least eight weeks and it really did ease away the lingering aches and pains.'

In the meantime Hildegard had arrived back in Europe with the heavy box of exposed film from Tashigang, leaving Christian sitting up there, as usual, in 'their' village. Julie and I had yet to make the transition; that gentle Tibetan atmosphere which had absorbed us so completely lingered still. Gradually, we pulled ourselves back to our dream mountain ... a double journey back in time, Julie said, first coming back to this side of K2, and secondly renewing the friendship with our Italian companions; of the many nationalities she had met on her enterprises, she always held the Italians in special affection for their warmth and their ability to turn a group into a happy, caring family. 'It made no difference to them – or me – that I was not Italian. Nor that I was the only woman mountaineer,' she wrote.

We were still within reach of villages. Bright, shining green oases would emerge from time to time out of the barren mountains, owing their existence to near-horizontal irrigation channels, some even 1,000 metres long, testament to the many generations who had dug into the stony flanks of this narrow valley. The water comes from the mountain torrents, which find their source high in the snowfields and glaciers. Askole – at around 3,000 metres – is the last village on this difficult and sometimes dangerous approach to the Baltoro mountains. For more than one hundred kilometres you move a good deal along sandy goat-tracks, now and then passing beneath huge blocks of rock, poised in precarious equilibrium on the shifting slopes; you proceed within reach of tall walls of compacted stones, loose conglomerate, and have to traverse enormous gravel slopes which slide under your feet without warning. You have to keep your eyes open! There are icy side streams to be crossed before the final forty-kilometre stretch on the mighty Baltoro glacier. Altogether, this approach to one of the wildest corners of the world takes between ten and fourteen days.

The local Baltis can earn about £5 a day as porters, carrying loads for up to six to eight hours. Weighing 25–30 kilos each (50–60 pounds), the loads are made up of boxes, plastic drums or the duffelbags which hold the equipment and food for the walk-in. 'Their shoulders must ache where the mountaineering rope or homespun woollen twine bites through their thin cotton suits' – yet these people live on just chapatis, salt tea and sometimes a few lentils.

To get to K2 is an adventure in itself, as we knew from earlier expeditions. This time, Julie said, 'I am more scared of tripping and injuring myself on the walk-in than of the daunting prospect of climbing thousands of feet up the second highest mountain in the world.' Inexorably, our mountain of mountains draws closer ... Julie, again: '... K2! K2! echoed through my thoughts with every footstep. K2! K2! Such a stupid name for the world's second highest mountain. I pushed it out of my brain with thoughts of my family and home, half a world away, but like a repetitive marching chant, it always crept back to haunt me, just as it has done for several years ... In my case it is a passion ... many people would argue that I must be mad to love a mountain, but K2 is no ordinary peak.'

It was the most beautiful approach we had ever experienced. The five Baltis accompanying us were friendly and helpful. Now and then along the way, when we encountered over two hundred porters of a big expedition, we would be more than ever delighted with the intimate atmosphere we enjoyed by being so small a group.

When, at the wide circus that is Concordia, junction of the giant rivers of ice, we saw K2 rise in front of us, contentment descended on us both.

We were home.

THE VILLAGE ON THE MORAINE

TODAY'S CLIMBING JUNGLE: GIANT EXPEDITIONS VERSUS THE SOLO SPEED MERCHANTS

Iridescent, blue-black bodies of giant bumble-bees cluster together, wings held out stiffly. They are drinking. With them on the damp, quartz sand are over a hundred brimstone butterflies, like yachts at a regatta, their wings barely moving and mostly folded. Only now and then does one butterfly open its delicately veined, lemon wings and gently adjust its position before closing them again. Thin proboscises uncoil to dip between the tiny fragments of rock that make up the sandy bar of the river. Here and there, single much larger insects have settled, sleek as black velvet and with elegant sickle-curved wings, conspicuous by their darkness in the bright multitude. All might be exotic jungle blossoms around the river. The dense throng on the sandbank reflects the multiplicity of life in the forest beyond. And you don't think, in that moment, of the thousands that perish every time a forest giant falls to the ground, of the struggle for light, of the continuous growth and disappearance, of the birth of new species, the tenacious survival of old ones, of the balance of perpetual life which depends on, and evolves from, all this …

The island of insects on the sandbank seems a haven of contentment. They are all drinking.

Base Camp at the foot of K2 was on the moraine, a long, curving sandbank in the kilometre-wide bed of the Godwin-Austen glacier, at a height of 5,000 metres; and by its very altitude alone had nothing in common with swarming butterflies on an Orinoco sandbank in the Venezuelan jungle. Yet the gaudy tents shone happily among the rubble of the moraine, grouped in patterns of colour according to the expedition to which they belonged – as if different types of butterflies had lighted together on a favoured spot. The silent, crystal mountain world beamed its influence over the camp, just as the jungle held thrall over the sandy islet in the river.

It, too, appeared a haven of contentment: from tent to tent, mountaineers of different nationality invited each other to tea, were ready to offer assistance. They sat together, exchanging stories, drinking. Everything had changed in the thirty years since Hermann Buhl and I made our lonely way up here. But the convivial picture on the moraine concealed deep division between opposing and conflicting styles of expedition. All were represented, from the classic to the most modern. People whose views on how to tackle a big mountain were at complete variance had come together: climbers with opposing ideas on strategy, risk and safety, climbers of varying degrees of 'hardness' and experience, according to their background and how they perceive the mountain scene. To call modern mountaineering a 'jungle' is not, I am convinced, over-stating the sort of thing that is now happening in the Himalayas.

Will it ever find a natural balance? It is impossible to predict

Expedition trash on the Baltoro glacier. The Mountain Wilderness Movement, since its foundation in 1987 in Biella, has been active in the search for solutions to protect the mountain environment.

because the situation itself is an artificial one. People who don't like to delve too deeply into the causes of problems believe it can all be resolved through fraternal equability. But things are not usually that simple … especially once you are on the mountain itself. Apart from the camaraderie engendered at Base Camp, there are few positive aspects to several expeditions sharing the same route.

It is only when climbers come to recognize the dangers inherent in too much togetherness – and to face them openly and with courage – that they will be able to drink their tea together as real companions, and not as victims of an illusion.

Even in 1979 when I went to Gasherbrum II, the sublime isolation of the Baltoro was already over: about a dozen expeditions gradually gathered at the foot of the big mountains. We visited one another from mountain to mountain, base camp to base camp, exchanging invitations to share Tyrolean bacon dumplings, Japanese fish, French delicacies, Spanish ham and red wine. The Baltoro had changed, but in a friendly way. Yet those who had known it in its pristine loveliness could not but help feel a little sad.

In 1984, when I returned again, twelve expeditions were to be found on just one of those mountains: Broad Peak. How astonished Hermann Buhl would have been to see his West Spur now: tents all over the place, and fixed ropes, too – and not just to safeguard the extremely steep and sheer ice wall, as we had them in 1957. The route itself had changed substantially and a good deal of the West Spur was laced with fixed belays …

You couldn't rely on them, however. Even first-class mountaineers like Peter Habeler and Wojciech Kurtyka nearly came to grief when old fixed ropes gave way or anchors pulled out. On the other hand, the large number of climbers on the mountain provided an illusion of greater safety. Some felt it safe to wait in an improvised bivouac above the gap at 7,800 metres, only to finish up with heavy frostbite. Broad Peak, though technically not a difficult mountain, had by no means become a safe one.

And the fact that it was *said* to be easy could well have had something to do with that.

Could a similar situation develop on K2? The multicoloured dots of the extended tent village, the island of butterflies, reminded me of the series of base camps at the foot of Broad Peak in 1984. But K2 was infinitely more difficult – and so much higher. A mountain on top of a mountain … What would happen? Most of the mountaineers were optimistic – the colourful Base Camp was a friendly, hospitable place to be in, never boring. It had its own, very positive, atmosphere.

We are sitting with the Casarottos – Renato, tall as a tree, and Goretta, his graceful wife – in their spacious grey-blue frame-tent. It is as large as a room and in the corner houses another, smaller tent, a shining red triangle – their bedroom. Along one of the walls stands a row of plastic drums full of gear and food. There is still space enough to sit comfortably in one corner and enjoy Goretta's home-baked cake (quite extraordinary at this height of about 5,000 metres). Renato talks of his past and why he has come to K2 this summer. He is among the world's best mountaineers, one of his famous first ascents being that of the difficult northern summit of Broad Peak in 1983, which he climbed solo. He has been to K2 before – in 1979 when he took part in an expedition led by Reinhold Messner. The very imaginative route they chose then followed first the SSW ridge, then ran up higher to the right. It had been 'discovered' by Messner, and christened by him the 'Magic Line'. For various reasons, however, and much against Renato's will, the expedition subsequently switched attention to the Abruzzi Ridge, by which Reinhold Messner and Michl Dacher finally made it to the summit. Renato, for whom the abandoned SSW Ridge remained the real goal, always felt there was an old score to settle: he wanted to climb it solo. But now he was faced with having to share the route not only with the Italians of Quota 8,000 and an American expedition which had diverted from its original objective, but also – last but not least – with a Polish expedition, expected shortly. For a soloist, the prospect of so many others moving up and down 'his' route was very frustrating – despite the fact he was on good terms with everyone involved, and that some of the climbers were friends of his. (This is where the image of the jungle leaps so vividly to mind: lianas fighting their way up a jungle tree, clinging to the trunk and to each other, obliviously.)

It is clear that two big groups working together can proceed more quickly and with less outlay than if they went independently. The practical advantage of such a joint enterprise is also felt by anyone who later follows the same route, for the fixed ropes are rarely, if ever, removed. Whoever comes afterwards will at any rate find pitons in place and tent platforms left by his predecessors. You could say that the first ascent of the route results from the 'collaboration' of everyone who has ever been on it. Some people accept this combined system happily enough – others despise it and prefer to tackle unsullied mountains on their own; reality hardly ever satisfies everyone's expectations!

Similar problems and developments of routes can be found time and again in the history of the first major ascents in the Alps.

In 1979 a French team spent four months on the SSW Ridge and came very close to the summit. They failed by about 200 metres. In its upper section their route did not follow the 'Magic Line', going to the left of it – but all the same, the name stuck in the minds of many mountaineers.

Certainly, the position Renato found himself in on the overcrowded ridge held little attraction for him as a solo climber.

There was another party, too, which was not at all enthusiastic to find other people on 'its' route; this was the Austrian expedition which arrived later than most of the others. These climbers actually thought they would have the Abruzzi Ridge to themselves, and were amazed to see the huge village of tents at the foot of K2. Their first reaction was to stake out a perimeter fence, in the form of a light blue climbing rope, all around their patch, like a prospector's claim. The message was that everyone else should keep out. Other villagers watched with secret delight …

However, the Austrian soul is quite adaptable. Soon Julie and the rebuffed 'star' Diemberger stepped over the blue line, bringing a guitar, and in a matter of minutes we were all sitting round, singing and drinking beer. And I let some of the young ones know how lonely and beautiful it had been here in the 'good old days'.

Austrian yodellers are an attraction all over the world. Immediately we were joined by the dark, stocky South Koreans (who also held a permit for the Abruzzi). Though they were shy at first, I managed to encourage them to some tentative yodelling – an Austro-Korean mixture is pretty exotic.

With nineteen members, the Koreans were the largest expedition in the place. They, too, came a little later than the rest, at the beginning of the fourth week of June. They put up a lot of tents, had high-altitude porters and intended to climb with oxygen. To our eyes, they were the epitome of the big classic expedition to an eight-thousander. At the same time, however, they were fully equipped with modern gear – not for nothing do the big sports equipment specialists from all over the world get their goods manufactured cheaply in Korea. Solar batteries fed three video cameras, which were operated by a TV crew from Seoul. You could even 'go to the cinema' in the Korean quarter: they showed films of the history of K2 climbs and attempts, and later put on the James Bond movie, *Diamonds are Forever*. There was even an 'adult documentary' from California! The Koreans generously took their show on tour, moving up and down the moraine, from camp to camp – to see James Bond people even came down from the British Base Camp a quarter of an hour away at the edge of the Savoia glacier, starting point for the North-West Ridge. If you spend two or three months in rock and ice, entertainment is always welcome. With increasing frequency, Alan Rouse, Jim Curran, the Burgess twins and other British climbers would come over from their splendid isolation behind the Gilkey Memorial to visit the rest of us on what they called 'The Strip'. Did they, I wonder, see anything there to remind them of Las Vegas besides the bright lights and colours?

Up to this point there had been no bad incidents, apart from when an Italian journalist, who wanted to take pictures of K2 from the Windy Gap, fell into a crevasse while wearing skis. He jammed on a bridge only five metres down. But he certainly had strong nerves: before he let Julie and me haul him out, he sent up a camera for us to take several pictures of him in his hole. 'After all,' he said enthusiastically, 'an occasion like this doesn't come along very often in life.'

All in all, there were fourteen different undertakings represented on K2 that season. Ten were expeditions: the Franco-international team of Maurice Barrard on the Abruzzi, as well as the Austrians and Koreans; Quota 8,000 had also paid for the Abruzzi Ridge along with the SSW Ridge; Renato Casarotto's solo attempt was destined for the SSW Ridge as well, as were American and Polish expeditions. Then there were the British on the North-West Ridge, and Herrligkoffer's international expedition, which was aiming for the South Face – all of these on the Pakistani side of K2! Only one expedition, the American, attempted K2 from the Chinese side.

In addition, there were three small independently operating teams on the Abruzzi: the two Basques, Julie and myself, and two Swiss, Fuster and Zemp. The latter really belonged to Herrligkoffer's expedition, but had decided to try the Abruzzi even though their permit did not allow them to. (They were not the only ones asked to pay a retrospective fee of 45,000 rupees in Islamabad!) Finally, there was the Yugoslav soloist, Tomo Cesen, who opted on

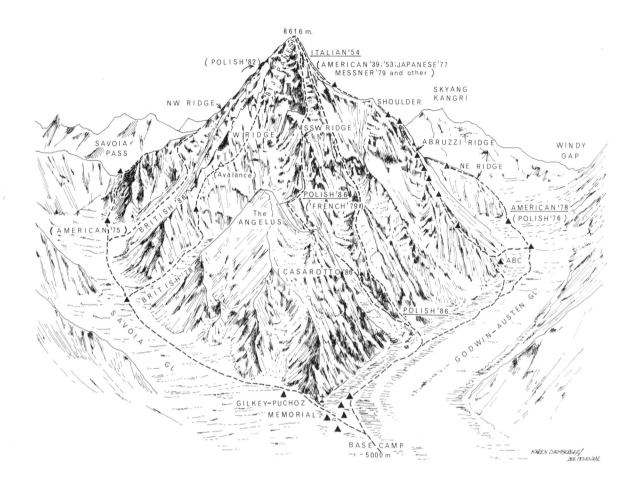

8616 m.

(POLISH '82)   ITALIAN '54
               (AMERICAN '39, '53, JAPANESE '77
                 MESSNER '79 and other)

                                    SKYANG
                                    KANGRI

NW RIDGE   SHOULDER

SAVOIA   SSW RIDGE   ABRUZZI RIDGE   WINDY
 PASS   GAP
           W RIDGE   NE RIDGE
         (Avalance)

                                    POLISH '86
                                    (FRENCH '79)

           The   AMERICAN '78
         ANGELUS   (POLISH '76)

(AMERICAN '75)

BRITISH '86   ABC

BRITISH '78   (CASAROTTO '86)

SAVOIA   POLISH '86   GODWIN-AUSTEN GL.

   GL.

                                                   GODWIN-AUSTEN GL.

GILKEY-PUCHOZ
  MEMORIAL

                 BASE CAMP
                  ~5000 m   KAREN DIEMBERGER /
                                                 DEE MOLENAAR

K2 from the South West (expeditions which reached the summit as first ascents are underlined).

sight to attempt a bold new route to the Shoulder – and succeeded.

It is understandable that the Ministry of Tourism, faced with such a massive demand for permits (between a third and a half seek to climb 8,000-metre peaks), some years ago formulated strict rules and regulations for expeditions, in order to exercise control over the situation in conjunction with their liaison officers. However, some of these regulations seem to have been drafted on a 'green' table, as we say in Austria – that is, theoretically, with little regard to practicalities; others (really useful ones for the protection of wildlife and the environment) are very often only half-heartedly insisted upon, or neglected. The legal ramifications of this often yield strange fruit.

Take the case of the German encampment on the moraine, which found itself unintentionally breaking the rules. This group of tents served as Base Camp for K2, while one hour away, at the foot of Broad Peak, Dr Karl Maria Herrligkoffer had his main Base Camp, for the expedition held permits for both peaks. Under the terms of the rules, however, only one base camp is allowed per expedition! Their Pakistani liaison officer was very firm on that. It seemed insoluble – and then, Eureka! a way out suggested itself. The Base Camp for K2 could simply be officially renamed Camp I – whereupon the problem vanished! The tents were no longer 'unlawful'. Even on the Baltoro glacier you can meet the galloping horse of bureaucracy!

Outside the Germans' large and comfortable mess tent, where we sometimes sat to enjoy fantastic dumplings, sauerkraut and delicious stewed bilberries, was parked a symbol of German efficiency, a special 'bicycle' – an ergometer. You could adjust it so that it required more or less energy to operate and then pedal away to your heart's content. It was one of Herrligkoffer's favourite toys – and I knew it of old. In 1978 the same machine had stood at 5,300 metres at the foot of Everest; good old Karl even allowed me a go on it – as an experiment. I see the eyes of doctors shine!

Even if you never caught him on the bicycle, present in this camp was the man who was without doubt the strongest on the Himalayan climbing scene: Jerzy Kukuczka. With his Polish ropemate Tadeusz Piotrowski, he was part of the international German expedition. In the race to be the first to climb all the eight-thousanders, Jurek, as he was known, was close on the heels of the great Reinhold; and even if each of them made out there was no competition, it was far from certain at that time which of the two would pull it off first. (Reinhold Messner completed all fourteen that autumn, 1986; Kukuczka made it about a year later.)

This friendly, rather silent Pole, with the fresh face of a country boy and clear eyes that reflected calm and circumspection, had a very special objective on K2: the unclimbed Direttissima, or Central Rib, on the South Face. His partner in this ambitious enterprise, the bearded Tadeusz Piotrowski, was even quieter, as silent as K2 itself: he was, as we say in Austria, a rock of a man, one of the best Polish winter-mountaineers, and quite imperturbable. Although the pair had for the moment the nominal support of the two Swiss, a German and 'Little Karim' (there has even been a film made about that legendary Hunza!), no one in Base Camp was under any illusions but that it would be the two Poles, on their own, who would solve the real problems of the route – and in pure Alpine style. Giant seracs threatened the central part of the route with falling ice and after that the angle became breathtakingly steep, up combined rock and ice, and leading directly to the 'exit' originally projected for the Magic Line, where icy couloirs and rust-coloured barriers of rock barred the way. 'A mousetrap, that exit, if the weather breaks,' commented that old fox of the Himalayas, Norman Dyhrenfurth. Yes, Norman! Such a pleasure to meet him again. We both 'live' in Salzburg, yet travel so much that we never see one another there. We went to Dhaulagiri together in 1960, when Norman shot the expedition film to which I contributed the summit sequences. It was an adventurous trip, in the course of which a ski-plane was used for the first time high in the Himalayas, to land supplies and people on the North East Col of Dhaulagiri. Ernst Saxer and Emil Wick successfully made the highest glacier landing of the world (at about 6,000 metres, according to the latest measurements). Not long after that, however, the aeroplane crashed, although luckily both pilots survived. Despite the resultant chaos, eight of us managed to reach the summit. At the time, this first ascent might well have been the highest without using oxygen (but we cannot know for sure, without knowing the full story of what happened to Mallory and Irvine on Everest).

This time Norman was filming the Herrligkoffer expedition. He was in good company. There were about a dozen cameramen and assistants at the foot of the mountain covering the various expeditions. Higher up, however, on the mountain, there were but few!

The strenuous and dangerous business of filming at high altitude requires not only considerable dedication, but also a special way of thinking and behaving that is not found in many mountaineers. You need to be able to withstand storms for longer, have a higher number of depots, and be prepared to move less hurriedly, with extreme patience and strength. You could compare it to being a sailor: you cannot leave the boat when the fun stops. To be creative when climbing a mountain needs a style of its own.

This is why Julie and I, while belonging to the Quota 8,000 expedition, have been granted total independence. Our goal is to climb K2 by the Abruzzi Ridge, and to make a film of the various aspects involved when so many expeditions jostle together on a mountain. Of course, our own climb will be part of it, as will the history of the mountain. Quota 8,000, on the other hand, has no other thought but to go all out for the SSW Ridge. At least, for the time being it hasn't.

Meanwhile, we are treated to a diversionary sensation: the young Frenchman Benoît Chamoux, who is also a member of our expedition, climbs Broad Peak in a single day. He is not the first to do so: the Pole Wielicki did the same in 1984. Julie and I were on the mountain when his team broke the trail. (There is no other way for such speed records: the 'mountain sprinter' can obviously carry hardly anything. Trailbreaking, high camps and back-up in the case of weather breakdown – all these are in the hands of the collaborating team ahead of him.) Nevertheless, it is an enormous sporting achievement.

Opinions differ over its relevance from a mountaineering point of view. An ascent like this can never, for instance, be compared with Reinhold Messner's solo climb of a new route up the Diamir Face of Nanga Parbat, nor indeed with Renato Casarotto's fiercely persistent, months-long struggle for the SSW Ridge of K2. The unladen sprinter follows a route prepared by mountaineers who without doubt did carry loads and therefore in all probability employed fixed ropes as well; for him the route is a measured race track, an uphill obstacle course. Freed of route-finding and weight-carrying, he can concentrate all his energies into finding his own most effective rhythm for optimal performance. Certainly it's adventurous, but it has little in common with mountaineering. At the same time, it can't be ignored that this obsessive preoccupation with speed for its own sake rubs off on everything else.

Benoît returned safely from his adventure, thinner than ever (if that is possible), and with his face alight with joy. The first thing he wanted was his picture taken with the Grandfather of Broad Peak! Of course, he got it. And the point I really want to make is that he never once lorded it over the rest of the team. Later, he produced an even more astonishing performance: he climbed K2 in similar manner by the Abruzzi Ridge, again in a single day. Not bad, for a scrap of a boy! I know other top mountaineers who are, like him, vegetarian. I go in for muesli myself, but I also pack my solid smoked bacon, my *Bresaola* (air-dried meat) and a block of hard Parmesan cheese, then I know I have the best basis to keep me in altitude trim. Mountain ibexes may live solely on grass, but the snow leopard – which has been seen as high as 6,000 metres – certainly doesn't go around just eating potatoes. Both ways of life have proved efficient at altitude, nutritionally.

What I find really remarkable are the incredible lengths to which Benoît will go to realize his ambitions. Sheer precision sets our youngest 'bloom' in the expedition jungle apart from many of his counterparts. He never improvises. The currently widely-held attitude, 'We'll make it – somehow' – whether in reference to acclimatization or to preparation for an ascent – is dangerous and hard to stop. So often climbers discuss different styles – whether to climb with or without oxygen, to go on big or small expeditions, take or reject high-altitude porters – ignoring the fact that all these styles work if they are properly applied. But if the attention to detail is not there, a lot will be in the hands of chance.

The Pakistani liaison officers in our 'township' may have felt this – regularly they all met together with their highest ranking officer, a major. And the expedition leaders? They can solve problems of collaboration and logistics on the mountain by discussion and consensus. Did they always? Sufficiently? Certainly everyone had the best intentions … but a critical eye on the strategies applied in 1986 would discover more than one 'black hole', and the close proximity of different enterprises will always mean extra risk, however positive the human dimension. That was one of the lessons of this summer on K2.

Taking a stroll along the moraine – it is quite impossible to film for longer than an hour at a time – it was interesting to listen to the opinions of the medical doctors. That they can never agree I know from many expeditions. One thing is sure: back in 1957 (and later) we all regularly took Vitamin B12 for a fast increase of red blood cells, important for the transport of oxygen around the body; but now this has been discontinued because the blood becomes too thick, the haematocrit rises, and with it the danger of frostbite. Nowadays, the view is that it is better to give Vitamin E. Dilution of the blood, which about ten years ago was thought to be the key for better eight-thousander climbing, is no longer taken seriously by anyone: a French doctor once assured me that it was much too dangerous and would need a hospital on site to make sure it was done safely. And as for wonder drugs like Diamox, designed to speed up acclimatization and guard against mountain sickness, there was almost unanimous agreement at a recent medical congress in London that it would be unwise to take it if you had already had any degree of acclimatization. For then you would be likely to fall sick and become subject to a kind of over-acclimatization. The mountain doctor, Urs Wiget, told me that in case of a wrong diagnosis of oedema, taking a diuretic (which is what this is) could rob the body of precious liquid, already seriously diminished at altitude. This could so easily prove fatal to someone whose blood was already thicker than normal. I feel an obligation at least to warn against the thoughtless consumption of pills which a well-meaning friend might pull out of his pocket at 8,000 metres. That goes for all sorts of medicine – you should only ever take drugs under the direction of a doctor.

Once on Dhaulagiri, after taking some preparation to increase circulation, all of us felt the benefit of really warm feet, but in exchange, our fitness had totally gone. And I missed out on the summit of Nanga Parbat when in the dark I took some pills in mistake for aspirin. I cannot speak for medical science, but it is clear that how a person reacts at 8,000 metres and how much a body can endure, are still imperfectly known. In my opinion, medicines should only be taken at altitude if there is no other alternative, and above all, only for getting *down*, not up.

Acclimatization is of supreme importance. This takes at least three weeks for an eight-thousander. But let us hear what a well-known mountain doctor has to say on the subject …

THREATS POSED TO HEALTH BY HIGH ALTITUDE

by Franz Berghold

Even if the human body is not fundamentally equipped for living and mountaineering at extreme heights, it can adapt astonishingly well and even accomplish remarkable physical performances – so long as one follows the 'rules of the game' governing climbing (and staying at) high altitude. But what happens in those cases where such adaptation cannot be achieved?

It is necessary to distinguish between direct and indirect damage or disturbance to a person's health.

A variety of disturbances that are collectively known as acute mountain sickness result directly from difficulties in adapting to the decreasing amount of oxygen which can be absorbed through respiration as one goes higher. In extreme cases a person may develop the very serious high-altitude pulmonary oedema (HAPE) or high-altitude cerebral oedema (HACE). Pulmonary oedema occurs most frequently between 3,500 and 5,000 metres; fluid from the tissues seeps into the lungs, from which a characteristic gurgling sound can be noticed; at the same time, the victim is desperately gasping for air, has difficulty remaining upright and becomes increasingly confused and unable to understand conversation. Swift transport to a lower altitude usually produces dramatic improvement.

Cerebral oedema, on the other hand, is usually met at very extreme altitude. It is characterized by dullness or lethargy, impaired co-ordination, confusion and ultimately unconsciousness. Unfortunately, even a rapid descent to lower altitude may not lead to improvement. This condition occurs less frequently than high-altitude pulmonary oedema, but is more likely to prove fatal. The immediate causes of both these high-altitude oedema conditions are so far improperly known, and no really convincing drug therapy exists. For instance, a doctor treating high-altitude pulmonary oedema in the same way as he would treat pulmonary oedema which has occurred in connection with other illnesses may find that not only does the patient not improve as normal, he may even get alarmingly worse.

Fortunately, however, and contrary to widespread belief, high-altitude pulmonary and cerebral oedema are not common. Much more frequent are several dangerous indirect disturbances, about which far too little is known and which are far too little taken into account. One is the inevitable and enormous loss of fluid from the body during high-altitude climbing, which poses a significantly greater threat than the lack of oxygen itself. By perspiration and, above all, by respiration, the body loses several litres of liquid per day; the consequence is an increasing thickening of the blood which can lead in turn to a series of extremely dangerous effects. I will list only the most frequent: strokes, pulmonary embolism/thrombosis, acute heart failure. At altitude, deaths from these causes occur more frequently than those from the better-known HAPE or HACE.

High-altitude deterioration, the slow 'dying' of the body at altitude, also probably derives primarily from an increased loss of fluid, even when in connection with persistent oxygen deficiency. There is no total agreement about this among specialists, but one thing is now clear: at extreme high altitude, the main cause of severe and fatal disturbances to health stem from the loss of liquid from the body. And it is a vicious circle: the increasing density of the blood due to fluid-loss slows down the delivery of oxygen to the body's cells. The lack of oxygen, already felt as a result of altitude, is made thereby worse. Yet oxygen is absolutely essential to all performance.

Lack of oxygen coupled with increasing density of the blood results more than anything in a dangerous decrease in efficiency. This affects not only the muscles but above all – and this is generally not given enough attention – it affects mental performance. *The significantly* high accident risk at extreme altitude *(on the highest peaks of the world, nine times more people die from accidents than from altitude sickness)* is more than likely due to the fact that at extreme heights the brain – *in comparison to the muscles – is relatively poorly supplied with oxygen. This could explain why high-altitude climbers often perform irrational acts, make wildly inaccurate estimates and take alpinistic decisions that, lower down, would cause any mountaineer to shake his head. It goes without saying, therefore, that the risk of accident rises enormously, out of all proportion to the objective circumstances, extreme as these may be.*

Finally, a brief mention of some of the relatively harmless disturbances that can be experienced at great height: peripheral oedema *(fluid retention, causing swelling of an arm, a leg or the face, usually noticed on waking),* retinal haemorrhage, disturbed breathing patterns during sleep. *'Harmless' in this context means 'not posing an immediate threat'. Such symptoms should at any rate be considered a warning that the sufferer is having difficulties adapting to high altitude. You cannot die from*

*sub-cutaneous oedema, nor from disturbed breathing at night, however
dramatic they may appear, nor do retinal haemorrhages presage blindness,
but people affected by these conditions should watch out that they do not
later run into far more serious problems, such as outlined above.*

*More details on this subject can be obtained from Dr Charles Clarke at the
Mountain Medicine Data Centre, St Bartholomew's Hospital, London EC1,
or from the following books:*
Medical Handbook for Mountaineers *by Peter Steele (Constable, 1988)*
Going Higher, the Story of Man and Altitude, *by Charles S. Houston
(American Alpine Club, 1988).*
High Altitude and Man *by John B. West and Sukhamay Lahiri
(American Physiological Society, 1984)*
High Altitude Medicine and Physiology *by Michael Ward, James
Milledge and John West (Chapman and Hall, 1989)*

But back to 'natural medicine':* remembering Hermann Buhl's
'sleeping draught', three weeks ago Julie and I mixed sugar and
glacier water into the beer kit we had brought from England, and put
the 24-litre barrel to ferment in the warmest place we could find –
the Italian mess tent, a giant red and blue dome in which twenty
people can sit together. We have three of these huge dome-tents
with 'street lighting' in between – quite apart from the electric light
inside the tents – all fed by silvery, shimmering solar cells. Then,
like a row of small condominiums, come the colourful, peaked,
individual tents of the Italians. It's all a bit too loud for Julie and me
– we kept catching snatches of voices from Bergamo, Milan or
Genoa on our tapes – so that we have set our tent some distance
away on top of a conical moraine hill, with a wonderful view (day
and night) over the Quota 8,000 centre, for all the world like a space
station on Mars. Of course the electric extension cable was not long
enough to reach us, and we have to make do with candlelight – but
no matter.

The black barrel incubating our beer is a source of great interest to
the whole village. Time and again someone will come, talk about
the weather, K2 and the route – and then, casting an innocent glance
in the direction of the barrel, enquire on the state of the brew. Willi
Bauer insists on regular tastings to monitor its progress, so that we
assume he must have been a food chemist in some other incar-
nation. Finally, our beer is ready and turns out to be a foaming,
overwhelming success. From as far away as Chogolisa, people

arrive to talk about the weather … A good thing Julie brought along a second beer kit. We have enough time for another fermentation.

Sometimes, when I am sitting on top of the moraine hill at my tripod waiting for avalanche shots or taking long-lens views of camp life, I will notice that Julie is missing. Then I know that she has either walked over to the ice towers with her Japanese sword, to practise or to meditate, or wandered across to pass the time of day with Norman Dyhrenfurth, the old film-maker, whose stories of storms, Himalayan attempts, the search for the yeti, and many other adventures she enjoys so much. Norman is pleased to be visited by such an almost perennially cheerful butterfly, before she flutters on to see Goretta and Renato, or Mari and Josema – our Basque friends from Everest – or, helpful as always, gives some tips on sync-sound filming to the Italian cameraman who has not yet mastered it. Except for when aikido or budo draws her to the ice towers and the marvellous glacier tables, she is never gone for long. We'll meet sooner or later somewhere among the tents on the moraine. But if she takes the long Japanese sword and crosses the glacier stream in order to meditate, to sink into the core of her being amidst the icy landscape – or to perform the difficult, exacting martial arts moves – a ritualistic exchange with an invisible opponent – then I always leave her alone, I do not enter her circle.

Only once did she take me along.

'I have two passions,' she used to say. 'Mountains and the martial arts.'

It was good to be with her.

SUCCESS AND TRAGEDY – RUSSIAN ROULETTE?

If I did not think so much, study and plan the climb so carefully, I would have been dead long ago.
(Tomo Cesen, in Trento, 1990, after his successful solo ascent of Lhotse South Face)

Seen from some angles, the contours of K2 exhibit the perfect harmony of a triangle with the dimensions of the 'golden section'. From above, it demonstrates the amazing symmetry of a cut diamond. Perhaps, indeed, one should call it the Himalayan Koh-i-noor after the celebrated diamond, the 'mountain of light', which similarly has been an instrument of fortune and disaster.

From a geographical point of view, the mountain rises from the centre of the highest mountain masses of Asia, and when you look on a map, the display of its ridges and spurs and ribs reminds you of nothing so much as a compass rose.

On 20 June the weather is beautiful and Julie and I sit looking out from our tent at Camp 1 at 6,150 metres on the South-East Rib, the steep Abruzzi Ridge. 'Good luck! All the best for the summit!' we shout after Mari and Josema, our Basque friends, as they set off up into the snow and stone desert of the wide ridge with slow, measured steps and bent under the weight of their enormous packs. They are carrying everything they need for an ascent of K2. It is an emotional moment. Julie and I originally hoped to go with them, and in our imaginations picture ourselves flanking our friends as they climb higher, fired by the same irresistible urge to stand on top of this mountain, the siren call which overrides all the stresses and struggles involved. What is it that makes us like this – have we been bewitched by the shimmer of the great crystal? Are we caught in its spell? Or are we simply happy in what we're doing? Why do people call this the mountain of mountains? Nobody can really explain, but Julie and I are not the only ones to have felt its pull ... this inexplicable lure which keeps drawing us back.

We are a little sad, as we watch our friends dwindling away in the wilderness of rust-coloured rocks and towers above us. It's a shame not to be with them, especially as we share the same style and attitude towards climbing, but we arrived at Base Camp three weeks later than Mari and Josema, and are still insufficiently acclimatized. You need to build up to climbing at high altitude.

The view from here over the endless parallel ribbons which overlay the Karakoram glaciers, following their gentle curves and giving them their characteristic, regular pattern, is overwhelming – and as familiar to us now as if we had always lived here. Two years ago we clambered up and down this spur so many times; and close by, we climbed our first eight-thousander together – there it stands, now, just in front of us. Yes, we are perfectly at home here. Yet we have to prepare for our ascent, have to establish points of support – supply depots, which we must keep pushing higher and higher and eventually turn into camps – before we dare venture beyond the 8,000-metre line. Our eyes continue to follow the two bowed figures … are Mari and Josema embarking on one of the great days of their lives? Will they achieve their dream? And will they come back safely? We wish it from the bottom of our hearts.

Higher on the spur, a group of four are moving up together: Maurice and Liliane Barrard, Wanda Rutkiewicz and Michel Parmentier. They were the first this year to get started on the SE route. How long will they take? No new ropes have been fixed on the Abruzzi yet, and the old ones – if they are usable at all – will mostly be buried under snow. An ascent now, the way our friends are doing it, will be more or less in West Alpine style – even here. The effort required is infinitely greater than later on in the season when a big expedition will have newly roped the bulk of the spur. Then, even if climbing without the help of porters or the use of bottled oxygen, the Alpine-style ascent only really starts below the mighty shoulder of K2, beyond Camp 3. Julie and I have experience of both methods and can appreciate the differences. In the circumstances, it is difficult to estimate how long it will take Maurice Barrard and his three companions, or indeed Mari and Josema. Nobody attempting a 'lightning dash' later in the season should compare his climbing time with that of earlier ascents when the route is in a very different state. For everyone, however, the trick is to try and co-ordinate his own performance, the conditions on the mountain and the weather to hit just the right day for going to the summit.

Luck in life almost always depends on being ready at the right moment. As Mari and Josema finally disappeared among the ramparts of the ridge, I remarked to Julie, 'Let's hope their summit day will be the right one.' And it was.

Choice of day, however, is not the only consideration.

Paris, spring 1986: 'I have serious misgivings about the serac wall on that hanging glacier,' Maurice confides, pointing to a photograph of the summit pyramid. 'It is definitely worse now than it was in 1979. Look at this latest shot: the fracture zone along this great balcony bit looks to have more cracks than ever. Heaven knows how much will come off and funnel down through the Bottleneck. My inclination is to try to the left, up that rock barrier – then, who knows ...' (he smiles enigmatically) '... afterwards we might be able to get from the summit onto the ridge along which we almost made it last time. I know the way down from there ...'

His big, searching eyes above the grey moustache in his chiselled features show no emotion; you would never guess he had just put forward the idea of doing the first traverse of K2. Maurice Barrard is a dyed-in-the-wool mountaineer, a man of enormous experience: in 1980 he climbed Hidden Peak (8,068 metres) with a single companion, by a new route, Alpine-style; in 1982 he and his wife Liliane stood on top of another eight-thousander, Gasherbrum II; and in 1984 Nanga Parbat became their mountain. Over the last few years, they have made many great ascents. In 1985 he and Liliane came within a hair's breadth of the summit of Makalu: they were only about forty metres from the top, but there was such a storm, they did not dare enter the 'magic stronghold' of the summit itself. They would have been blown away.

Maurice is both audacious and cautious. He knows when he has to turn back. More than once he has proved that two people alone can climb well at altitude – even when one of them is a woman!

Your luck will hold as long as you follow your own rhythm ... but when that harmony is disturbed by the ripples of some outside force, then it can be threatened. Certainly he knows that.

Ever since we arrived at Base Camp, Julie and I have both had the feeling that something is wrong with Maurice. Liliane appears calm and strong, but Maurice is only a shadow of himself. We can't think what the reason can be. Perhaps he has overtaxed himself on the mountain? Is it having all these other people around that affects his rhythm? Is he disturbed by the obvious tension between Wanda and Michel?

One day, we were skiing up towards the icefall as they made their way back from the Abruzzi: they could not see us as we had just dropped off the normal 'track' to deposit our skis among the ice towers and, after a short rest, to pick up our two loads again to carry up to ABC (Advanced Base Camp) beyond the icefall. We caught a glimpse of them crossing the flat patch below the avalanche cone and were shocked at what we saw: not because Michel was moving quickly and Wanda was already way ahead – no, because trailing the calm, upright, walking figure of Liliane, came a stooped and tired Maurice, like an old man. That really did give us cause for alarm. We could not believe it was him – a man with all his successes. A mystery – and yet it seemed to us that he was the only person who could find the way to lift himself out of his 'trough'. Perhaps he simply did not have the opportunity, or did not allow himself to do so.

We had never met Michel Parmentier, a lively Parisian journalist, before. All we knew of him was that he had climbed Kangchenjunga. But Wanda Rutkiewicz – 'die Wanda' – was a familiar face. I had first climbed with this tough, but always graceful, Polish woman on Everest in 1978. Time and again we have helped each other, as for instance on the South Col, when the day before her summit bid she found herself without a sleeping bag. I lent her mine and passed rather a cool night at 8,000 metres. The tables were reversed on Nanga Parbat, when Wanda left a tent for Julie and me above the Kinshofer Face. She did indeed reach the top of Nanga Parbat, and now her target was K2 – as yet still unclimbed by a woman. Wanda, ambitious and very determined, had Broad Peak on her shopping list this summer as well, and wanted to leave immediately after that to go on to Makalu! I got the impression that she had allowed herself to get caught in the eight-thousander race. But, well, if that's what she wants ...

One thing I did notice: she seemed lonely and less happy than on earlier occasions. The reason or the result of the way her life was going, I never knew. We never talked about it, even when we chatted together in Base Camp. It is just that when you have known someone for so long, you are aware of subtle changes.

The major difference was that Wanda was no longer part of her Polish women's team – as in 1984 and 1985 when she climbed with Krystyna Palmowska, Anna Czerwinska and 'Mrowka' Dobroslawa Wolf. She was now a lone operator, joining here and there where opportunity offered. In the past couple of years, Julie and I had enjoyed getting to know this happy, collaborative little group. We had been with them here on K2 and on Nanga Parbat. 'Mrowka', 'Anka' and 'Krysiu' should soon be arriving this summer, too, this time as part of a mixed Polish expedition under the leadership of Janusz Majer. Their target would be the SSW Ridge. We were looking forward to seeing them ... but then the dark shadow fell.

The first Black Day of the summer was the 21st of June.

All of a sudden, at 5.30 A.M., we hear a sinister roar from the direction of the Magic Line. Julie and I rush out of the tent and realize that an enormous avalanche has detached itself from the snow flank below the Negrotto Saddle and swept down the entire face. Only grey ice remains. A ragged line marks the edge where the giant snow slab tore away. It goes right across the route! Was anybody on it? Who might have been up there? Base Camp is a hive of agitation ... soon we learn that two Americans, Alan Pennington and John Smolich, were climbing up the Negrotto Saddle. They have disappeared, buried under thousands of tons of snow in the basin at the foot of the wall.

Alan's body was discovered the same day, but no trace was ever found of John.

His friends buried Alan at the Gilkey memorial cairn, a rocky spot on top of a small hill near Base Camp where some flowers bloom and patches of moss grow in the sand. It was originally erected to the memory of Art Gilkey, who disappeared on the mountain in 1953, but it has since served as a cemetery for other victims, or more often as a memorial cairn with plaques for those who die or disappear in storms high on the mountain, and whose bodies are never recovered. K2 had claimed twelve lives before this summer, over the years. Much less, it's true, than Everest or Nanga Parbat but it still came as a shock to everyone. What would be the after-effects?

In my life, luckily, I have only rarely been confronted with death on the mountain, which considering the thirty years I have been climbing is remarkable. But I do know what it means.

If somebody dies during the course of an expedition, one of the first thoughts to emerge is, naturally, should one go on or not? On the one hand, you know that in the mountains risk to life is ever-present. While on the other, the death of a person – how shall I put it? – shatters the dream with which you set out. What you eventually do depends on various factors – the same person may

1. A harsh life in a wild environment: Balti locals on a rope-bridge made of woven twigs.

2. The ocean of peaks of the Karakoram, crested and pointed, and (3) a huge ice tower in the Shaksgam valley.

make different decisions given different circumstances: it certainly makes a difference whether the victim was your friend or somebody you hardly knew. Even if it is your best friend who dies on a mountain, you cannot foresee what you will do afterwards. If the summit for which you were striving was a treasured ambition of your friend, you may decide to go on just because of that. But you cannot say for sure: always, there are the two possibilities – turn back or go on. And everybody, when such a thing happens, reflects long and hard over what to do.

The Americans decided to break off their expedition. And Quota 8,000 decided as an immediate consequence of this terrible event to give up the SSW Ridge, its stated objective, and turn instead to the Abruzzi Ridge.

It seemed to me that all further climbing up towards the Negrotto Saddle would be like Russian roulette for a while yet; there were still large sections of overhanging snow and ice higher on the route. Even if the same huge rock was no longer poised there to be loosened by the sun's first rays and come slicing down from above the Saddle, cutting through the surface tension, the equilibrium had doubtless been disturbed. (It had looked so safe, too; there were even fixed ropes attached to it.) Julie and I were happy, therefore, with the change of plan by our two leaders, Agostino da Polenza and Gianni Calcagno. Even without it, we would not have gone up this route again for filming.

Climbers know that reaching a summit always involves risk, but they do try to keep that risk to a minimum. If a certain danger is known, you can usually avoid it. But that still leaves the less definable hazards – some more or less so than others – and a certain residual risk has always to be accepted or no one would ever climb a mountain at all. I do not believe that those who have survived on big mountains are simply better than those who have died. Luck, certainly, comes into it. But errors committed do have their weight, as do caution and experience.

There are some situations where you cannot avoid the Russian roulette element – as for instance every step you take on the moving Khumbu Icefall on Mount Everest – but they are, thank God, the exception rather than the rule. Those who've mastered the rules of the 'game' – for want of a better word – stand the best chance of surviving: yet without good fortune, nobody can make it. Fate is a vital ingredient.

*   *   *

The tense atmosphere that persisted after the disaster was aggra-
vated by a completely unexpected turn of events: mail-runners
arrived at Base Camp with instructions from the tourist authorities
in Skardu to stop immediately any attempts on the Abruzzi Ridge
for which permits were not held. It was a reasonable, tidy-minded
intention, but everyone knew that in 1979 Reinhold Messner's
Magic Line expedition had experienced no problems about changing their route – the royalty paid for the permit being considered a
'peak fee', rather than a 'route fee'. Those deemed 'illegal' amongst
us were considerably agitated by the news; after all, they too had
paid for K2. Even Quota 8,000 received one of the letters. However,
since Agostino as well as Gianni had paid full K2 royalty fees – one
was meant for the normal route – they believed themselves the
victims of a mix-up in the paperwork at the Ministry of Tourism,
and insisted that their switch to the Abruzzi Ridge was valid. They
would clear up any misunderstanding on their way back through
Islamabad (which they only succeeded in doing, in fact, thanks to
the friendly intervention of General Qamar Ali Mirza, President of
the Pakistan Alpine Club). If Quota 8,000 had given in, it would
have hit our plans too.

Everyone wondered who was supplying the tourist authorities in
Skardu with their information about the Abruzzi Ridge. As a direct
consequence of these events several climbers were banned from the
mountains of Pakistan for four years.

Fortunately, Julie and I were on good terms with the liaison
officers, none of whom objected to our presence on the Abruzzi.
They also respected the film-work we were doing.

Then, 23 June brought the first summit successes – Wanda, Michel,
Liliane and Maurice stood on the highest snow crest of K2. The
weather was marvellous. They were rewarded with an indescribable
view, thousands of peaks at their feet. And while they had been
clambering to the top from a bivouac at 8,300 metres, Mari and
Josema were making their own, quite separate summit attempt:
from a final camp at 8,000 metres (which they considered a 'must'
to get back to after their assault), they too – somewhat later on this
radiant day – reached the top and there, overjoyed, hoisted aloft the
Basque flag.

Later, Wanda told me that these were moments of sheer ecstasy
for all of them, chasing everything else from their minds: a
euphoria, impossible to describe, held them all … Perhaps that was

the reason why Wanda and her three companions – unlike the Basques – only came down 300 metres that day to pass another night at their bivouac site ...

Considering what happened afterwards, this fatal decision appeared incomprehensible to everyone in Base Camp. But, then, we were not up there.

Tullio Vidoni, however, *was* high on the mountain at approximately 7,700 metres. With three companions from Quota 8,000 he had set out to attempt a summit dash, taking advantage of the initial fine weather period. In a report in *Alpinismo* (the journal of the Club Alpino Accademico Italiano) in 1987, he graphically recalls the later developments: 'Because of the squally conditions, we could barely make out the tents of the Barrard couple or of Michel Parmentier and Wanda Rutkiewicz, who had by now spent many days on the mountain; and when we reached the spot, there were Michel and Wanda coming down, both of them extremely tired. They told us they had been to the summit two days ago with the Barrards and two Spaniards ... They started descending this morning and had made it down despite the appalling weather conditions; the Barrards, however, were worn out and had decided to rest for some hours longer.' (Wanda told me later that she had seen them, for the last time, descending just below the balcony, the big ice overhang. She also said she was herself fighting the effects of two and a half sleeping pills, which she had taken during the night.) Tullio continues:

> With the greatest difficulty, Gianni and I tried to set up our tent and, judging by the swearing, which was swallowed by the gusts of wind, it seemed that Agostino and Benoît were not having an easy time of it either. I couldn't help thinking of those two other poor people up there, higher than us, without gas or food. Once our shelter was up and we started arranging ourselves inside, Wanda appeared and asked us to climb up and search for her friends.
>
> It was seven o'clock at night, quite dark, and in such an inferno it would have been madness to go out, and to no avail. We tried to make her see this, but she kept insisting for a long while more, before giving up on us. Though recognizing our impotence – there really was nothing we could do – we were beset by a feeling of guilt which nagged at us all night long. It was a sleepless night between the wind and snow lashing the tents, between the ever-diminishing hope of

finding the Barrards still alive and, last but not least, worries about our own situation, for the snow was still falling and the danger increasing. Not only was it impossible to climb up, it was not going to be easy making it down.

Finally morning arrived: the weather was terrible. Snow was still coming down and it was foggy. Impossible to think of going up, and so we decided, all four of us, to descend. Wanda joined us, but Michel opted to stay: he still harboured slight hopes for the couple. His decision made us feel even worse: it seemed as if we were abandoning the situation. I descended last, with Wanda in front of me. She was moving so slowly that within a few moments I had completely lost sight of my other companions.

Wanda did not have any ski-sticks, so I gave her one of mine. After a few steps, she asked for the other one as well, but I refused. Now that the slope was so steep, we kept sinking in up to our waists; the densely falling snow cancelled out the tracks of my friends. We met the two Spaniards dismantling their tent, and Wanda sat down and announced she would descend with them, so I left them together and with great difficulty caught up with the others. At the end of the plateau, we now had to find the spur.

While we waited, hoping it would clear enough for us to see something, we picked out the indistinct figures of Wanda and the two Spaniards slowly coming down and then stopping. Meanwhile, we succeeded after some effort in finally finding the way onto the spur; after calling in vain back to Wanda and the others, we assumed they had decided to sit it out in the tent waiting for better weather and so we started to go down. However, I left my ski-stick pushed firmly into the snow to mark the beginning of the spur so that they would not have the same trouble we had in locating the right way to go.

That whole day long, snow and wind assailed the mountain – and us. We reached Base Camp towards evening. Wanda and the two Spaniards came in exhausted two days later.

... Michel was still on the mountain, in radio contact with Benoît, who performed a real miracle in talking him down across the snow plateau to the start of the spur.

Unfortunately, we don't know what happened to the Barrards ...

Hesitatingly at first, but by and by with more conviction, we accepted that they would never come back. It was hard to come to terms with – a great shock to all of us. Everybody liked them.

Was Maurice right in his belief that the balcony was coming

down piece by piece – and were they hit by one such section? It is more likely that they lost their way in the storm coming over the Shoulder. Liliane's body was later discovered in avalanche debris at the foot of the mountain, directly below the Shoulder, but Maurice's has never been found. I did not take part in the search which found Liliane. Later, an unauthorized picture of her body was printed in a magazine. In my mind I remember her only as she was, bright and lively.

In the course of a few years, Maurice and Liliane stood together on top of three beautiful mountains, among the highest in the world; they were a team of two, and their mountaineering had much in common with Julie's and mine. We felt very close to them and had hoped, one day, to climb with them. Neither of us felt like going to Liliane's funeral. Only later, in our own time and peace, did we visit the place. Something hung in the air, unsaid ...

'They're coming! Mari and Josema! They'll be in camp in a couple of minutes!' The call echoes from tent to tent. Renato hurries towards them, the rest follow, we and many more. We are so relieved they have made it, overjoyed they are still alive.

But if it wasn't for their eyes and smiles, we would hardly recognize them. They're haggard and wrinkled, and must have lost a quarter of their weight. Walking prunes, the pair of them, two gnomes, horrible to behold and with almost no voices; yet at the same time, to us, so familiar, so dear and precious. They fell into Renato's arms, and now we hug them, too.

Next morning Mari whispers in a voice only slowly returning to normal: 'We have left our tent at Camp 2 for you. We knew you would have plenty to carry already with all the film gear.' It was a great gift, saving as it did the transport of one tent to 6,700 metres. But at the same time, we still have three of our own tents on the ridge.

Mari tells me a good deal about the events higher up, yet there are still questions unanswered. Could sleeping pills have played a part in the fatal decision of the Barrard group to bivouac for a second time at 8,300 metres? What do we really know about the extent and duration of the effects (and side effects) of medication on people climbing without oxygen at extreme heights? How often may it have been chemistry that was ultimately responsible for people dying on high mountains – indirectly, without anyone being aware of it?

In the afternoon, Julie films an interview with our Basque friend:

ME: Mari, what was it like up there?
MARI: Up there? Hard to describe. Climbing up was such an exertion, and the thought that you had to get down again never left you. Thinking of the descent becomes such an obsession that you can't really imagine what the summit will be like. At any rate, when we got there, it was some summit – like a mountain on top of a mountain. It was wonderful! Because the weather was so gorgeous and – I don't know – the sensation I had most was that we'd made it come true, the greatest dream of my life, the high point of my mountaineering career. And perhaps, because I was so happy, that made me a little bit crazy ...
ME (*pointing to the blue blisters on Mari's frostbitten fingers*): And that? Was it worth that?
MARI (*thinking hard before he speaks*): Yes, to me, it was worth it – for K2. Things like this: they'll get better. Perhaps if it had meant amputations, whole fingers lost, then I'm not so sure what I would think. It would certainly not be worth losing a whole hand, but something small like this, yes, it's worth that to have climbed K2. You might even be prepared to give more than that ...

Quota 8,000 has another go, making the most of a few days of fine weather and first-class snow conditions. On 5 July Gianni Calcagno, Tullio Vidoni, Soro Dorotei, Martino Moretti, Joska Rakoncaj (his second time up, he climbed the North Spur two years ago) and Benoît Chamoux reach the summit. Benoît, as usual, started later than the others, climbing through the night, and joined up with his team-mates just as they headed for the summit: this way he succeeds in climbing K2 in an incredible twenty-three hours. Our Swiss friends Beda Fuster and Rolf Zemp also make it to the top.

On the same day, Julie and I reach the Shoulder of K2 and set up there our blue Ultimate tunnel-tent, ready for an attempt the following morning. We can see tiny figures moving above us – incredibly slowly, giving the impression of struggle in the extremely thin air. In preparation for their return, we open a sort of *osteria* on the Shoulder. For two hours, into that evening, we are brewing up for our summiteers who straggle in one by one, having stumbled down, taking plenty of rests on the way. They have raging thirsts and are totally dehydrated. Soro, who returns first, speaks of the incredible heat of the 'altitude sun' striking the steep face of the summit. He is the only one who does not stop for a drink, descending immediately over the nearby ice-barrier to the Italian assault camp below, set up for this dash.

The following day we gamble away our chance by making a late start and carrying too much (knowing that we will eventually need to bivouac). Eight people coming down the summit pyramid, in many places using the trail they had broken on the way up, have left something of a trench and quite often it is necessary to make new steps. Also, I waste some time putting in two awkward pitons, which I think will be necessary for belaying when we return along the traverse below the giant balcony. By four o'clock in the afternoon we have put the difficult part behind us and have a clear passage to the top. But now, with only a little more than 350 metres to go, we don't care to risk a high bivouac; for a biting, icy cold has descended with the shadows and we turn back. Tired and disappointed, we reach our camp. Next day, the weather does not look good enough for the summit. We wait. But on 8 July it is no better. Ah, well, down we go then!

Shortly before we leave, we open our *osteria* once more, as Alfred Imitzer appears, the leader of the Austrian expedition. He is planning to make a solo attempt, but pretty soon he comes back, and quickly heads off down again. It is clear that the weather is about to break. We dismantle the camp, anchoring everything down to make a depot, and start the descent. It takes us to the 10th to fight our way through the heavy storm, unaware that high on the mountain, another tragedy is playing itself out.

Despite the bad weather, on 8 July, Jurek Kukuczka and Tadeusz Piotrowski both reached the summit of K2. It was the greatest success of the summer: the first climb of the South Face. They started on 3 July and after a straightforward climb set up their small lightweight tent under a vertical rock barrier, about the size of a

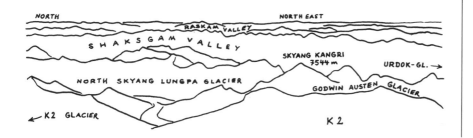

View from the summit of K2, 8,616 metres, towards Sinkiang, the Shaksgam Valley and to the North and North East (see photo 7 between pages 168 and 169).

house. Once above it, they had only to join the summit snow slopes of the Abruzzi Ridge. Back in Base Camp afterwards Jurek told us that the rock barrier was extremely difficult – Grade 5 or 6. In the end, they had no choice but to leave everything behind: tent, sleeping bags, equipment. In stiff winds and welling clouds, they finally stood on the summit and were able to make it down to the Barrard bivouac site at 8,300 metres. Next day they reached the Shoulder, and on the morning of 10 July tried to continue to Camp 3, above the Abruzzi Ridge, hoping above all to find something there to drink: they had been without liquid for almost three days and had already spent two nights in the open.

They were slowly making their way down a steep ice slope below the Shoulder – Jurek ahead – when all of a sudden, Tadeusz lost one of his crampons. He tried to hold himself in the steep ice with his ice-axe, but before Jurek could do anything to help him, Tadeusz lost his second crampon as well while banging it into the wall in an attempt to get the front points to grip. He fell with full force onto Jurek, who braced, but could barely keep his own footing. Unable to catch his companion, Jurek watched with horror as Tadeusz hurtled into the depths. Shattered, Jurek finally reached Base Camp on 12 July. He and Tadeusz had achieved the finest climb of the summer, but at great cost.

I was curious to know how Tadeusz came to lose his crampons. Were they the modern quick-release type, which I know from experience do not always offer total security? For if you wear them over thickly iced gaiters, you may unexpectedly step out of them. But to my surprise Jurek said no, Tadeusz had been wearing the old classic strap bindings. There is then only one explanation: in his exhaustion he either did not fasten them properly or did not notice them working loose.

The two men had made a superhuman effort. Wanda remarked, 'The thing we always say about Jurek is that he can live for days on a diet of Himalayan rocks and come out fit the other end.' Just him, though. Tadeusz was never found.

JULIE HAS DOUBTS

After a push to 8,000 metres, you need at least a week in Base Camp to recover before you can begin to think of another summit attempt. That was something Hermann, Marcus, Fritz and I learned years ago on Broad Peak, when effectively we climbed the mountain twice – apart from the small difference in height between the two ends of the summit 'roof' – and it is something I have seen confirmed time and time again. It is nonsense to suggest that you are 'played out' for the rest of an expedition after once forcing your way above 8,000 metres. Quite the opposite: you usually feel much better the second time you go to those final heights. Many mountaineers will confirm this.

However, it is important to relax properly before your next try. And to do that in Base Camp, or even lower. The necessary interval between two attempts will vary from one individual to another, but it will rarely be less than a week.

Julie and I, on 8 July, had left our assault camp in place as a depot for another attempt. We had completed the very hard and difficult descent and arrived tired, but in reasonable shape, at the foot of the mountain. Route finding on the steep slopes below the Shoulder had been nerve-racking and we had spent two nights in storm-buffeted tents with hardly a wink of sleep, worrying about snowslides and the threat of avalanches. But after two expeditions on this spur we were on familiar ground. A high-altitude porter from the Korean expedition, who had fought his way down from Camp 2 through the same storm a little ahead of us, was sitting now in Base Camp with heavily bandaged hands having sustained bad frostbite to all his fingers. (The Korean doctor, Dr Duke Whan Chung, was eventually able to save them fortunately.)

No, getting fit again for another attempt was not a problem, especially as the unstable weather left more than enough time for rest and relaxation. Three weeks passed without offering any real promise.

But the mountain had claimed five victims. It made us all sit up and think very hard – Julie and me, no less than the others. We tried, as they did, to come to terms in some way with what had happened, to find explanations rather than to put it all down to an act of God. Mountains never 'want' to kill anybody, especially not K2. It seemed incomprehensible. In 1984 Peter Habeler had called this icy giant a 'benign' mountain, and I must confess I had always had the same feeling. It was all very hard to understand. Was there suddenly some curse on the mountain?

Julie and I were nowhere near finished with our filming, even if our Quota 8,000 companions were now packing up. We would have to remain to do that at least, whether or not we got another chance at the summit.

I noticed that Julie showed less than her usual enthusiasm. She was withdrawn, and I could understand how she must be feeling. On the other hand … there was the mountain, still standing there, enigmatically concealing itself with shifting veils, shimmering through the clouds.

Matters hung like that for a while.

Despite the shadow the dreadful events had cast over the camp, there were occasionally spontaneous good moments. People cannot suppress their positive characteristics indefinitely. Julie and I continued working on the film, trying to capture the atmosphere of this waiting period (which everyone handled in his own way). We shot the Koreans at their board games and various mountaineers endlessly checking their weight on rusty, unreliable scales (it is nothing to lose 15 or 20 kilos on an expedition); with synchronized sound, we filmed the two Austrians, Hannes Wieser and Alfred Imitzer, engaged in the long-winded process of moving their tent a few metres – as you have to after weeks of ice melting out from the stones all around but not from the shade of the tent, so that it finished up on a plinth, like a monument. The floor can be over a metre above the ground outside, and perched on this, your available space diminishes as the tent develops a list towards the south like a drunken castle.

Other things, too, told of the long time – close on two months now – that had elapsed since our arrival: mountaineers with scissors heroically tackling their matted, overhanging growths of hair and beard in order to widen their fields of vision … and Krystyna, 'Krysiu' our blonde Polish friend, who with a shy smile would always fill the vodka glasses whenever she saw me arriving so that I could drink a toast with the (unshaven) Old Man of the Mountains, the Polish leader Janusz Majer, or with 'Voytek', Wojciech Wroz, who had been to 8,000 metres on K2 twice in recent years, from different sides, or with the girls – small, active, dark-haired 'Mrowka' (the Ant), and quiet 'Anka', both of whom we knew from earlier enterprises. The Poles had their teeth well into the Magic Line – the SSW Ridge – and were making progress even during this bad weather …

The only other person battling away up there was Renato – lone, indefatigable, Renato Casarotto. He began his third serious push for the summit on 12 July, promising Goretta that this would be his final attempt. After that, they would return home. She remained, as ever, in their tent on the moraine, maintaining contact with him several times a day over the radio.

It was the beginning of the third week of July, and Renato was already high on his ridge, when Julie and I were able to record a discussion between him and his wife, which highlighted Renato Casarotto's drastic situation. Goretta was sitting in front of us, radio in hand; Renato himself could not be seen up amongst the swirling clouds which encircled the sharp edge of the ridge and the streaming white banners issuing from the rust-coloured turrets …

RENATO (*over the walkie-talkie*): Ciao, Goretta. I arrived in Camp 3 at five o'clock. It's blowing a gale up here! The weather – well, let's hope it improves. Let's hope the wind from China clears the sky and gives me a chance of getting up this time. *Passo!* Over!

GORETTA: Yes, but I don't really know. The altimeter looks good, but I can see that the wind is tremendous up there, where you are. We'll know better tomorrow.

RENATO: Right. *Va bene.* But the little tent up here, it's full – absolutely stuffed full with snow and ice! It's taken me an hour to get it all out. A real epic: everything is soaked. I forgot to close the side-flaps last time, that's what did it, that's how all the snow got inside. *Cambio!*

GORETTA: And you? How are you feeling, Renato?

RENATO: I'm OK … fine, really. So far. But I'm tired now, and so

fed up with this whole business that I'd love to jack it in, come
down, get away from here …

GORETTA: That has to be *your* decision, Renato. *Va bene*, Renato –
let's speak again, later …

RENATO: *Va bene!* You call me!

GORETTA: *Va bene! Ciao!*

Julie steps into frame and claps her hands to synchronize the sound
and pictures (we did the same at the start of the discussion). 'End
board!' she says (though we're not using the clapper-board), then
turns to Goretta and whispers a gentle *'Grazie!'* That wraps it up for
today. I put the camera away and go back, with Julie, to our tent.

It was one or two days after that, on 16 July, that we learned that
Renato had definitely given up. It was a great shame – he was so
high, something like 8,300 metres. All of us down in Base really felt
for him, had been willing him to succeed on his SSW Ridge, but
after two months even the indomitable Renato had now had
enough. Would he be returning to Base Camp that night?

Goretta expected to hear over the evening radio link. She
imagined him to be on the ridge above the Negrotto Col as he was
still quite high the last time she had spoken to him. I was standing
beside our tent with Michael Messner – perhaps we were talking
about the weather, a frequent topic of conversation. Thoughtfully, I
looked up towards the great glacier cirque at the foot of the steep
slope coming down towards us from the Negrotto Col – it was a
whole tangle of crevasses and threatening seracs, an elongated cone
of large chunks of avalanched ice with narrow white passages
between. No, the whole approach to the Magic Line has never held
any attraction for me! All of a sudden, I fancied I could see a small
dot in the middle of that chaos. It was moving fast as I squinted
through half-closed lids towards the spot, about two kilometres
away, and yes, the dot was actually more of a comma. Somebody
was coming down at high speed from Camp 1 and heading towards
the seracs, the humpy world of the icefall above the rock buttress
about half an hour from Base Camp. Was that Renato?

Now the comma was moving forward almost horizontally across
the plateau – there! Then, suddenly, it vanished. Wiped out. I
rubbed my eyes in amazement and peered again. Nothing. Nothing
at all. Yet I hadn't dreamt it, had I?

Alarm bells began ringing in my head. Why had that tiny figure disappeared so abruptly? There one minute, gone the next? When somebody is shielded from sight by the undulations of the glacier, it's not like that. Or were my eyes simply playing me tricks?

'Michei, did you see anyone – there?' I pointed to the spot, wanting to be sure.

'Yes – there's someone coming down, on the glacier.' So I hadn't imagined it – the figure.

'I think … oh, I don't know … ' I faltered. 'He vanished so suddenly, that's all. As if he'd been swallowed up … just as if he'd fallen into a crevasse.' There! I'd said it, and added, 'But I can't be sure.' Now at least the anxiety was shared.

'Whoever it was,' Michei sought to reassure me, 'He's bound to be down in half an hour. Perhaps a little bit more.' It was no good. The worry kept eating away.

It seemed absurd that I could have glanced up at the very moment someone disappeared: it was too much of a coincidence. Yet increasingly I felt that's what had happened. Could it have been Renato? I dared not tell Goretta my terrible suspicion – but at the same time, I could not just do nothing.

I hurried to her tent. She was sitting outside and looked up at my approach.

'Ciao, Kurt. What's the matter?'

'Renato – where is he now?' I tried to sound as calm as I could.

'Still on the ridge.'

For a moment, I felt relief. Then fear clutched at my heart again: *somebody* was on the glacier … Michei saw it, too … if not Renato, then who …?

Something must have happened …

'It's just that I saw someone, something, further down.' I didn't want to say more than that.

'No, it couldn't have been Renato.' Goretta was positive, but her clear blue eyes continued quietly to scan my face. 'I'll be speaking to him in a few minutes, anyway … at seven o'clock.'

Was it a Pole, then, I had seen in the cirque? Should I run across to the Polish tents – tell them? Probably nothing had happened at all. In a short while, someone would come stumbling along the moraine. No! I have to tell them right away. Just in case …

'Goretta, why don't you try now … with the walkie-talkie?'

She looked at me searchingly, a bit surprised. '*E va bene*,' she said, and picking up the handset, called Renato …

The next moments will stay with me forever. Renato's words,

desperate, tumbled out of the receiver. He was at the bottom of a crevasse, in a very bad way. That much I gathered from the excited Veneto dialect. Tiny Goretta was shaking with tears. 'We'll get him out fast,' I tried to console her. 'I know exactly where he is … ' She could not be comforted. Grief-stricken, she kept repeating, 'He's dying!' Over and over: 'He's dying!' 'No, no, he won't die – we'll be up there in no time.' I took the walkie-talkie from her: 'Renato! Hold on, we're on our way. I know where you are!' *'Fai presto, Kurt, fai presto,'* Renato implored. Come quickly!

Perhaps he was jammed between the crevasse walls. If that was the case, there wasn't a moment to lose.

Within seconds Base Camp became an anthill. Everybody began running around gathering what was needed to help Renato. 'Rope! Where's a rope?' Then the desperate search. With the ever-increasing emphasis on unroped climbing in the Himalayas – apart, that is, from fixed rope belays – you can sometimes find yourself in the ridiculous position of not being able to find any rope in Base Camp once the rolls of fixed line have been taken to the foot of the mountain.

To rescue Renato, Julie and I took the only rope that was handy, our *Geh-seil* (the rope we used when we were climbing together), a couple of ice screws and ran off. Later, we gave it all to Agostino, who could move faster than we could.

We scrambled, gasping, across rocks in the twilight. Agostino, with the walkie-talkie in his hand, kept up a continuous conversation with Renato, talking to him like a father, willing him to live. He would not be alone for much longer, Agostino assured him, we were all running to help him … as fast as it was possible to run at 5,000 metres. Not knowing how far down the crevasse we would find him, certain only that it was bad and he was injured, we forced ourselves on, stumbling, fighting for breath, up to the edge of the glacier. Every precious minute counted.

To get back to the question of ropes, it would be a good idea for expeditions to keep an emergency rescue kit always ready at Base Camp, so that time is not lost getting things together. In Renato's case, however, we were with him very quickly despite delays, hardly one hour after receiving his call for help from the crevasse. I told Gianni, who was quicker than I, where I thought Renato was, and he hurried ahead with Little Karim. They found him almost immediately when, in answer to their yells, a faint voice issued from a narrow and particularly deep crevasse.

Renato had broken through a snow bridge on the normal route we always took in that place. He was literally only five minutes from the end of the glacier. Moving so fast – as I had seen him – there was probably quite a weight of momentum behind each downward step, so that he thrust harder into the surface than he would have done if travelling more slowly. On the other hand, his speed was insufficient to carry him across to the other side of the crevasse. He probably did not see it coming up, his mind on other things, disappointed no doubt at having had to give up on the SSW Ridge, and in a hurry to get shot of the place now that the months of struggle and hope and disillusion were behind him. In conditions like those, how easy not to see the tell-tale depression in the surface of the snow, a faintly outlined, elongated groove which the path crossed. To one side the crevasse had always been open. The snow at that time of day was wet, heavy and deep, not yet reconsolidated by the evening cold.

As fast as we could, we built up an anchorage point, then Gianni went down on the rope – deeper and deeper. It could have been forty metres that Renato had fallen, going obliquely at first, and then straight down. It was an 'A-crevasse', that treacherous form of fissure you get in depressions and on even, flat glacier surfaces, where the opening is narrow but it gets wider and wider, the deeper it goes. As Gianni told it afterwards, Renato was crouching on the flat bottom of the crevasse, leaning against his rucksack in total darkness, with water running everywhere. He embraced Gianni – or tried to. It must have been a moment of indescribable relief for him.

In the light of his head-torch, Gianni put the harness on Renato, who showed no obvious signs of injury. All the same, the force of so great a fall must surely have caused severe internal damage. He was dying, *tutto rotto*, he had told Goretta on the radio.

God knows, at that moment, hope lived once more in all of us. In Renato too, perhaps, when we started to pull him out. He was quite lucid talking to Gianni, helping himself as much as he could.

But this sense of relief that he was moving upwards out of the crevasse despite his pain, was the last he knew. Before he even reached the overhanging lip of the icy abyss, which we only managed to haul him over with the greatest struggle, he lost consciousness. Despite placing two ice-axes under the rope where it cut into the snow at the edge of the crevasse, it took us several attempts, and all our efforts, to get Renato to the surface. Immediately we muffled him in sleeping bags to keep him warm.

Finally, Gianni was back up beside us.

Renato lay perfectly still on his down bed. We feared the worst. Carefully, we shone the torch into his eyes. His pupils narrowed. He was alive!

Everyone apart from Gianni and me now descended to organize further help. Julie wanted to alert her British compatriots and take care of Goretta.

Shortly after they left, Gianni shone the torch once more into Renato's eyes.

He was dead.

All night long I stood or crouched there, gazing into the darkness, listening to the stones falling from the faces above the cirque, feeling the movements of air …

Now and then Gianni would change position. Neither of us spoke. I could see the wandering of lights across the glacier, along the moraine, and another light which was moving slowly much higher up, on Broad Peak. Some time soon the British would arrive with their doctor, but it would be too late. Nothing could be done any more. Renato was a still, dark contour in the slope at our side. At some point in the night Gianni interrupted the silence to suggest that, if Goretta agreed, we should bury Renato here in the crevasse on his mountain.

I thought of his life. The only consolation was that he had really lived it. As he wanted to. Not many do that … Poor Goretta – she does not know yet, but she probably senses what has happened. I'm glad Julie is with her.

Then I think of us, Julie and me: we have always had a tacit agreement that neither should press the other, if he, or she, did not want to go on. And we have kept it like that. I have the feeling too that now, after this night with Goretta, after Renato's death, that Julie might no longer want to continue … And she shall not, if she doesn't want to. Everybody decides for himself.

Another thought presses in: if one of us at least were to get to the top this time, the thing would be finished. Otherwise K2 would remain the unattained dream: sooner or later we would come back and try again. In my heart, I now felt it was time for us to direct ourselves towards new targets … beyond the great peaks. Could we do this without having satisfactorily concluded the past? I knew that Julie still had Everest in mind, she spoke also of Makalu:

1. Kurt, snowblind, waiting out a storm at 7,000 metres (during the descent with Julie from their first eight-tnousander together).

2. An avalanche falls from the ice castle of Broad Peak (8,047 metres or, measured more recently by GPS, 8,060 metres).

3. Julie and (4) our first eight-thousander together – among the clouds and whirling ice crystals.

5. Setting prayer flags in the cave of the holy water (Julie in front of the huge ice mushroom) and (6) a Tibetan ceremony in 'Ne' with *Tormas* and one hundred and eight butter-lamps.

7. Tashigang – an island for nineteen families at 2,000 metres in the moun-tain rain forest, and (8) Julie with some of the village children.

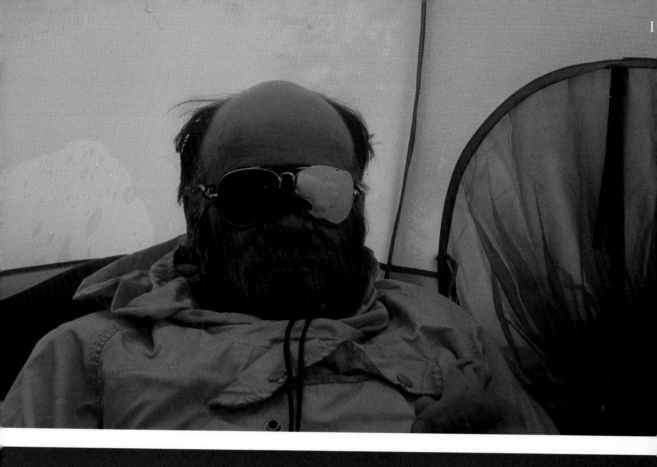

4

3

5

6

probably neither she nor I would ever escape from the charmed circle of big mountains. During the next five years, we would almost certainly still go now and then to the highest mountains in the world, but my understanding was that we had to go further, into the valleys between and beyond them, to the deserts, to the great forests, had to live with those people who are there, describing their existence with our films – as we had done with Tashigang …

If just one of us, as a conclusion of our first years together, reached the summit of K2 – wouldn't that be fulfilment for both? Even if only one trod the dream summit? Only one made the dream come true?

I will try it.

As I expected, after Renato's death Julie had no further desire to climb K2 this year, not in this black summer. Did that mean never again, at all?

I was thinking a lot about it, but saw no direct connection between Renato's accident and an ascent by us of the Abruzzi Ridge. Come again next year? That would be our fourth expedition to K2. Again I told myself, if the weather grants you another chance, Kurt, go it alone. If one of us makes it, the mountain won't block our future any longer.

'Don't you think, with all these other people, the situation up there could get out of control?' Julie asked me this once when we were speaking about the possibilities of the ridge. How likely was it that an ascent of the Abruzzi could really get out of hand? Could anybody, after all these fatal accidents, embark on a gamble? I was optimistic. 'If you are self-sufficient,' I said, 'you just don't get yourself involved.' After all, if things snarl up too much, you can always go down. That was my belief. I was wrong. *Four* times, later, Julie and I tried to counter the developing tragedy, consciously or subconsciously, with everything in our power. Yet in vain. Was that fate? Can things happen no matter what you do? Thinking of K2, I still have not found a definite answer, not even today.

Sometimes I returned in my mind to 1984, and whenever I did, I saw us wandering in bright sunshine along the Baltoro glacier towards Skardu, having climbed Broad Peak after eight weeks of siege on K2, where we had been repulsed time and again by storms. Then, on our return, there was suddenly the most glorious weather, for two whole weeks. Yes, we could have climbed the mountain! In

9. High altitude camp at 7,700 metres, below the K2 Shoulder. In the background is the icy roof of Chogolisa and, in the foreground, the mighty crests of Broad Peak. Later on, the barrier above the camp gave way … racing down to the glacier as the 'teapot' avalanche.

10–15. The village on the moraine – starting point and rest place for at least two months (c. 5,000 metres, at the base of K2). (10) a Korean tries our beer. (11) Mrowka, 'the ant' from Poland, is reading (behind her are Anka and Krystyna). (12) Alan is happy, as the weather is improving. (13) Goretta talks via radio to Renato, her husband, up on the SSW ridge. (14) the Austrian group in front of the mess tent: on the left, 'Mandi' Ehrengruber; above him, Alfred Imitzer and Willi Bauer; on the right, Hannes Wieser. (15) Relaxing in front of the Casarotto Base are Renato, Josema, Kurt and Julie.

our joy of doing our first eight-thousander together, we had no regrets. Yet it is true: we could have done it – then. So what if we got the same conditions now …?

Certainly, most of me would have liked nothing better than to wander back into a green world … But I can't go away yet, I told myself. Whether in the end Julie decides to have another try or not, we can't leave yet. The film is not finished: we have only exposed about half our stock, 2,000 metres, so far. So we must stay for that, and, yes, if by the time that's finished, no other chance for a go at the summit comes up, I'll have to accept it. And I will, calmly. But supposing a chance does present itself, then I want to take it.

Did Julie know somehow in her heart of hearts that she would die up there? This was the only time in many years that she showed a hesitation to push into the unknown – even though, in the end, she still decided to go. I remember once on Nanga Parbat, just before setting out one day, having an urgent compulsion to make out my will – I only had time to scribble my signature on a piece of blank paper for my wife … and then I came back alive anyway. But is there a sixth sense that gives you a presentiment of the end, once you are close to it? As if a comet on collision course with a planet were conscious of the fact – or perhaps more aptly, a spaceship, conscious through its instruments before the crew were aware of the impending danger. Would the crew react to the warning – in time? The inner voices of individuals vary, even given the same situation, perhaps because their destined courses may be different. I am no fatalist, because most of what happens depends ultimately on decisions taken.

THE ICE AVALANCHE AND THE RIDDLE OF THE TEAPOT

Bilberries are a wonderful fruit – especially on the Baltoro glacier. Contentedly, I sit in my sleeping bag spooning them into my mouth.

Hey! What's that? A great rumble of thunder?

'Quick – an avalanche!' gasps Julie, ripping open the entrance to the tent.

'Coming …' Drawing half a breath, I toss the bilberries into a corner and almost tumble headfirst out of the tent in my tiger-spring for the camera, which as always stands at the ready outside. Eye to the view-finder … press the button … motor running … clouds of snow powder, gigantic, thundering, welling, rolling, exploding out of themselves. Again and again, exploding.

Hundreds of metres high they are! This avalanche must have poured down all of two thousand metres and it is still growing, billowing around and below the Abruzzi. Now the swelling powder clouds blot out the ridge, gobble its features. Whew, it *is* a giant. Just what our film needs. In high excitement, I hold my breath and keep my finger on the button – not daring to move for fear of ruining the shot – until at last I am forced to struggle for air. 'That was gorgeous!' I pant to Julie, who is in the tent behind me.

'Mmm – wasn't it!' Her face has appeared in the entrance; she has her camera in her hand, and must surely have got some good pictures. She disappears again.

Only now I notice that I am barefoot, and in my underwear; in my giant leap through the tent door, I have stubbed two toes on the loose stones of the moraine.

Avalanches have an imperious command. Especially for cameramen. It's cool, I now realize. I climb back into the sleeping bag. The sky is covered. The avalanche is still mushrooming out of the clouds which wrap the Abruzzi Spur. But a cameraman can't be disturbed by bad weather. When avalanches come – any avalanche – then your finger must be on the button – even if the end of the world is on the way.

It's true, I grunt to myself, changing the magazine, the best a cameraman can hope is that his wedding night is safe from avalanches – then at least the light will not be good enough!

My bilberries! Did they survive?

'There are some cherries left,' Julie offers sweetly from inside the tent. 'Do you want any?'

Cherries, now? Didn't I just stuff myself with bilberries? But cherries on the Baltoro glacier – who could refuse? Of course I want some!

The Germans bequeathed us all these wonderful delicacies when they left, since when Julie and I have really enjoyed ourselves. Mushrooms, goulash in gravy, casseroles, sauerkraut, sour pickles, cod's roe, anchovy rings, smoked herrings and other tins of fish, crispbread ... a heavenly cranberry *compote*: I have to stop ... my mouth is watering too much even as I remember it.

Not that we had any complaints about the catering of our Italian friends; they had fantastic ham, all sorts of olives, and always mountains of spaghetti; but regularly when Julie and I went to the Abruzzi Ridge where we looked after ourselves at ABC (Advanced Base Camp, at 5,300 metres, at the foot of the mountain), or even to the high-altitude camps, we felt much healthier. In Base Camp, sooner or later, we all went down with upset stomachs. Julie believed she had finally discovered the source in the brownish sediment at the bottom of the water drum; but Gianni, our second in command, has come to a rather different conclusion – he now thinks it must have been the cleaning-powder, which he says was used too liberally. As not all, but several of the Italians were hit, like us, with statistical regularity, it remains a mystery what it could have been. But perhaps it is possible to acclimatize, even to this?

Whatever the reason, we had now recovered, and felt increasingly better as each day passed. Steve Boyer, the doctor of the American expedition, had given us some green vitamin tablets – a poisonous green – as well as tiny white tablets which contained folic acid; without those, he said, it wouldn't matter what we swallowed, it would have no effect. So I don't know whether our physical uplift was due to the long rest in Base Camp, to the American pills, or to the first-class German cuisine. Perhaps it was a combination of all three.

*   *   *

There remained one shadow, however: sometimes Julie was homesick, it seemed to me. She kept pressing to order the porters for the trip out. So we did; with the gentle help of Captain Neer Khan, liaison officer to the Austrians, we fixed our departure for 5 August. I could sense Julie's relief. The matter was cleared, done, and her customary cheerfulness returned.

Base Camp was now smaller. In some way, you felt the loss of all those who had gone home. One of them was Norman – Norman Dyhrenfurth – he had looked very tired when he left. Even though his expedition was successful, for him it had not been without personal disappointment: the leader, Dr Karl Herrligkoffer, before flying out from Base Camp (by helicopter), had deputed his personal major-domo, a Hunza who spoke quite good German, to be provisional leader in his stead. Being passed over like this must have given Norman several sleepless, angry nights.

For with his many years of Himalayan experience, Norman could certainly have handled a job like that. But perhaps old mountain lions are always a bit testy with one another. Julie and I got on well with both of them. We visited Herrligkoffer in the Broad Peak Base Camp on his seventieth birthday; and Norman I have held in high esteem ever since our Dhaulagiri expedition of 1960. Having never been on an expedition with Herrligkoffer, I cannot make any judgement, except to remark that he has given many mountaineers their first chance to go to the Himalayas.

It was a cordial goodbye. Julie and I were both sad to see Norman leave.

Whatever else happens, we have at any rate to finish the filming. For climbing footage, it will be enough that we can still go as far as Camp 2. We might not be able to get much higher anyway in this weather. But there are things to film, too, at the foot of the spur – like the old oxygen bottle from the year 1954, weathered now to a rusty orange, which we discovered between the ice and rocks there. It had, so the barely legible inscription informed us, belonged to the first climbers of the mountain, the 'Italian expedition under the leadership of Professor Ardito Desio'. On 31 July that year, Lino Lacedelli and Achille Compagnoni reached the summit of K2. Respectfully we weighed the elderly bottle in our hands, and carried it back to our tent at Advanced Base Camp. That we must certainly have on film, and the marvellous ice towers all around there!

*   *   *

... *Ratsch!* ... *ratsch!* ... *ratsch!* ... *ratsch!* go our skis on the wide glacier. We are on our way to the ice fall, climbing on special short skis with skins attached. Once there, we will leave the skis as usual close to the first ice towers, and continue on foot to ABC. When we come down, it is always such a pleasure to be able to shoot home from there and not to have to trudge all the way back.

It is darkish, with, here and there under the clouds, a glint of grey-blue ice on the massive flank of K2. We are now at the edge of the kilometre-wide surface from which the clouds of ice powder rose in the giant avalanche. I see a crushed gas cylinder lying on the ground, all bent and scratched. Enormous forces have been at work here – mighty blocks litter the area, and everywhere are strewn bits of ice, small and large, with comet tails of snowdust behind them.

Ratsch, ratsch, ratsch, ratsch ... we hurry away; no place, this, to linger.

Hell, what's this lying here? An old teapot, squashed completely flat!

Ratsch, ratsch, ratsch, ratsch – I hurry on. Suddenly, an idea strikes me. That teapot could illustrate the power of an avalanche better than a hundred words. 'Julie, you go on,' I shout. 'I'll just nip back and get the teapot for the film.' 'OK!' She glides on.

I hurry back. The pot has been squashed very artistically. Aluminium: it really doesn't look that old. Anyway, it's good to have it – we'll film it up at ABC. I stuff it into my rucksack and race to catch up with Julie.

We have almost reached the end of the avalanche zone. As we clear the brow of a hillock we spot three figures spaced out along the foot of the avalanche cone. They are looking for something. They must be Balti porters on their way back to Base Camp. Their loads will have been deposited near the first ice cliff.

They must have found something – two appear to be carrying bits and pieces in their hands, but I can't tell what. Is it the remains of a tent? That is interesting. We stop and call across. The three porters approach us slowly.

There is no reason to be particularly concerned if bits of old expedition gear come down the mountain here – it happens all the time. But for some reason I am curious. Is it the orange piece of cloth which one of them is holding? I've seen something like that before, somewhere. Yes, on the other side of K2 at a height of 7,600 metres we found a torn Japanese tent, and each of us brought home a strip as a memento of the North Spur. Mine is hanging on the wall beside a big picture of K2.

But didn't Quota 8,000 also have such tents? The same colour?

Thoughtfully, I finger the piece of cloth handed to me by the first of the Balti porters, who now stands in front of me. Hmm, I hand it back to him, still uncertain what it can be.

'That looks like Austrian gear!' I hear Julie's clear voice. She is turning a red jersey over in her hands. The front is all ripped.

What's an Austrian pullover doing here – if that is what it is? Julie points emphatically towards the garment, 'It's theirs, I'm almost sure of it. Give it to the Austrians in Base Camp!' She hands it back to one of the three porters. We recognize him: one of the Balti cooks, a cheerful fellow we first met at ABC, where his favourite saying always was, 'The Koreans have everything; they are very, very rich.'

The third Balti on his way back towards Base Camp has nothing in his hands – and immediately after that he is not on his way back to Base Camp any more, either; because, to our surprise, we discover that his load is made up of our own gear from ABC – all stuff we still need! A misunderstanding: this morning we described to him a kitbag we wanted him to fetch down – for a princely bonus – and he has got the message confused, 'mixed it up with a Radetzky march,' as the saying goes in Salzburg. He is not at all pleased to have to carry the whole load back up to ABC again, but that has become his destiny. I wonder darkly what's in the heavy loads of the other two, but it is none of my business. They are porters to the Koreans.

Towards evening we reach ABC, and the Balti, no longer keen to carry down our kitbag, vanishes hastily. My mind is still trying to make sense of the torn pullover and the scrap of orange fabric, but we cannot be absolutely certain that the tent is Italian, nor the pullover Austrian. Why should they be?

We pass a marvellous evening, brew enormous quantities of tea and feast on cranberry *compote*. We are alone with the ice towers, content and happy.

Next day we film the old oxygen bottle. I 'find' it in the scree and, with 'astonishment', pick it up, turn it over slowly, weighing it in my hands and running my fingers up and down its weathered surface – that will do fine for voicing over the history of the first climb.

Similarly, you can juxtapose cookers or double boots – the old and the new – very effectively: my old heavy leather double boots from

Everest – which I am still wearing because they are so comfortable and because my left knee can't cope with the new man-made materials which haven't the flexibility of leather – set against Julie's modern, lightweight, plastic double boots. And with the film in mind, I have also brought along a petrol mini-stove developed decades ago by grand old master Borde for the Swiss army, and which my friends and I used back in the fifties when we did the Peuterey Ridge Integrale on Mont Blanc, the Eiger North Face, the Walker Spur and God knows what else. Even today, when your gas cartridges run out, there isn't a country anywhere in Asia where you can't find petrol, and so I can still cook with it.

Demonstrating that on film, in conjunction with a camping gaz cooker, is not difficult. We want to make tea anyway. Perhaps I should add that the petrol stove used to be known in mountaineering circles as the Borde Bomb, because if not treated with a proper respect it had the nasty habit of exploding in your face!

Finally, from the rucksack, I pull out the bashed teapot …

'Wow!' says Julie. 'That's really taken a beating!'

It certainly has: it looks as if a furious regiment of mountain goats had trampled on it or terrible claws mauled it; it has been crushed, kicked, bent, scratched. I let my camera roll as Julie scrutinizes it curiously. Her concentration, as she tries to imagine its story (faithfully following the film director's instructions), looks real enough. 'OK, you can stop,' I tell her. 'That's enough.' But Julie doesn't look up. Her gaze seems to bore into the aluminium.

'There's a name written on this,' she says at last. And bites her lip.

'A name?' I, too, can now make out faint letters.

'M–A–N–D–I,' Julie reads slowly, a deep crease between her eyebrows. Mandi: that can't be anything but the name of who it belonged to. It sounds Italian, but I don't know anyone with that name. One of the earlier expeditions?

Suddenly I have the feeling I do know the name from somewhere. Could it be an Austrian surname? Does the teapot belong to the Austrians? A picture of the pullover we saw yesterday flashes into my mind – teapot and pullover, of course, there's a connection.

And the orange bits of cloth? Suddenly, I understand. The Quota 8,000 tents which had been under the ice barrier at about 7,750 metres, the tents of our friends which they left up there below the Shoulder, they were exactly this colour. The ice avalanche could easily have broken off from up there. All at once I remember an old

Japanese fixed rope, black and yellow, frozen into the ice, on which I was able to put my weight carefully, yet which at a second try, without offering any resistance, came away in my hands. Obviously there were slow movements up there, continuously changing the ice, movements which even a strong rope could not resist. I remember also a crevasse in the ice barrier above that camp, and that enormous 'balcony' weighing many tons which hung over your head when you stood by the tents. Such a good wind-shelter it offered!

If the Austrians left gear up there, then the puzzle is solved. It is clear what happened: everything up there, left by any of us, will now have vanished. We must tell the Austrians right away.

Alfred Imitzer, Willi Bauer, Hannes Wieser, Manfred Ehrengruber … all are deeply despondent. Their top camp has been wiped out. Willi's expensive cameras will all be smashed – they will obviously have lost everything they stashed up there in the Italian tents. This was to have been their highest support camp, essential to their plans, and the avalanche has smashed it. It's a terrible blow for them.

Nevertheless, they are grateful to us for bringing the news. The teapot question at least is solved: 'Mandi' refers to Manfred Ehrengruber, and he confirms he left it at the support camp, Camp 4.

At first nobody can find the pullover. Didn't the porters hand it over? Nothing seems to be known about it. Only after the Austrians' liaison officer conducts a lightning search among the kitchen personnel – Hunzas and Baltis – does the thing show up. It turns out to belong to Willi Bauer.

A day later I am standing with him and Alfred Imitzer on the moraine, looking up at the mountain. From here only part of the route is visible. I am terribly worried that the avalanche might also have destroyed Camp 3. That, too, would have been in a direct line with falling ice from the seracs below the Shoulder. I try to convince Willi and Alfred that if they are planning a further attempt, they should take into account that Camp 3 might not be there either. I am most insistent. Something inside me tells me I have to get this home to them. Even at the risk of being thought an old prophet of doom with my admonishing finger, they must know my fears. Their next camp down is more than 2,000 metres from the summit – and without Camp 3 …

Alfred, I notice, hesitates; he has always given weight to what I have had to say. But Willi pooh-poohs the whole idea with an airy wave of his hand: 'If the avalanche had hit 3, then it would have taken quite a different line from where you found the pot.' 'But, Willi, avalanches can divide as well. Camp 3 could easily have been wiped out.' I almost beg him to take notice. But in vain. When Willi Bauer makes up his mind, that's it.

Even Alfred now seems more inclined to listen to Willi.

We separate ... none of us is very happy.

Perhaps it's a storm in a teapot anyway and there is no chance of going for the summit again – not in this miserable weather ...

THE DECISION – WE GO TOGETHER

Willi Bauer taps his altimeter. The weather is getting better. In the British camp they are packing to leave: only Alan Rouse and Jim Curran, the cameraman, will stay behind. Alan wants to have one more go at the mountain, this time by the Abruzzi Ridge, and with Mrowka, the Polish girl. If we are indeed to be granted one last chance, it looks as if it is coming up now. The Koreans are already preparing for another attempt. I am pleased that Alan will be on our route: I first met him on my lecture tours in Britain, and have always admired his dynamism. Julie knows him too, of course, he is one of the best British mountaineers. Secretly, I wonder whether this, together with the general renewal of activity, will influence her to change her mind about going up again. I love life no less than she does, and have no intention of risking my neck – not even for the mountain of my dreams – but we know this route well enough now, certainly as far as the Shoulder; it is only beyond that the question of 'yes' or 'no' arises. If we get that far, and things don't work out, well, we just come down again. If the weather breaks, we turn back. The only way it could go wrong is for there to be a sudden change during our summit bid, when we're already very high ... but, some degree of risk is inevitable – always.

I don't mention any of this to Julie – she knows it well enough herself – but I have the feeling that she is chewing things over. It could not be otherwise; I know her too well. Wouldn't it be best simply to take everything we need for our filming up to Camp 2 – which we have to do anyway – and just in case, take along whatever else would be necessary for an attempt on the summit? That's what I think we should do. And, watching Julie out of the corner of my eye, I see that is what she seems to be doing ... Again, I tell myself that a decision does not have to be taken now; it will depend on the weather, on the circumstances … in the last resort, it is up to how we feel when we're up there. Somehow, without Julie having said a word, I form the impression that she has had a change of heart.

Yesterday, when Willi Bauer asked me vaguely whether, if the worst came to the worst, he and I might tackle the summit together, I gave an equally vague response. But now I make the point of going over to speak to him. 'Willi, I think Julie probably wants to go after all.' He shakes his head thoughtfully, then laughs, 'Oh, well … ' and shrugs his shoulders. Later on, I see him heading out of Base Camp towards the Abruzzi with three other Austrians. It is 28 July. As for Julie and myself, we have a last-minute hitch: five porters suddenly turn up who could carry some of our gear out to Skardu. We ought not to miss this opportunity – you never know here whether you will really see porters when you expect them. Captain Neer Khan, liaison officer to the Austrians, one of the friendliest and most helpful people I have ever met on an expedition, helps us to negotiate with them. Finally, we see the small group on its way, under the charge of a wild-looking, bearded Balti, a giant of a man who carries, as a 'special load', the big movie camera in its metal case. No matter how we try to hurry, Julie and I do not get away until almost evening. And then, at the very last moment, I forget to bring my sunglasses, which are hanging at the entrance of our Phazor dome-tent. I only notice it that night on our arrival at ABC. With the walkie-talkie out of order, there is no way of reaching Alfred, who might have brought them up for me when he comes later; however, Heli, an extreme skier in the Austrian party, is good enough to lend me his spare pair. He must have given up his plans for skiing down from the Shoulder, I suppose … but not the summit apparently. I do have one pair of skier's dark storm goggles, but would never set out without a pair of normal snow goggles as a spare. So, I am very grateful to him for saving me a trek back.

It is dusk when we climb through the icefall.

Julie says suddenly, 'I told Jim we had to get our cameras down from Camp 2 … which isn't true.'

'That's all right – it's not his affair, what we do,' I reassure her. Julie ought not to worry over the odd white lie – she gave the diplomatic answer, that's all.

Maintaining an easy pace, we continue up through the icefall towards ABC.

We go on cooking late into the night. Again and again I feel my way down to the small stream at the foot of the boulder slope to fetch water. Stars are twinkling high above me … I wonder what that means? Finally, we close the door of our tent and drop fast asleep in no time – so deeply asleep that we do not hear the Austrians make their early start. Clearly they want to climb straight up to 2, leapfrogging Camp 1. Some of them do not have much time before they are due to catch their return flight from Islamabad. We have a relaxed morning in the sun; I film the Austrians higher up on the spur, and Broad Peak bathed in sunshine, and the ice towers. To get to Camp 1, we don't have to leave until noon or early in the afternoon.

We will take along the small 16mm movie camera and maybe a dozen magazines for it … but they are very heavy. Add all the other equipment, gas, food – even if we do have some stashed higher up – and it's quite a load. We don't need sound, so I am surprised to see Julie loading her mini tape-recorder, and wonder if she intends dictating her diary into it, or something for the movie? Unless … More and more, as she carefully checks, arranges, prepares everything with her usual precision, I become convinced that my companion, like me, has more in mind than a simple film trip to Camp 2. I have felt this ever since Base Camp, but have not dared pin hopes on it: now I can see with my eyes that it's true. We will go up together – as always. We will make our attempt together. I am deeply moved. So, in the end, she did decide to come after all.

Without realizing it, I have stopped my own packing to watch her: as if she feels my gaze, Julie suddenly says in a low voice, 'I know I didn't want to go up any more … but I've changed my mind.'

I am silent, unable to find words. Now she has said it. There is no doubt any more. We shall attempt the summit together. The happiness that surges through me is beyond words, as if all the years of my life were concentrating here in this single moment. Everything that we have experienced together on K2 floods back to fuse with this moment – to create an entity, a oneness. I would have tried it alone, was ready to, but somehow that would have been absurd. Perhaps I would not have got far before turning back; I don't know … Now I am just indescribably happy. We are no longer divided, as it seemed to me sometimes we were during this period of indecision. I know, too, that since we will now be together, it will be much easier to turn back, if there's a reason for it – that will be no problem; it is just that the two of us are together, on our way for a final try, and that alone makes me so happy.

'It may divide you forever … ' The thought comes like a bolt from the blue. For a moment, I am struck rigid with astonishment, then joy and high spirits drive away all forebodings: what on earth could separate us, since we will, as always, be on the one rope – and if the summit is not possible, we will turn around …

I put the thought out of my mind. Now, we have to concentrate very thoroughly and precisely. We have to be extremely realistic. Since the avalanche broke off at the ice barrier, below the Shoulder, we have to consider that associated shock waves might have caused other snowfields to collapse also. In the worst instance, it could have brought down everything right up onto the Shoulder. But even if Camp 3 has been destroyed, it will not matter to us since we do not have anything there. Our depot – in a duffel bag at the foot of a bluish serac, a little further up – does not contain very much, either, and we know we have lost the few not very important items we had stowed inside the Italian tent which was torn away by the avalanche. None of these is very serious – but what about our depot on the Shoulder itself? Our whole Camp 4? Is that still intact?

To be on the safe side, we have to assume it no longer exists. So: our green bivouac tunnel tent is hanging in the duffel bag at the rock tower below House's Chimney – we can get that from there; sleeping bags, however, we will have to bring along from here. Also from here, we must take our thick woollen balaclavas, the gloves, head-torches, batteries, a stove, enough gas, some food … Everything else is already on the spur.

But bigger and bigger grows the pile of things that should go with us: I left my warm Javelin over-gaiters up on the Shoulder in case of another try – they might have gone, I'll need some more. So I pack an orange pair of Japanese full-gaiters which we bought in the bazaar in Kathmandu on our way back from Tashigang. Julie's down trousers were up on the Shoulder too, so I see to it that we take mine along for her, just in case. Three pairs of gloves each, spare socks, the thin silk balaclavas. What a good thing we doubled up on almost everything. When I finally try and hoist my rucksack, I can hardly shift it off the ground. 'A pig of a bloody load!' Even Julie's pack is unbearably heavy. So we empty the bags and start again. Finally, we reduce the film magazines by half, but not much else can be jettisoned (it's only when we're climbing that I notice my down trousers were left behind in camp after all). On top of everything, we take an extra load, just for today, to give us some luxury on the way up to Camp 1 – juices and tinned fruit salad. And since, just before we get there, there's a wall where we can get good pictures of ourselves struggling, heavily laden, through some rust-coloured, vertical rocks, with crampons scratching the slabs, we shoot off two of the magazines here. We can leave the exposed magazines behind in the next camp to be picked up on the way down. So, that only leaves three more for higher up … If we do go for the summit, how high will we tote the movie camera, anyway? We can always take slides.

Julie's familiar cheeky expression is back, the understanding between us, all as it ever has been – the crisis of uncertainty over. I take a deep breath, not just because of the heavy load on my shoulders … happiness goes with us. Whether or not we make it to the top, this will be a fitting ending. Even if the weather stops us going higher than the Shoulder, and the whole struggle is for nothing, we can return home then with no complaints. Better to have tried and not made it than to have not tried, to have wasted the opportunity …

Good God! Is that Camp 1? The Korean tents topple forlornly like old toadstools. The sun's powerful rays have melted away much of the snow, including that underneath the tents. Our tent, too, has developed an alarming tilt; lying inside is like being in a bed from which somebody has stolen two of the legs. For security, I lash a rope to the nearest rock, passing it through the entrance, and we both sleep belayed in our harnesses. It doesn't seem worth the effort of taking it down and putting it up again, flattening out another platform and all that – and Julie says she doesn't mind. I simply stuff extra rocks under her side for support. We are used to a bit of discomfort.

It's a bit stormy during the night, but nothing too bad; higher up, however, as we learn in the morning, it must have been much worse. We can't believe our eyes suddenly to see two tired figures stumbling down across the steep slope of snow and rock beneath the towers, close to where House's Chimney makes a deep cleft in the shining yellow barrier of rock. They're Austrians … not Willi – I would have recognized him immediately from his short, stocky figure – it must be two of the young lads. And yes – when they get closer we see it is Siegfried Wasserbauer and Helmut Steinmassl. They have both decided to pack it in. It was terribly stormy up there, they tell us, and anyway – one of them makes a deprecatory gesture – 'Enough is enough,' he says laconically. Julie and I make tea and the other two start taking down one of their tents to take back to Base Camp. Suddenly I hear *'Kreuzbirnbam!'*, one of those all-purpose Austrian oaths, followed by laughter. 'The tent is full of water! It's unbelievable!' I jump to take a look and call Julie, too. I certainly have never seen anything like this: the tent is like a filled bath-tub! Condensation? Powder snow – blown in and then melted? 'Well, there's one thing you *can* say: your tent's certainly water-proof!' I grin at my compatriots: 'Especially the lower half!'

How on earth to get rid of so much water? There must be nearly 30 litres in there. 'Seems a pity to waste it – you could take the highest bath in the world!' I ought not to joke at my friends' expense. 'Best thing would be to stab it with a knife, on the downhill side, close to the ground … ' As I offer my helpful advice, I'm already standing by with the movie camera … The Swiss Army knife stabs at the swollen belly, then a jet of water spurts into space in a high curve, to finish as a stream running down the slope. Water sports above the Godwin-Austen glacier! They couldn't have had more fun at the noble water games in Salzburg's Hellbrunn Castle, where Arch-bishop Markus Sittikus regularly soaked his guests. When the tent is finally drained, the two poor lads still have to scoop out armfuls of ice that the morning sun had not yet had the chance to melt. Only then could they roll up their no longer perfect, but still basically watertight, tent. Meanwhile the tea is ready and we all have a drink together before they begin their descent. As they leave, they present me with a burner from one of their Husch stoves; this will fit onto the extremely lightweight gas cylinder I got from Alfred in Base Camp, which I plan to use on the summit day. Alfred didn't have any burners in Base Camp and told me to keep my eye open for one on the mountain. After struggling with too much weight on our first summit attempt, this time I have worked everything out to the last gram, with the pedantry of a Benoît Chamoux.

A Husch cylinder with burner weighs far less than a camping Gaz stove – that will be our standby in case we bivouac on the summit assault. Julie will go with just a hip-bag for the final day, and I with a superlight Japanese rucksack, which will hold all we need (that, too, came from the bazaar in Kathmandu). For the time being, however, we are both pack mules. That's why we decide to leave the heavy 16mm camera here and to shoot off all the remaining film magazines before we go. Already another subject has presented himself. Hannes Wieser, twinkle-eyed and laughing as usual and wearing his customary black hat, swings into view over the crest of

1. Uigur tribesman, Khur Ben, habitually crossing the mountain desert with his camels, contemplates the singularity of the mountain climber.

2. Shaksgam valley in the dry season, with camels.

3. Julie after the four months of our first K2 expedition.

snow below camp. It means that Willi and Mandi (proprietor of the teapot) will soon have company – if they haven't already gone on. Alfred, too, has arrived, tall as a tree and full of energy (he was here even before Hannes). We film each other, drinking tea, and Julie looks up at 'her' Broad Peak. She seems a little tired after the night in our tilted tent, but her eyes shine with that imperturbable spirit, which has already seen her through so much. Soon we will climb up to our tent at Camp 2. We are collecting our stuff together. The camera and the films we will leave hanging inside a small bag under the roof of this dome tent, well up off the ground – heeding the warning of the Austrians' 'bath-tub'.

By the time we are about 100 metres above the camp, we look back: a multicoloured group has appeared. It must be the Koreans and their high-altitude porters. With so many people coming, we get a move on.

Having picked up the bivouac tent and some gas from our rock-tower depot, I struggle under my heavy load through House's Chimney. I can understand why high-altitude porters often refuse to climb without fixed ropes. Only when you have done the job – for that's what it is – yourself, can you understand the problems. Anyone who is familiar with Alpine-style climbing in the Himalayas knows from experience – from his own oversized rucksack – how much effort the mountaineer is spared by having a porter. Even with other styles of climbing, there is still plenty of opportunity to find out what ferrying loads is all about. Almost everyone who reaches a Himalayan summit has got there by dint of very hard work.

There is no doubt that without the help of high-altitude porters – above all, the Sherpas, but also the hardy Hunzas – many expeditions would never have reached their goals. These mountain people have a strength which would do credit to a mountain buffalo – were there such a thing. 'Himalayan tigers' is the traditional epithet for Sherpas, but nobody has yet come up with the perfect synonym, either for the men from the East (*Shar* = East, *pa* = people) who until the fifteenth century lived in Kham in eastern Tibet, from where after decades of migration – 2,000 kilometres across the high plateau – they came over the Himalayas to settle in the high valleys of Nepal and Sikkim; or for the wild Hunzas from the high valley of the same name in northwestern Pakistan, who defended their independence so fiercely and successfully for so long and were

4. Mountain rescue near crevasse camp on the north spur.

5. A human 'pack-animal', loaded up. Himalayan mountaineering is quite often strenuous but the fascination makes it easier to bear.

6. The first award for our 'highest film team'. We are proud and happy (festival in San Sebastian, 1983).

7. An everyday side of film-life – here we are, doing the best we can in the pouring rain of the Lake District.

notorious until the end of the nineteenth century for making surprise raids on camel caravans crossing the Karakoram Pass. Courage as well as strength characterizes both Sherpas and Hunzas, and it's not surprising that quite often their bodies have developed an incredible tolerance to high altitude, exceeding that of many expedition mountaineers. There are Sherpas whose bravery has become legendary – several have died trying to rescue their 'sahibs' on Himalayan ventures. And still today, avalanches, storms, rescue missions regularly claim victims from among their number. In 1939, here on K2, Pasang Kikuli died together with two other Sherpas, after climbing the Abruzzi Spur in bad weather to bring down the sick and exhausted Dudley Wolfe from one of the high camps; they disappeared in the storm. These people look at mountains and at mountaineering with different eyes from us. I have already told of Nawang Tenzing, my friend and rope companion of several expeditions. With him I went to the summit of Makalu; and with Nawang Dorje I climbed Dhaulagiri. I am not certain whether my third indigenous partner for an ascent of an eight-thousander was a Hunza or not. Fayazz Hussain and I climbed Gasherbrum II together; he was our liaison officer – I feel quite sure that the dynamic Fayazz must have come from the mountain area in northwestern Pakistan. In all three cases we enjoyed a good relationship, were friends and remained so.

Unfortunately, attempts on the part of the expedition participants to understand the world of the locals remain sketchy – that's if any attempt is made at all. Only when you speak the language – even a little – when you try to understand their life and their religion, do certain things become clear in your mind; and you are not surprised when, for instance, someone like brave Pasang Dawa Lama (who later stood on the top of Cho Oyu with Herbert Tichy), having climbed to almost 8,400 metres here on K2 in 1939, resisted going any higher for fear of the evil spirits that come out at night – something which cost Fritz Wiessner the summit. You could say that fleeing from night demons indicates a very sound sense of self-preservation.

As well as such legendary figures, there are also some very ordinary mortals amongst these mountain people. Throughout one expedition, Julie and I couldn't help wondering whether the Balti who came with the glowing recommendation of one famous mountaineer was really the man he said he was – or his brother. At least he was happy and an outstanding singer!

High-altitude porters are paid according to rules laid down for expeditions by the government. Besides their wages they must be supplied with a complete mountaineering outfit; but if you give this too early, they scurry off to the bazaar and sell it all. Sometimes they show up with old tattered gear from other trips. You should not be angry – because these people are not rich – and of course it's natural to try to make good money out of the equipment. In fact, you can buy the most modern equipment the world has to offer in the bazaar in Kathmandu! In Pakistan, such things are more usually shared out within families; I did not find much in the bazaars there. For these people, the lure to possess things from the faraway and 'exotic' countries of the mountaineers, as well as curiosity and vanity, besides just simple poverty, leads to desires being awakened that are mostly impossible to satisfy – a shining tubular steel ski-stick here can give its owner a prestige akin to the possession of a Porsche … at least he thinks so.

Except when you are on the mountain, in the real throes of the climb, you should not take it too tragically if things disappear. Such petty offences are the exception rather than the rule, and it is balanced by the fact that they themselves willingly offer you what little they have. Hunzas for instance are famous for the greatest generosity and honesty. Towards the end of an expedition, however, you can find on several Himalayan peaks that the mountain becomes a sort of goldmine for the locals … the conservationists' target of a 'clean mountain' could easily become reality without much effort, provided a little time and encouragement were devoted to it. Travellers to the Himalayas will notice that the less an area has been visited by strangers, the less likely it is that they lose even the smallest items – quite the reverse, for often it is you that will be given gifts. At a later stage of a place being opened to outsiders, locals may be too timid to ask for items which to them seem to represent 'riches beyond measure', but which they would nevertheless like to have; perhaps then, something might disappear.

It didn't matter much that our good Hayat in the Hindu Kush filched a few packets of nuts for his children; he was a bit uncomfortable when Tona silently gave him a whole boxful. With Musheraf it was rather more difficult: he had an incredible talent for invention when it came to explanations of what had become of our ski-sticks: they fell into crevasses, into mountain streams, they rolled down the steep slopes – but he was such a fantastic man, so full of energy for our climbs, and again and again would generously bring us fresh apples from his village, which was three days' walk away. He obviously had a good number of friends with fruit trees – all of whom had an insatiable need for ski-sticks! In the end we came to a mutual and good-natured understanding, overlooking his little foibles by regarding them rather as a 'ski-stick tax'. Musheraf turned a little red in the face when I told him that I should hang on to one stick at least for the journey back. Since then, I always carry an abundance of ski-sticks on expeditions.

Apropos of which, each of us, Julie and I, have one ski-stick firmly fixed onto our rucksacks! This certainly makes climbing up through House's Chimney very awkward, but the end is almost in sight now. Even though we both know it by heart (in two years we have climbed up here about a dozen times), the chimney remains a struggle when you are heavily loaded, despite the fixed ropes and the old metal caving ladder. Gasping for breath, I take another rest …

In 1954, the Italians installed one of their winches here – a sort of rope hoist to ferry up their material. The rock barrier reaches a height of eighty metres, and the great chimney of ochre-coloured dolomitic rock cuts through it at this point in an oblique line; in difficulty, it is not dissimilar to a section of the big curving couloir on the Matterhorn North Face. Towards the end, it grows so narrow that my huge rucksack keeps snagging against the wall. Chunks of ice rain down into the depths.

At last I'm through, and call down to Julie that she can follow. She has been sheltering behind a projecting rock out of the line of fire of all those ice chunks and stones I have set off during my ascent. Her reply floats up: she's climbing. Apart from this almost vertical cliff, the Abruzzi Ridge has an average inclination of forty-three degrees. Above about 7,000 metres, on the slabs of the Black Pyramid, the angle steepens to fifty to fifty-five degrees, and only after 2,000 metres of height gain from the foot of the mountain, do you get the more gentle slopes of the so-called Shoulder. Today – as distinct from in 1954 – only the highest snow shoulder just below the summit pyramid (between about 7,800 and 8,000 metres) is referred to by this name. Higher up, it gets very steep again – all the way to the summit!

Camp 2 … 6,700 metres … we've almost made it! Already I can see the friendly red glow of our Basque tent up there, sheltering in the lee of a high rocky islet and dug into the fairly steep, packed snow which coats the gravel slope. Nowadays, this airy position with its panoramic views over Concordia and the wild Baltoro peaks serves as Camp 2 for most expeditions, although originally it used to be Camp 5. The first climbers established a total of nine camps – something which had advantages and disadvantages.

Julie and I climb the last few steps together and hurry towards the camp, full of anticipation – and relief that for today at least the effort is over.

Whatever's happened to our tent? Christopher Columbus! It's a Spanish caravel in full sail, run aground in the snow! Fantasy. 'Don't exaggerate,' I scold myself. 'When it's only the top sail you see.'

Blown snow, which the wind has collected from the mountainsides over the last three weeks, has built up against the tent, causing the fabric to yield, wherever possible, under the pressure; the top of the tent, however, being secured by a rope to an anchorage in the slope higher up, could not give – and now the whole structure is a series of undulating curves, between pressure and tension, like some untitled creation of a modern artist –

Untitled? No – it has to be 'The Spanish Caravel'! In my time, I've seen an enormous variety of names given to the untitled works of great artists (artists who may or may not be a 'name' in their own right)! The only people who might possibly object to naming this particular opus after a Spanish sailing ship, could be our Basque friends from whom we acquired it.

'Half an hour's work,' says Julie drily; then laughing, she nods at the tent meaningfully. Half an hour of shovelling before we can live in here again … that should do it. She knows how much I enjoy spade-work – even as a student in Vienna, long before we met, I often exhausted my energy in this way. Shovelling enlarges your breathing passages – essential for mountaineering, I console myself. Soon chunks of snow are flying out over the slope, blocks of snow are smashing and rolling down the mountain until they become smaller and smaller balls and in time they dissolve entirely to dust. While I am digging away, Julie pulls strongly at the fabric, readjusts the tent poles and guys: luckily, nothing is broken.

Finally, it's done: how beautiful, if you have really worked hard for your hours of peace, to be lying in your sleeping bag, sipping your soup, looking effortlessly from the door down over the whole world – we have left it open on purpose. Once more we are having a really good time.

But now we're tired; we lean our heads against the snow wall behind the fabric and fall asleep, content and happy. Quite early for us – it's only afternoon.

Herds of stampeding buffaloes? What is it? Alien yells disturb our idyll. Am I dreaming of a Western? Red River Raid, perhaps? An ambush?

'*Patsch!*' Swearing, I sit up; something has hit me on the head. '*Porca miseria!*' I yell out loud. Three more blocks of snow have thundered against the side of the tent.

'Calm down,' Julie soothes; 'it's the Koreans' altitude porters.' Outside, there is a moment's quiet, then comes the sound of loud laughter and foreign voices joking – at least now only small chunks are hitting the tent.

'The blessed shovel must needs serve the community … ' I do my best to remain objective, and bury my head in the sleeping bag. Of course, there are others, like me, who enjoy shovelling – but now, not a metre away from me, a Hunza's ice-axe begins pounding the ground. Closer and closer – he's already touching the tent, for goodness' sake – one false stroke and he'll have a hole in my head. I explode, leaping up again. '*Himmelkreuzdonnerwetter!* Watch out for the tent!' I bellow. Outside an invisible Korean intervenes, and the metallic hammering close to the tent ceases; I am grateful to him for that. But the general noise goes on for hours – the clattering of pots, shouts, slurping, laughing, moaning, snoring – a high-altitude symphony. At times it's overlaid by the reverberating movements of someone crossing the slope and hanging onto the tents and fixed ropes for support … or hacking new snow for cooking.

Julie has long since disappeared deep inside her sleeping bag. She has a way of overcoming situations like this without losing her equanimity: an ability that I admire and envy. No sleep comes my way.

Then I remember something: up here in 1984 we had to sit out two days of violent storms, during which we read Herbert Tichy's *Weisse Wolken über Gelber Erde* (White Clouds over a Yellow Land), gusts battering the tent as I translated, and Julie listening as best she could over the clamour of the wind. K2 was giving us a good piece of its mind, then, on storm trumpets that were far louder than this. With such thoughts, I finally drop asleep despite the Hunza symphony.

PUSHING TO GREAT HEIGHTS

Whichever way you climb, with or without high-altitude porters, whether or not you adopt Alpine style, you have to conserve all the energy you can. You should climb only after you have become totally acclimatized and without carrying too much weight. (The higher you are, the more you feel it.) If you share out a group's equipment in a sensible manner, and if you build up depots beforehand, you can reduce the average weight carried; the same applies to the division of exhausting work like trail-breaking, not only when you're going Alpine style, but also, for instance, when employing what is known as the Hanns-Schell technique, where the person in the lead makes use of the group's only oxygen apparatus, handing over the set when he hands over the lead. That way supplementary oxygen goes only to the person breaking trail.

On K2 I cannot see any disadvantage in climbing up slowly and conserving energy on the first half of the mountain; in my opinion you then arrive at a great height in better condition than if you had 'run'. However, from 7,000 to 7,500 metres onwards (the latter being the height at which the so-called Death Zone starts) the number of days given to climbing and descending should be kept as low as possible. The actual height at which you make the transition will vary a little from person to person. If someone has adopted a special tactic which involves carrying practically nothing, then he might do it in a different way – like Benoît Chamoux, who was working in tandem with a group that started a day ahead of him, so that going up to join his friends he climbed at a pre-determined rate, with practically no stops at all, enabling him to maintain the same rhythm all the way to the top, climbing night and day. However, dire consequences would befall anyone wanting to break records in this way who had not made all the necessary preparations; blind dedication to speed alone is incompatible with safety and is, I feel, already having negative side effects.

But if you have to carry more to enable you safely to spend longer on the upper half of the mountain, you should – and will prefer to – climb more slowly. There is the danger that essential food and equipment will be left behind in the interests of gaining speed … and that actually reduces the safety of all the people on the mountain at that time.

Normally, an ascent using supplementary oxygen cannot be carried out, or does not make sense, without high-altitude porters. When climbing without oxygen and without such porters – in the West Alpine style of Hermann Buhl – everything that is going to be needed should be transported up and cached in depots or high camps before the top is stormed. Nowadays, the modern Alpine-style mountaineer often tries to omit this phase (the pure West Alpine style without fixed camps, as used by Hermann Buhl and me on Chogolisa in 1957, is referred to as Alpine style today) and so he sometimes arrives at great altitude insufficiently acclimatized. If a route is planned to be done in pure Alpine style, then you need to prepare yourself, train and practise on another route or another mountain beforehand. The much quoted ascent of Hidden Peak by Messner and Habeler in 1975 – two mountaineers on their own with a mobile high camp – was an admirable performance, but it was not pioneering: the technique they used was not new, nor was it correct to claim this as the first eight-thousander to be climbed in West Alpine style – for Hermann Buhl set both these precedents. He pioneered both the idea and the name for it. Even Reinhold Messner only followed the tracks of Hermann Buhl in that respect (the attempt on Chogolisa and the ascent of Skil Brum in 1957 were already examples of perfect Alpine style and no different from that used on Hidden Peak).

That K2 with its great altitude and steepness deserves its title of 'mountain of mountains' has been proved many times over the years, not just because of its extraordinary beauty, but also for being 'a mountain above other mountains'. In comparison to K2, fellow eight-thousanders in the Karakoram – Broad Peak, Gasherbrum II and Hidden Peak – and all the higher seven-thousanders, are still a 'full storey below' this giant. Whatever applies for them is only part of the story for K2. There, the mountaineer experiences his few minutes' worth or half an hour of summit joy at the most only one or two ropes' lengths above 8,000 metres; whereas on K2, an equivalent height just brings him to the last high camp. A decisive difference: it means that anyone on K2 has to be able to stay above 8,000 metres for very much longer – for days longer.

THE KOREAN TENT

The rocks of the Black Pyramid: split by frost, glued back together by ice – a structure made up of fragments, and steep enough in places to lean against; shattered slabs, with here and there vertical breaks like giant steps.

The porter column scratches, clanks and pants its way across the rocks above us, punctuated every now and again by a shout, in a Korean voice or some Hunza dialect. We follow close on the heels of the porters, but don't intend climbing as far as Camp 3. We can imagine what the overcrowding will be like there – we won't find any of the peace and quiet a mountaineer needs just before an eight-thousander. There will be no opportunity for concentration, for imagination, for focusing every last fibre of being on what lies ahead. Hermann Buhl identified this phase as decisive before any big mountaineering effort – we often talked about it. The whole night before a big climb he sometimes spent in a state between waking and sleeping: a kind of trance, Hermann used to say, completely dedicated to the mountain.

For my own part, I prefer some sleep before setting out … 'We will overnight in the 7,000-metre camp, and continue climbing tomorrow,' I tell myself. Michel Parmentier's lightweight *parapluie* tent, which he donated to us when he left, should be up there inside Wanda's tent; it's a little dome that you erect in the same way as opening an umbrella, and it holds two people – just. Julie is clearly already looking forward to this magic contraption – as if in some way it shared the Gallic allure of its owner. (The suave French journalist talks altogether too much to my way of thinking, but I guess that goes with the job – really I suppose I shouldn't mind.) I have more confidence in our own narrow but uncomplicated British bivouac tent – a streamlined, dark-green tunnel with a front extension in which you can cook – even if you have to lie down to do so – and this does not even weigh one and a half kilograms. Of course, it *is* a bit tight for two (very tight, Julie says!), but remarkably stable. It stood the test well on our Broad Peak climb, but Julie claims that you can't move once you're inside it. So I guess that for the summit, we will be exchanging this tent I have tied onto my rucksack for the one with the French chic. If our depot on the Shoulder of K2 is still in existence, as we hope but rather doubt, then we will also have our blue Ultimate tunnel tent. This has proved itself stormproof, and in the event that it's there, we will certainly use that.

Suddenly the column stops in its tracks – dissent, a cacophony of voices. 'What's the matter?' I yell upwards.

'Camp 3, finish!' calls back a Hunza, letting his heavy load slide from his shoulders and crash on to the rocks; he has obviously lost all motivation. Camp 3, finish – gone!

Of course – the avalanche. The same thundering cloud of ice and snow that brought down Mandi's teapot, that squashed and battered it so unrecognizably under the force of the ice blocks, as well as ripping Willi's sweater, the same avalanche that carried away the tatters of the Italians' tents from the assault camp at 7,700 metres and dumped them in the valley had then also, as I feared, got as far as Camp 3, and devastated that.

A figure appears: it's Mandi – Mandi Ehrengruber. Pale, with a ravaged expression and rapid movements, as if fear still stalked him. He must have spent a sleepless night on the site of the destroyed camp up there at 7,350 metres, exposed no doubt to the full blast of the icy winds from China and worried all the time about what else might come down from higher up the mountain.

He sees us and stops. 'Camp 3 is gone, Camp 4 as well,' he says dully. 'The whole serac wall above the Italian tents has come down. My God, you can't imagine what that slope looks like.' We regard him silently – his face tells more than volumes of words. His eyes wander.

'I've had enough,' he says at last, turning to face Julie and me again and shrugging his shoulders in resignation – so far as his rucksack allows. 'Every bloody thing's gone from up there.' He breathes heavily, 'All that effort for nothing.' Utter disappointment and tiredness sound in his voice. It alarms me. 'And Willi – what's he doing?' I ask. 'He found a Korean tent – the only one to escape damage. He's going on.' Well – Willi, I think, a lot more has to happen before this one gives up!

'What are the chances of more stuff coming down?'

'Plenty, I should think. Snow-slips, I'm sure, are still possible. It's difficult to tell.' He turns to leave, taking hold of the fixed rope. 'I've had a bellyful, any road—'

'Safe journey, Mandi – take care!' Julie calls after his fast-disappearing form.

I bite my lip. It's going to be chaos ahead.

Above us a great commotion has started up, yelling voices cut the air. The news has hit everyone like a bomb. We work our way up towards the group of gesticulating porters and the stunned Koreans trying to calm them down. But the porters have good reason to be upset; they have not just thrown their bags into the snow on a whim – they're frightened. They're afraid that the whole place which they are trying to reach will be destroyed. One is worried that he will not find any shelter for the night, others that they will no longer make it down again before nightfall. Above us rears the Black Pyramid with its notorious slabs, the most difficult section of the Abruzzi Ridge.

The leader of the porters pleads to turn back, insisting to the Koreans with increasing urgency that it is madness to go on. When his entreaties fall on deaf ears, his frustration finally spills over.

'You will all die!' he yells.

Even today, writing these lines, I can still hear the cry: it was at once a shriek of fear and a terrible warning. Arms uplifted in supplication; the wide-eyed, troubled stare; the note of pleading in the voice of the normally so cheerful and determined Mohammed Ali, as he begged and begged, 'Please, don't go on – you will all die!' That is something I will never forget.

The news from above had changed the situation at a stroke. Panic and desperation now reigned. Terror in the face of such forces of destruction as had been operating up there was written in almost every face. To know finally the full and devastating effect, the extent of the ice avalanche – which I had feared – was shattering. Even if Julie and I had no supply point within reach of the avalanche (apart from that almost empty duffel bag by the ice tower above Camp 3), we were still faced with the big question of what now should be done – and the Koreans, too, were scratching their heads. It was as if suddenly a dark star had risen over everybody on the ridge, as if its invisible light mingled with the sun's rays, which until a moment ago were playing so cheerfully on the steep ribs and crumbling towers of the Abruzzi. The ice of the serac cliffs far above us now took on a dangerous glint – the sunlight still beamed in the wide sky above the Baltoro mountains, but it no longer carried the promise of good fortune.

Had the falling ice been the pointing finger of Allah, warning the bearded leader of the porters? And why only him? Was the man a clairvoyant? My steps slowed. So compelling were his gestures, so vehement the words of Mohammed Ali, they certainly seemed like a voice from Beyond. I hesitated, glancing at Julie: 'We'll go as far as the 7,000-metre camp, shall we?' It was only a couple of ropes' lengths further on, tucked under a rock wall. My companion nodded earnestly, if a little thoughtfully. 'Of course,' she said. Both of us had now stopped.

Throughout the argument between the Koreans and their high-altitude porters – which language difficulties of necessity made a long-winded business – and while the former desperately tried to reach a compromise, I was thinking to myself: so, the ice avalanche has wiped out Camps 4 and 3. Willi is sitting in possession of the only remaining tent – a Korean tent – up at the site of Camp 3; and he, I guess, even if it's too late now, must be remembering my warning. The only Austrian tents that remain intact are those below House's Chimney at about 6,500 metres – 2,100 metres below the summit. By placing their faith in a more limited reach of the ice avalanche, the Austrians neglected to carry up with them any other tents – and who knows how much, if any, of their gear still exists in Camp 4 and Camp 3?

The Koreans on the other hand with such an array of porters will surely have spare tents for the summit push – and they are helpful people. But if their porters refuse to go any further, the Korean attack is finished. And we, what about us? Do we want to go on?

I'm not so much shocked about being proved right – I sensed that anyway – as about the possibility of further avalanche danger. What is the state of the snow surface on the slope below the Shoulder? How much will it have been affected by the falling masses of ice? And what if a vertical drop has been created in the serac wall, which cannot be overcome and necessitates a long and complicated detour? There are a lot of unknown factors above us. However, you can't judge them from the troubled face of one fleeing climber. Especially as Willi Bauer has remained up there, and I have the feeling that the weather is improving all the time. Mandi was appalled at what he saw and decided to give up – not without good reasons for the Austrian summit push is now almost certainly without a tent of its own and all its gear missing, swept away by the avalanche.

'Yes – this time I will see it through, however tough it turns out to be. It's the last chance!' Willi had said, down in Base Camp before setting out. That's why he is still up there ...

For Julie and me it makes the most sense if we take a look for ourselves and come to a decision after that.

The Koreans? They seem desperate, are still negotiating. 'If we go ahead' – Julie breaks into my thoughts – 'it may get their porters moving, too.' That's right, if we simply go on, it may be enough to budge the porters from this spot. They could at least climb up another section before turning round – some would make it up to Camp 3, almost certainly.

We say a few words of encouragement to the Koreans, then we tackle the mighty snow rib below the big, and in places vertical, rock wall on whose grey-black slabs further up swings a very ancient rope ladder. The snow rib is steep and continuous. We are breathing heavily under the weight of our overloaded packs. At the end of the second ropelength we traverse to the left, on to a snow-covered rock band, just below the wall – a bit to one side of the route. Looking back, we realize with satisfaction that the porters are on the move, they are climbing up.

'All sorted out!' Julie laughs. 'I think we gave them a hand, don't you?' She chuckles. A look of determination has come into her eyes. The Korean push continues, then! They overtake us with their porters, having passed the break-even point of the climb. For a while we still hear the scratching of their crampons, the shouts of the column, then silence settles. We are alone.

'Kurt – what do *you* think about the avalanche danger?' Julie asks out of the blue. I hesitate. 'I don't want to die, you know,' she says in a low voice – a moment of fear revealed in her eyes.

It touches me like a breath of the big mountain. 'Oh, Julie, we will go back immediately, if anything is wrong. I don't want to die, either!' I assure her, moved. Nobody must die!

The scene down there with the leader of the porters had its effect on her, too – I am still chewing it over myself. The avalanche danger? I don't feel I can comment on this until I have seen things at first hand; it's several days ago now since the ice fall happened. 'We'll take a look and decide then ...'

Julie seems reassured. I am, too, to some extent. We'll certainly not take any unnecessary risk … equally, though, we don't want to give up too easily.

'He-ey! Let's pick up that French tent, then!' Julie says abruptly, eyes alight with expectation.

I growl assent … the French tent of Michel Parmentier! Our gift horse – I had almost forgotten about it. He said we would find it inside Wanda's tent, up on this rocky ledge. 'You go and look,' commands Julie and points to the 7,000-metre Camp, as this intermediate post is called, with some overstatement. Wanda's dark green Goretex two-man tent, storm-crumpled and half-squashed by snow, sits on the narrow ledge at the foot of the vertical rock wall, carefully belayed. Immediately to one side of it there is a sheer drop down endless snowfields and ribs, about 1,700 metres to the Godwin-Austen glacier. Exactly how far, nobody knows, because the given heights of camps on the Abruzzi Ridge vary from one expedition report to another, sometimes by as much as one or two hundred metres. The so-called 7,000-metre Camp is perhaps only 6,900 metres high. But who worries about that – barometric heights, which in the end depend on the atmospheric pressure, are unreliable. On the dark green fabric of Wanda's shelter there is the bleached, barely legible inscription: 'highest film team in the world' – Julie's and my logo. We gave the tent to Wanda last summer on Nanga Parbat, after we had to give up only 600 metres below the summit when the weather broke and in our haste to get down had to abandon the tent Wanda had lent us then. Now – after her K2 success – Wanda doesn't need the tent any more: she told us to help ourselves to its contents. But for reasons of weight, we cannot take much; I find provisions, some gas, and *voilà!* – the carefully rolled-up, shining red French mini-tent! I see Julie's eyes shine as I pass it out to her, and cannot avoid thinking of the charming Michel, the noble benefactor. Truly, it can be set up with a couple of moves, very much like opening an umbrella which has a floor attached beneath it. The thing is light, you can sit inside and – if you first tuck your feet into the attached side-pocket specially designed for the purpose – even lie down. French *raffinement*, somewhat bizarre! To me, the spokes of the 'umbrella' seem a bit flimsy and the circular entrance-hole too small and close to the ground – all right perhaps for a svelte and elegant Frenchman (like Michel), but hardly adequate for a solid, unbendable, Austrian *Gugelhupf*-eater (like me)! However, during the long years with my rope-companion

I have come to recognize that when there's something she really sets her heart on resistance is useless ... (a trait which, in the occasional 'tugs-of-war' between us, we attribute to each other!)

As I gasp my way on all fours through the ridiculous entrance, I think to myself: 'Love is to accept an awkward French tent – even when you have a perfectly good British one ...'

While Julie is cooking and I am outside again, I suddenly see Hannes Wieser – unmistakable in his black hat – coming up at some speed. He's always cheerful is Hannes, everybody likes him. He tacks over towards us and I have the feeling that there's something on his mind. 'Have you a spare sleeping bag, by any chance? One of our people has stupidly taken two bags down with him!' he calls. We tell him no. 'But we can give you a bivvy tent, very good and very light. Considering that up there all your tents are gone ...' I add.

'No,' Hannes replies, 'I don't need the tent. Willi has agreed something with the Koreans over the radio. But do you have a stove? And gas?'

'Of course: a cooker and a gas cartridge you can have – the others we need ourselves; but provisions, if you need ...' In my mind's eye I see Camp 3 destroyed by the avalanche: anything, everything could have disappeared, been destroyed, swept away? It is clear Hannes and his friends plan to climb up to Camp 4 tomorrow – does he really not want the tent? As I hand him the cooker I say again, 'It's super light, our bivvy tent, and we don't need it. Really, you're welcome to have it ... you never know ... with the situation up there ...' But Hannes waves it away; a kilo more is a kilo more – that's true enough and I don't insist. Alfred is already way ahead and so he shouldn't waste time, says Hannes, pulling tight the strings of his rucksack. Then he climbs on, speedily and cheerful as ever, his black hat pushed to the back of his head.

We don't envy him the chaos up there, inevitable with so many people trying to re-establish the derelict Camp 3. The Koreans will surely put everything into a decisive push towards the summit now that good weather, finally, seems to be on the way; it could well be the last chance of the season.

Optimism starts to fire us, too, despite all the setbacks the mountain seems bent on throwing in our way. No, we don't want to force anything that should not be – we'll leave a definite decision open – but the weather seems good, we are in fine shape, and if, against our expectation, the summit remains forbidden to us this time too, then at least we shall have tried. We can go home with a totally different feeling. As for the thoroughness of our planning, we could hardly have done more. To begin with we will pass a calm and undisturbed night here – 7,000 metres is still a good height, if you are acclimatized.

Later I often thought back to this stage of the ascent, back to this day. We had already then had three chances of escaping the subsequent tragedy: first, there was the warning of the sirdar. It was irrational – logic demands reasons why one should give up, and there were none. But did Mohammed Ali hear an inner voice? Only a few days later he was fatally hit by a falling stone. It was below Camp 1 on the same Abruzzi Ridge on which he had warned the others so earnestly. Isn't the choice of destiny sometimes absurd?

Why didn't we hear the voice? Perhaps we did – but we didn't believe in it. Still, I see in front of me the man with his uplifted hands, with the imploring gestures, hear his voice. *Allah o akbar ...* we should have listened to him. But he was the one who died.

The second chance we might have had to escape fate came with the strike of the high-altitude porters. If they had persisted in their refusal to go on, it would have been unfortunate for the Koreans, for their attack would have failed: I hardly believe they would have entertained an Alpine-style push. (They were moving according to an exact plan, in the classic style of a big expedition, the strategy of which is determined from Base Camp.) The Austrians could then, without fuss or restriction, have simply taken over the only un-damaged tent in Camp 3 – the Korean one – for their own summit push. The fateful overcrowding would never have happened.

The third way we might have avoided the disastrous constellation on the K2 Shoulder would have been the introduction up there of our small bivvy tent, giving extra space for one or two people. The overcrowding would have been alleviated and the fatal con-sequences avoided. But who could have foreseen it? At that point – nobody. When Hannes Wieser refused our small tent, unwittingly we had all come one step closer to the deadly trap.

It was diabolic machinery, into the cogwheels of which all of us were imperceptibly but irretrievably being sucked – the mechanism being so complicated that it was not recognizable to the individual; every way that might have led us out eventually became blocked by the taking of single decisions, which by themselves would never have been so critical, but in their conjunction opened the death trap for seven people up at 8,000 metres. That two of them finally survived the hell of the days-long storm is a miracle – which ever way you look at it.

My hope is that by thinking through the individual elements in this chain reaction the lives of future mountaineers on K2 or on other mountains in the world may yet be saved. Perhaps they will realize in time that their situation is narrowing down in a similar way. It is for this reason that I go into all the detail, that I write about these events at all.

Julie and I spend a calm, recuperative afternoon and evening. It is so nice when you don't have to hurry, when you can really live with the mountain.

To live with the mountain – that's what always draws me back. It is something I have discovered with Julie – my rare companion – even if basically it is what I had been doing myself from the very beginning. Both of us have tried to understand how even among our best friends there is an increasing mania to make an expedition as short as possible, to climb the mountain as swiftly as possible, to start back as soon as possible. More and more people are caught by this disease: do they still love the mountain? They don't seem to 'live' it any more – or if they do, they 'live' it differently – perhaps only as an extension of themselves. It is understandable that sometimes for tactical reasons you have to move fast on the mountain – in certain situations, at certain sections during a climb or a descent. But with them, it seems to become a rule that dominates everything. Do we go to these wonderful places simply to fulfil a duty – and to get shot of them, the sooner the better?

Today is 1 August. A fantastic day. Luck is with us …

It has often proved the case on this great mountain that in order to put yourself into fine weather high up when going for the top, you have to commit yourself to the ascent in advance of it before you can be sure what the weather will do. Naturally, you may make a mistake and have started for nothing … but if you hang on until it is absolutely fine, conditions may turn bad again before you are up there.

But this time, Julie, we've got it right! Her eyes shine with happiness; I think we both glow – like the ocean of glittering peaks and glaciers around us, from way below our feet out to the distant horizon. Its reflection has lit up our faces. Amid that dazzling flood of light, there soars in front of us, still considerably higher than we are, the striking profile of Broad Peak, which seen from here presents its narrow side. The summit we shared ... Through the pleasure that wells within me, seeing it like this, I anticipate how beautiful it will be to stand at last on the top of K2. While Julie, above me, tackles the vertical serac wall below Camp 3 – because of the sideways pull on the fixed rope, only one of us can move along it at a time – I look out into Sinkiang: there in those savage valleys is where it all started ... now we are climbing to the very apex of the giant crystal that dominates that land.

7,200 metres! Heavily loaded, we pant our way up the steep icy wall. In spite of the ropes, it's a bloody hard struggle. But that's all part of the game. If only we could know that our depot on the Shoulder was still there, we could dump a whole lot of this gear in Camp 3. Whether it is, or not, will depend on where exactly the ice avalanche broke off, I suppose –

Of course when you carry a whole altitude camp on your back like this, you are heavily loaded. At least, under the weight, we can feel assured that we are fit, that the long rest period in Base Camp has done us good; also our acclimatization after so long here is better than ever before.

Julie is first to reach the top of the ice cliff and waits for me there. Gasping, I muscle up the last few metres, one hand on the grip of the jumar clamp, which I push, move after move, higher along the fixed rope, while at the same time forcing the front points of my crampons into the wall and giving myself additional support with the ultra-lightweight titanium ice axe in my other hand. All the equipment is far less heavy than it was in Hermann Buhl's time – jumars didn't exist then at all. Nor had the figure-of-eight been invented, this compact metal device with two holes in it: when abseiling, you pull a loop of rope through one hole and then pass it over the opposite end and snap the karabiner of your seat-harness into the other hole. Gently braking by means of the friction of the rope in the figure-of-eight, you then slide graciously into the depths ... with hardly any effort all. None of that existed.

We will deposit the two figures-of-eight in Camp 3 for our return. (Here we are at the last of the long sequence of fixed ropes on the Abruzzi.) I have reached the top now, too – and immediately notice that both the ski-sticks I left there last time I came down have disappeared. I curse – but Julie shrugs her shoulders: we have each taken the precaution of bringing up an extra one. We detach them from the rucksacks. Up to here, a ski-stick is useless ballast, but from now on it is enormously important. Standing on the gentle snow slope above the ice wall while we rope up, I cast my eyes upwards: the Shoulder of the mountain looks unchanged – nothing has happened up there. Those tons of ice must have detached themselves from the steep face just below it … there … where the tents of Quota 8,000 stood at 7,700 metres, making up the camp which the Austrians took over as their highest stronghold after the return of the Italians. Before that, tucked into the sheltered position at the foot of the vertical to overhanging ice cliffs, there had been the tents of the two Swiss, as well as Michel Parmentier's, Wanda's, and that of the two Barrards. The entire ice barrier, the height of a house, has collapsed along its full width. It was sheer good fortune that nobody was up there when it happened …

Critically, I observe the sheared surface left by the fall: it looks smooth enough and there are no new horizontal fractures visible above it. No apparent danger, then, at present …

Everything must be buried beneath it, under blocks of ice several metres thick – if anything remained here at all, that is – and I think of Willi's torn pullover and Mandi's squashed teapot which we found 2,000 metres lower down, at the foot of the mountain, vivid testimony of the power with which the ice thundered down …

Slowly we plod up the slope to Camp 3, oppressed by the realization of how destructive the ice avalanche had been, even here: all that is left of the Austrian camp are tattered rags. A grey-green block of ice, the size of a table, came to a halt just short of the campsite, leaving a deep, scoured track behind it: it stands lopsidely now on the slope. The whole area looks terrible, as do the surfaces above: trenches, clefts … missiles of ice must have raced into the abyss, hurtling over the snow like speed boats; dice, the size of houses, rolled down the steep slopes, breaking into thousands of fragments, leaving furrows and depressions in their wake … The friendly slope we trudged up on our first attempt is now completely disfigured by scars and pock-marks.

It's a wonder that one of the Korean tents survived this inferno – probably only because it was rolled up, and not erected. But the prudent Koreans have now had new tents brought up with their high-altitude porters, and have put them up. They are in their camp now, but nothing can be seen of Willi, Hannes and Alfred, who must have gone on this morning, to the Shoulder.

In the snow I notice a bundle of bamboo wands, for marking the slope above Camp 3, and am surprised that no one has set them up yet. Maybe because the weather is so fine? I know how much store Kim, the expedition leader, sets by them: we will take care of it.

Kim Byung-Joon is thirty-seven years old, and has always appeared to me as an open, sympathetic character, a man of prudence and precision. Not a single decision does he take lightly; the events during the ascent, the decisive radio contacts between Base Camp and the mountain, his anxieties – all faithfully detailed in his book of the expedition – are proof of that. After the 'teapot avalanche', he too was highly worried about the fate of Camp 3: unlike 2, which remained unharmed, it could not be seen with binoculars. One of the Korean mountaineers gave it a 50 per cent chance of survival, but the deputy leader, Chang Bong-Wan, reckoned it had only 10 per cent and concluded from this: '... we have to change our plan.' Kim Byung-Joon, who had divided his members into an attack team and several support groups, therefore decided 'to have all necessary material carried up once more to Camp 3, in order to make sure that the attacking party has everything at its disposal above Camp 3.' The attitude of the Austrian members towards their last summit push cannot have been unanimous, otherwise much remains simply inexplicable: they all knew that the avalanche had carried important material to the foot of the mountain. 'Yet it appears that they did not carry up sufficient supplies to replace the loss when they made their summit try,' Adams Carter later adjudged in the American *Alpine Journal*. One other point worth making is that, according to their report, it was Willi Bauer who informed the Koreans that the highest camps on the mountain were probably wrecked.

Camp 3, 7,350 metres on 1 August: Julie and I discover an old, unused platform between two red Korean dome tents and have our French *parapluie* set up in no time at all. Perhaps it was not such a bad exchange after all – I start warming towards this intricate contraption. In our own tent, which we deposited at the intermediate camp, it would not have been possible to sit upright as we are now doing. In addition to our ice-axes, an ownerless snow piton serves to anchor the tent in place of my ski-sticks which disappeared from the edge of the ice cliff. But all this is little more than a morale booster. We obviously hope that after the avalanche disaster, several days ago now, nothing much else should come down for a bit; nevertheless, I remember that I have never felt very easy in this place.

All of a sudden, I jump up: one of the Koreans is filming with a small 16mm summit camera. It is like a sting of conscience, for my own camera has been left lower down. Cameramen are all terribly jealous of each other, and it is the first time that I have seen the Koreans filming on the mountain. Then I calm down: you can't have everything! After all, there's only the two of us, and no high-altitude porters. We will use our shots from the first summit push, backing them up with still photographs. There are more Koreans, all familiar faces from our time together in Base Camp, but with the exception of a very lively, curly-headed climber, I never remember who is who. Almost all of them are called Kim, or Chang, or Joon, with an additional name tacked on, difficult to keep in mind. They are dark-skinned and almost constantly smiling, their movements fluid, and without exception they are friendly and helpful – spitting images of one another to the unaccustomed eye ...

Except for the one with the black curls! He nods in my direction cheerfully. 'Hello!' he beams, sparkling, impish eyes dancing with enthusiasm. Is it the summit he has in mind – or our beer barrel? Or the possibility of celebrating both in a forthcoming feast? He is the one who in Base Camp most frequently takes up our 'secret' invitations to beer-tasting – 'secret' only among the Koreans. After every sip, 'Curlyhead' casts a prudent glance over his shoulder towards Kim's tent because, conscious of his responsibility as expedition leader, Kim deposited all the team's alcohol in Paiju during the approach march. Since then, the Koreans have been sitting on the dry side of the moraine.

With the exception of this merry (and occasionally 'damp') curlyhead, then, it is difficult to distinguish one quicksilver Korean from another. How many of them are there up here – in and outside the tents? Four? Five? Six? Hard to say: if they are not all standing side by side, you have no idea.

To one of them, I hand a small nylon pouch containing our figures-of-eight for the descent along with some other bits and pieces, asking him if they would mind keeping them in the tent for us. 'No problem,' he smiles. I know I can rely on them: once they even brought my exposed films down from the mountain. I wonder if we shall go to the summit together? It rather looks like it. While we are shooting off photographs of one another – with seracs and the ocean of peaks in the background – one of them tells me: 'Austrians today Camp 4, tomorrow summit; we tomorrow Camp 4 ... and next day summit ... I think.' He smiles timidly. Yes, you can never be quite sure of that.

So that's the plan! Willi, Hannes and Alfred to have their summit day, followed by the Koreans a day later – on the same day as us, in other words, and the same day as Alan Rouse (who has meanwhile turned up, to the enthusiastic welcome of Julie) together with Mrowka, one of the Polish women. The slim, lively Briton and his diminutive companion have much in common: the same bright eyes and strong glance, the same determination and energy. I notice it as they install their tent on the slope diagonally above us, first shovelling free a space. They too have arrived heavily loaded, having all they need with them.

One question still burns in my soul: is our depot still on the Shoulder, or has it vanished? The avalanche broke off below there, but who knows? Thoughtfully, I look up.

'Three porters up there ... today ... coming down,' says a friendly Korean at my side, following my gaze. Fantastic! They will almost certainly have seen whether our depot is there or not. First-class high-altitude porters to go to 8,000 metres ... you won't find many around here. So, six people have climbed up today to establish Camp 4.

While Julie chats with Alan, I make tea. Suddenly, I hear a shout and raise my head – up there in a landscape of light and shadow, creeping veils of cloud and the wind-sculpted snow formations, three figures have appeared. They are coming back – the porters. We'll soon know about the depot! They approach fast: two powerful young Hunza lads and – I notice with slight misgivings – the Balti cook, who failed to hand over Willi's torn pullover to the Austrians and subsequently got a real dressing down from the liaison officer.

Panting, the three arrive and throw their packs to the ground to one side of the Korean tents, just a few metres from us, a space apparently set aside for the high-altitude porters. 'Did you see any material on the Shoulder?' I can hardly wait for the answer. It would save such a terrible sweat tomorrow if our things were still there.

But I am to be disappointed: 'No depot on the Shoulder,' replies the Balti cook with conviction. His ski-sticks look suspiciously like those which disappeared lower down. Forget it, Kurt ... The bad news is our depot is gone. It's true we have brought up enough spares to set up a new camp – but the sleeping bags we had left up there were better than these, and the tent bigger and more solid. Nothing we can do about it.

Probably all the stuff, cached near the rim of the Shoulder, was

simply smothered by drifting snow. It will almost certainly still
be there, somewhere; we anchored it so well, that I doubt it would
have been blown off by a storm. All the same, we have to consider it
lost ...

The presence of the Balti cook has caused me to think. There have
been one or two instances where members of this basically honor-
able profession have damaged the reputation of Himalayan cooks. I
know it from my own experience. It is definitely not a good idea to
use cooks as high-altitude porters, even if sometimes you find
exceptional men among them.

In the Himalayas, the profession of expedition cook is quite often
practised by people who, thanks to their abilities not only in
preparing dishes but also in procuring provisions as well as demonstrating very necessary and multi-faceted organizational talents,
prefer to earn their money this way rather than by the highly
strenuous chore of carrying loads. Usually they are quite good
businessmen, too, so it is as well to keep an eye on the Base Camp
cook when you're close to villages: sometimes, on a return march,
we've discovered we could buy a great deal of our own provisions in
shops along the way! High-altitude porters, you will find, are
usually honest and high camps not seriously endangered. Nevertheless, according to the principle that 'nothing must be wasted',
depots on a mountain could be interpreted as abandoned, and may
not be so safe.

I heard of one case where a whole high-altitude camp was cleared
by people from the valley. On the Diamir Face of Nanga Parbat, it is
worth protecting the fixed ropes on the lower third of the ascent
route by striking a bargain to agree a date after which the agile
shepherds of the villages at the foot of the mountain are allowed to
come and cut them off.

All the same, I have not completely given up hope of finding our
depot ...

Julie and I are quite naturally upset at the news of its loss; if we
had not brought up all that extra gear three days ago, we would be
left now with no option but to go down. Even so, instead of a 'light
winged' ascent tomorrow, we have now to hump heavy loads again.
But we have no idea that another and much worse shock awaits us
on the Shoulder ...

Until this moment, I have not given a thought to any possible
mix-up of the Austrian and Korean summit assaults, even though I
knew that the Austrians no longer had a tent of their own up there.

*   *   *

Then we forget about all that! The morning comes up!

It is a dream day. There are high spirits all round. Such fantastic weather! It couldn't be better. Views into the farthest distances. I start to believe in Providence – this time we have guessed it right: tomorrow we really will be on top. The lost depot has become insignificant – all that counts is the weather.

At last – our K2! What we can see of it from here is little, but we sense the mountain. Julie's deep joy is apparent in her fast, determined movements as she packs the rucksack, as well as in the small, cheeky smile she throws at me – yes, it's trembling, vibrating in the air, happiness, luck, this is one of those days when the world is yours, when you think your whole life is worth it because such a day exists. Today … it's sparkling and shining, twinkling from all sides in the morning sun – seracs, ice cliffs – it is a flood of light, everywhere, which catches, grasps you and carries you away, out to shimmering glaciers, glistening firn-shields, blue pinnacles; out into the sea of Karakoram peaks where countless tiny ice-patches gleam like silvery fishes, to ridges blown clear by storms, marvellously engraved, iridescent surfaces, frozen glacier lakes, fluted faces like delicate icy plumage; yes, it would be difficult to draw enough breath to enumerate all that flows towards you: there is the feeling of leaning against the big mountain, while at the same time floating high above the world and in the midst of it – almost as if you are at the centre of a crystal sphere, inside which images of life are mirroring, refracting, repeating themselves in bewitching variety.

On days like this you start to see things differently. Suddenly, you understand how a mountain has come to be called Mother Goddess of the World, another the Fish's Tail or a third the Place of Giants, and the *why* – the laborious explanation – you don't even need, for all exists on a different plane.

These are the days of name-giving.

It was a lucky moment on such a magic day when man saw with his soul to the other side of things … when someone – nobody knows who or when – recognized in an ice-covered, shimmering, twin-headed peak of the Himalayas the two-pointed form of the Fish's Tail and named it accordingly: *Machha Puchhare*; even today, it is still a holy mountain. The villagers at the foot of Nanga Parbat call the icy massif, whose wide spaces echo repeatedly with the growl of enormous avalanches, as if from the sound of titanic voices, the Place of Giants – *Diamir*. So we were told by Sheraman Chan, the wild shepherd, one of few there who dare to climb the steep faces. And the distant peak, a pyramid in the dark sky of the Himalayas, regarded with awe by all who have seen it: Mother Goddess of the Earth, many Tibetans call it – *Chomolungma*. But it bears several names, as do other peaks in the 'Abode of Snow'.

And K2? This enormous, enigmatic mountain on which we creep higher – with its strict crystalline regularity? Today I feel intuitively that I understand why it is known merely as 'big mountain' – *Chogori*: it is unapproachable, even for a name-giver.

And tomorrow? *'La tela khor re, e nyima che shar'*, Drugpa Aba will have sung an hour ago, over a thousand kilometres to the east, in Tashigang – today, like every morning. Tomorrow, too. '… And so it is turning … the great sun is coming up … the sun of a great day … in the five colours … may nothing change … may luck remain … may nothing change … may everything bloom …' It is his prayer, this song.

The happy laughter of the Koreans preparing for their climb pulls me back into the present. Their child-like pleasure, manifested in a fast sequence of lively gestures and excited sounds, fits perfectly the atmosphere of this sunny day. And while the snow is sparkling and we sip the last cup of tea, the carousel of peaks, of which we are a part, 'turns' from minute to minute, slowly and imperceptibly in the light … *La tela khor re …*

Broad Peak, a dark-blue silhouette in the flood of morning sunlight, soars like the mighty fin of a jumping dolphin who has playfully dipped his smooth snout into the Godwin-Austen glacier at our feet, while his curved body suddenly, under some magic spell, remains frozen in the air between the Baltoro and K2.

The shimmering trapeze of Chogolisa, like an iceberg, could have drifted here from some northern sea: it's 'the great hunting ground' of the ibex hunters on its southern approaches; British explorers later called the shining apparition Bride Peak, clad from head to foot as it is in a fantastic, folded drapery of snow which flows down into gently billowing, silken waves.

Hang on a minute, Kurt! Haven't you forgotten that Broad Peak, your dolphin, has three dorsal fins? Pretty unusual, that, wouldn't you say? Yes, well, from this angle you only see one, the nearest, so hopefully no marine biologist will complain.

And what of the 'ocean' of peaks – is that sheer fantasy, too? During one of our excursions from Suget Jangal, Julie and I found thousands of sea-urchin spines on top of a brown hill; we discovered corals in the Shaksgam valley; a fossilized whelk at the edge of the northern Gasherbrum glacier; I even came across a nautilus shell on the moraine of the Baltoro … this really *was* once an ancient ocean.

Only the waves have changed: the crested ocean of peaks …

Yet even they are not rigid. *La tela khor re* … eternal motion.

Amid such a seascape, you may find the hermit crab – a mountaineer with his tent on his back. Several, in fact. So, not much changes. Sometimes two or three will be carrying one 'shell' between them.

Not far to the north rises Skyang Kangri, 7,544 metres, a shining yellow, three-tiered upheaval of crystalline marble, originally known as Staircase Peak – every step rises between three and five hundred metres. By its side – way down, yet even so at 6,000 metres – we see Windy Gap, from where in 1909 Vittorio Sella, expedition photographer to the Duke of the Abruzzi, took pictures of the still virgin K2. That year it was attempted for the first time by the Abruzzi Ridge route. Sella used sheet film, 20×25cm, rather than his celebrated 'Alpine Camera', which was as big and heavy as a beer-crate and operated with 30×40cm plates. Glass plates like these would never have survived seven weeks of transport through this rugged wilderness. Vittorio Sella's photographs have never been surpassed for sharpness nor – even today – for beauty. He has immortalized the spirit of this mountain, the indescribable essence of K2.

Looking out into the distance, I see to the north the ranges of the Kun Lun, pale yellow and grey, some of the peaks snow-covered; they are beyond the deeply incised Shaksgam trench, which separates the very individual mountain country of the Sinkiang desert from the Karakoram. Yet further out, like distant surf, lies a white, crested line on the horizon. Is that Tien Shan, the Celestial Mountains – or could it be the Pamir? Or is it just as likely to be clouds?

'Look!' Julie points over to the Shaksgam, to a certain corner of the valley, at a rusty brown, rather insignificant rocky pinnacle. Only we two know that we were the first humans to stand on top of it! This is our 'Heart Mountain'. Oh, good old Liu, with his worries about nameless, unclimbed peaks! Over there is 'Left Ear Peak', and there 'Right Ear Peak' – if you need good viewpoints for your camera, what on earth should you do but climb? Julie smiles roguishly: our name-giving had little in common with serious geography. And I had fallen in love up to my ears.

What are nameless mountains for … on such a name-day? That was a day like today.

'Look!' This time Julie is pointing downwards. 'We are definitely higher now!' A nameless dark peak far below us, about 7,000 metres high, on the opposite side of the Godwin-Austen glacier – we have had an eye on it for quite a while already. At its edge, at the base – even if we cannot see it from here – there is a small triangular lake, hemmed in by whalebacks of moraine. It is an intense green. We have wanted to go there for a long time – a really special, hidden lake it must be. It would only take a day. But how can we fit it in …? It will have to wait until next time, I guess – we have ordered porters to arrive on 5 August for the return march and already it is the 2nd.

So we have three days: just enough for the summit, for there is little sense anyway in staying longer in the so-called Death Zone above 7,500 metres, where regeneration is impossible even for the fully acclimatized. As for the weather, this time I have no worries; tomorrow will almost certainly be fine, and probably the next day too – going by the K2 weather pattern – and after that, we will already be on our way down …

I glance up. Shining, glistening slopes, with others a matt white: a variegated surface with, above it, the mighty curve of the Shoulder.

Out of the corner of my eye, I notice a bundle of bamboo sticks outside the nearest Korean tent. They remind me that during a recent chat I had with Kim, the expedition leader, I stressed that I felt trail-marking up on to the Shoulder was absolutely essential if he had no plans to fix ropes, always such a time-consuming and soul-destroying task. He was of the same opinion: so far, everybody who has been caught in a storm up there has experienced problems finding the way out.

Thoughtfully, my eyes wander over the wide, snowy curves above us: on those silent, still slopes, several people have already fought hard for their lives. Julie and I, too, struggled down with difficulty on our last attempt, and Wanda admitted to me that she had trouble steering herself through. It may well have been that Pasang Kikuli, Pasang Kitar and Pintso, who all disappeared after braving storm and snowfall in their vain attempt to rescue Dudley Wolfe from the 7,530-metre Camp, met their fate on these now-so-silent slopes. That was in 1939, on Fritz Wiessner's expedition. Tragedy also struck here in 1953: in a desperate battle against storm and gravity, American climbers tried to bring down their mortally sick comrade, Art Gilkey. A pulmonary embolism and thrombosis had left him unable to move. Before they could get him to the relative safety of Camp 7, he was swept away by an avalanche – and they, too, had a miraculous escape when Pete Schoening succeeded in holding his five companions after a multiple fall. Art Gilkey's death probably averted total tragedy.

I notice that only one of the bamboo sticks that the high-altitude porters have brought up bears a red pennant; the other marker flags have either been lost during the transport along the ridge or have not yet been fixed. No time to sort that out now … in any case, with this gorgeous weather the temptation to leave the sticks behind is almost overwhelming. I look at the bundle thoughtfully: they're no protection against avalanches, that's for sure. To put them in now, so near to the end of our time here, seems almost pedantic, an over-scrupulous precaution in the circumstances …

Then I think of Kim Byung-Joon: one of the difficulties on expeditions is that decisions taken down in Base Camp are not always executed higher up. Sometimes this is because it is impossible to do so under the prevailing conditions, but often, too, because at great height, people's priorities, their personal will, existing energy, the need to husband strength, are all different from those down at Base Camp. So it happens that in order to save effort, people tend to improvise in just those circumstances on the mountain where precision and pedantry would be of greatest importance. Kim Byung-Joon – we filmed this man with his impressive 'battle plan' – has taken care that the bamboo came up here; we will see to it that the markers are set out.

Among those getting ready for the ascent, I notice the two young, strong Hunza porters who were on the Shoulder yesterday; the Balti cook is not with them – evidently he will go down. And again, I see the Korean with his movie camera – it makes my fingers itch: the morning scene is beautiful, the atmosphere one of anticipation, the bright colours of the moving figures in the sunshine call to mind a host of excited, coloured butterflies, about to take wing into the beckoning, dazzling mountain world, which today emanates only fortune and pleasure – I so regret my camera being down in Camp 1. In my mind I am looking through the view-finder, following the gaudy yellow of our windsuits (sunflower colour – we both love it), like an inquisitive butterfly myself, then from the blue of the seracs I pan out into the distant Shaksgam, where perhaps in an oasis of that mountain desert the descendants of the thirteen sunflowers we planted are really blooming ... I can almost see them ...

Kurt, the most beautiful pans are those in one's head!

It's more important now that we make it up the mountain! Take the snow piton with you – you'll need that to anchor the tent. And pack the stove. Put on your crampons. Fold up the *parapluie*!

'Let's get this umbrella down, quick!' Julie, with a glance at the busy Koreans, echoes my thoughts. I temporarily interrupt my crampon-fixing: this umbrella is a real godsend – it's folded in a trice. The two little bears, our mascots which Julie has just tucked into her rucksack, have brought us luck indeed. Alan, too, has just taken down his small tent, and is busy packing up, together with Mrowka, 'the Ant'.

Julie and I are almost ready; the high-altitude porters are on their way and the Koreans just about to leave ... Oh, the bamboos! What will we do about them? I nearly forgot them altogether.

'Really, we ought to mark the section up to the Shoulder,' I remark to Alan, as he bends over his rucksack. He looks up: 'Yeah, I think we should, too. Chances are we won't need them but it's worth doing ...' he fetches a bundle of bamboo wands, and Julie too brings a dozen. We will set them up at intervals as we climb higher. After all, you never know.

'I'm glad we're going to be with Al,' Julie says as we set off. I am, too: the little episode with the bamboos has reinforced my faith that here is somebody who is helpful, and who pays more than lip-service to the principles of safety – he doesn't shirk effort. Instinctively, I recognize Alan as someone with both imagination and integrity ...

We are enveloped in the sound of our steps, single words in the air, the rustle of nylon suits as at every footfall, every move of the arm, the fabric rubs against itself ... After a bit, you get so used to this accompaniment that you cease to notice it and the great silence of the slope enfolds you once more – utterly.

I am careful not to put the sticks too close together, and notice Alan is being equally sparing. The slope is approximately three hundred metres high – it would be marvellous if we could eke them out for the whole distance.

We are short of three sticks. Earlier, I had called out to a Korean who was just about to start down from Camp 3, 'Please put *three sticks* in, till to *start of fix ropes!'* He looked at me, startled, and hesitated – probably not understanding my telegraphic English – and I stepped down towards him, pressing them into his hand. The rim above the drop, just below Camp 3, is lethal in fog; and even to locate the beginning of the fixed ropes, you really need markers, as we have all seen. Since Michel Parmentier's desperate odyssey in the fog, which he would never have survived without Benoît's cool-headed radio talk-down, we have all been acutely aware of that. The Korean needed no persuasion, therefore; we fumbled a few friendly words to one another, then he went down. As I turned to make my way upwards, I saw him planting the first stick.

One thing is clear to me: an Alpine-style climber could never bring anything more than the basic necessities up here, certainly not a bundle of bamboo sticks. For those, we must be thankful to the high-altitude porters.

There are ways that markers can help even when avalanches threaten: once a heavy snowfall has set in and you can see neither tracks nor surface features, you can – with their help – still evacuate swiftly. At the moment there is no avalanche danger, and the snow here has no real depth, but in the lee of the Shoulder, further up, it is bound to be deep; the six climbers who yesterday set up camp on the Shoulder for the Austrian and Korean summit attacks must have had to dig their way through for much of the route up there.

Here the slope offers no problems; it is only a moderate incline – a friendly ski slope in sunshine. The old scoring, left by the ice avalanche, doesn't seem all that menacing – if you don't think about it – and on a glorious day like this, it's hard to appreciate Mandi's panic. Naturally, everything always looks less serious with the sun on it – or was it the damaged camps that turned him back? Did it just suddenly come to him that by relying on their own means, the Austrians could not get any further? Or did he pick up a whiff of destiny …?

Events will always find different interpretations: and the good or bad outcome of a venture is all that is normally taken into account. Causality is so often ignored, the actual connections rarely being exposed. On the outcome alone – success or failure – a gambler might be made into a hero … and another man branded as a fantasist, as having overreached himself. But there comes a point, even for the most meticulous engineer of a technical wonder, when all he can do is pray that when his invention is put to the test, no screw will work loose … No amount of caution or precautions can divert the course of destiny or just 'switch it off'.

That is not to suggest that people should simply rely on destiny – hardly anybody does. When things go wrong, there are usually solid reasons why. It is certainly fate that determines the moment you join a motorway, but if, at that moment, somebody veers across the central reservation and rams into you because his steering has broken down, then technical failure has also come into play.

When Reinhold Messner and Jerzy Kukuczka survived fourteen eight-thousanders, it was principally thanks to their ability and experience. But they owed something to luck, too. Just how much, neither knew. Perhaps Mandi did hear 'the voice' – and interpreted the avalanche his own way. Perhaps he climbed down and is still alive today because of that. With the exception of Mandi, all the rest of us ended up in the invisible pull of the summit.

It seems to have been unstoppable – and in the centre of the fateful vortex stood a tent. Without the Korean tent which remained undamaged in Camp 3 – there is every probability that everyone could have got out of the deadly whirl in time.

Today, I often ask myself: why didn't the ice avalanche tear that Korean tent into pieces, too …? That it did not, that the tent was spared – that was fate.

While we climb the slope, planting our sticks, I keep noticing half-closed cracks in the surface – as if almost everything had been on the move. Is it possible that a small earthquake played some part in all this? I experienced something similar once on Everest below the Khumbu Icefall: many ice towers lost their tips and in Base Camp a glacier 'table', almost as big as a house, collapsed without warning.

Yes, it must have been fate that spared the Korean tent. To the Austrians – other than Mandi – this I am sure must have looked like a good sign; nevertheless, I am still surprised that they did not consider fetching an Austrian tent up from Camp 2 before continuing with their assault. In one hour, two at the most, Willi could have been down to their camp below House's Chimney … It would have meant then that everyone would have gone up to the Shoulder together, all forces united. Clearly, the Austrians could not then have stayed in the lead, they would have become part of the mixed group moving towards the summit. Why didn't they do that? The only consequence was that they would have lost a day – but *not* one in the Death Zone.

Perhaps Willi and his companions simply wanted to prevent their 'First Austrian Ascent' losing a valuable day – at any cost. But the day they thought they had won – won through an agreement struck with the Koreans, saving them the effort of bringing up one of their own tents through House's Chimney – proved illusory in the fulfilment of that agreement (which *according to Willi*, as well as allowing for the common use of the tent also called for them to fix ropes *'for the Koreans in the Bottleneck'*): on 2 August, the Austrians *lost* a day! Had they gone down for their own tent, they could certainly have reached the summit on 3 August: all forces – Austrian, Korean, British and Polish – would have made a single assault.

Yet at the time, I didn't have any headaches on that score: the Austrians had obviously agreed something useful with the Koreans and wanted to attack the summit on subsequent days. With that number of people, I quite naturally assumed that a tent-camp of corresponding size would be established on the Shoulder as a base for the two summit attempts.

1. Carrying is a part of everyday life for the local people of Baltistan, both men and women.

2. Nepo, a sacred mountain.

3. Hildegard, the ethnologist (my daughter): a different approach to living among the peaks and mountain people . . .

4. Two Tibetans, Drugpa Aba and the naksong, have completed their ceremony in honour of the mountain gods at the 'White Lake'.

7,700 metres: and above us to our left is where the ice avalanche detached itself: the newly exposed scar is clearly visible. Looking upwards, the massive bulk of the Shoulder conceals the summit pyramid of K2. It resembles a castle: there are the ramparts – namely the Shoulder with the ice barrier below it, which now, since the collapse of the ice wall above the old Italian camp, can only be penetrated by a single passageway: almost a month ago Beda Fuster and Rolf Zemp climbed steeply up to the right of where we are now, while Julie and I were able to reach the Shoulder directly from the Italian camp. Once you have surmounted these outer walls, you are standing on the Shoulder in front of the highest part of the castle, the summit cone with its threatening balcony – the keep, or last defence of this ice castle.

This time, after the bad experience of our first attempt, Julie and I want to get as close as we can to the summit stronghold – setting up our tent at about 8,000 metres so that we don't lose time un-necessarily in approaching the steep face on the morning of the push. At this level it takes an hour to gain a hundred metres of height – further up, you manage even less.

I have only one stick left – the bamboo with the red pennant. I

hesitate. Where shall I put it? The traverse to the right, close to the steep wall, passes a block of snow, like a huge pillow, standing as high as a man. From there, because of the curve in the slope, I cannot see any of our markers if I look back. It needs something here if we are to locate them. Past the snow pillow is the passage-way. I plant my bamboo stick. That's it, then – Alan, too, unfortunately, has come to the end of his sticks.

Deep snow … powder snow … with my face to the wall, holding the ski-stick at mid-height and repeatedly ramming in the ice-axe to haul myself up on, I work my way up the deeply furrowed track which leads directly over the ramparts. This was made yesterday. Julie is behind me, but we are only two in a long, human snake which burrows its way higher, taking time and stopping for plenty of rests. The slope is not too high, fortunately: forty to sixty metres at this steepness, then it eases off. Labouring heavily under our loads, which at this altitude seem to weigh us down more and more oppressively, we reach a small hill just in front of a giant crevasse. Here the track does a loop – it was obviously not clear which was the best way to get across; then I see: there's a bridge, and immediately afterwards, another steep slope – a tricky route-finding problem, it occurs to me, if a storm should blow up suddenly. A pity we have no sticks left … but a warning bell must have tweaked somebody else's conscience, too, for in the steep slope above the crevasse, just to the side of the tracks, a lonely snow piton has been stuck. A placebo, I grumble to myself – no more than that. But whoever left it there obviously had nothing better to use, either. I thought originally that this way through would lead directly to the campsite, or to the back of the Shoulder, without making any detours, but we emerge much higher than where we had our tent a month ago. And our depot? I have not totally given up on that. It would be nice to find it, even if – now that we have carried everything up again – it's of no great importance.

Suddenly I realize that the China Wind is blowing! Weakly, but there is it! Julie smiles when I tell her. The China Wind – it is like a sign of Providence – the good-weather wind.

Now we focus our whole attention on the snow rim of the Shoulder, which grows obviously closer with every step. Clearly I can see, a bit further down, the place where the white rim runs almost horizontally.

That's where our cache must be!

The summit pyramid, too, has now come into view and it begins

5. Above 7,200 metres, in the storm clouds on K2. A rope and ice axe are your life insurance at the edge of the vertical drop.

6. No water should penetrate the 25-kilo bags of flour used to make bread. 'Chapat-tis' provide the basic nutrition (and almost the only food) for the local Balti porters.

7. Success and uncertainty: to stand on the summit of K2 looking down from an incredible height is the dream. It may come true, once you have managed the Bottleneck. (8) Below the balcony . . . with a 'sky of ice' above. Even at this stage, success is not assured.

to rise above us at each step … but I see nothing of the Austrians. It is 13.00 hours …

At last – we've reached the edge. I look up at the steep face of the summit and above the ascending Koreans spot three tiny figures traversing below the giant overhang of the hanging glacier. What? No higher than that? I am taken aback, but it is definitely Willi, Hannes and Alfred! They will have to bivouac – or come back without the summit. What can have happened?

An uneasy feeling creeps over me.

Then my gaze slides lower – and my heart almost stops beating. All these people moving up the Shoulder, and there, at the edge of a small snow plateau, at 8,000 metres, sits forlornly – I do not trust my eyes – only one single tent.

'Quick! Let's look for our depot!' I shout to Julie and throw my pack to the ground. Silently, she follows my example; with just our ice-axes, we storm down along the edge …

We must find that tent!

The ground levels off – this must be it. Even if there's no sign of our ski-stick marker. I ram my ice-axe up to its hilt in the snow. Nothing. Julie does the same. We probe again and again, all around the area, until we are totally breathless. Nothing.

Again, I look up at the traverse below the ice balcony, then to the plateau, which the Koreans have now reached. I stare hard at the silhouette of the camp, but I haven't been mistaken: there is only the one Korean dome tent, which would normally shelter just three people. Where will they all stay? I still cannot believe there aren't two tents.

'Come on Julie, let's look again …' While, more intensely now than ever, we continue probing for our depot containing the blue tunnel tent, I reflect: I didn't see the porters bringing up a tent today, they had plenty to carry with other things for the Korean sum-miteers, including oxygen. The only other possibility is that the altitude porters brought up a second tent yesterday, which has not been erected yet. But nobody is doing anything about putting it up – so, there can't be another one!

Will the Austrians bivouac on their way to the summit, or coming back? It seems unavoidable, one way or the other, at the speed they're going. Perhaps they are fixing ropes. What were they thinking about yesterday, only to carry up this Korean tent? Did they believe they might get down as far as Camp 3, after going to the summit? Back to 7,350 metres? Such a thing would be practically unheard of!

Frantically I continue thrusting my axe into the snow, while a few metres away, Julie does the same on the flat surface near the rim of the Shoulder. But it's useless. There is no resistance, no yielding of fabric below the axe point, even though I am certain this is the right place.

Julie too is silent and worried. The situation is clear to both of us: there are almost a dozen people above us on the mountain, and so far they have only one tent between them.

That's an exaggeration, I tell myself: the two high-altitude porters will go down, and Alan and Mrowka have their own two-man tent – so that's four people less. One of the Koreans will probably go down, too, but three of them are sure to remain for the summit attack – and that means the tent will be fully occupied. But if they don't want to be faced with dangerous overcrowding should the Austrians retreat suddenly – dangerous in view of the heavy day in front of us tomorrow – then somehow or another an extra tent has to materialize. I keep probing.

I can't understand why we find nothing, not even the two ski-sticks that so securely anchored our enormous rucksack (which also contained two special sleeping bags), when the yellow-stained pee patch can still faintly be seen in the snow surface a few metres from where our tent was pitched. We can't – just can't – be looking in the wrong place. I wonder darkly about the Balti cook, who went down from Camp 3 this morning, but there have also been three weeks of snowstorms. 'Anything is possible,' says Julie, breathing hard and plumping herself down in the snow, 'but one thing is sure: here is nothing!' We give up the search.

THE KEY FACTOR –
A TENT

Somehow, somewhere, there must have been a misunderstanding or a breakdown of logic in the Austrian–Korean agreement: it is a fact that on 1 August the three-man Austrian summit team were not the only ones climbing up to Camp 4; three of the Koreans' high-altitude porters also went up but returned to Camp 3 the same day. On 2 August two of the Koreans' porters climbed again to Camp 4; with them went the three-man Korean summit team, as well as one or two other Koreans. That all these people only carried one single three-man tent to Camp 4 seems to me remarkably under-prepared. In my opinion it was a tactical error which could perhaps be excused as an oversight of the moment, and which I feel sure had its roots in the sudden and amazing entry of the Austrians onto the Korean scene. Even if you start from the premise that the Korean mountaineers carried only personal gear up to Camp 4, that still leaves the load capacity of five porters as well as the carrying potential of the three Austrians. After all, it was they who had made the offer of carrying the Korean tent from Camp 3 to the site of Camp 4! The load comprising the ropes for fixing would have been managed by one porter, and the total of four oxygen bottles by two more. But even if you make some allowance for the weight of gas and provisions, I cannot believe that it was not possible to carry up a second tent – at least on the following day. With that array of people, I had taken it for granted that is what would have happened and it was only the evidence of my own eyes on the Shoulder of K2 that taught me differently. It seems to me that the Koreans' strategy was simply confined within the limitations of their own summit attack – and would have worked perfectly, as such, with only the one tent, had they not become involved with the Austrians. Their comradely help towards the latter really demanded an enlargement of the capacity of Camp 4 – either they did not realize that, or it was not possible.

The Austrians on the other hand were not just receivers of comradely help: they probably broke the majority of the trail from Camp 3 to the Shoulder.

And the fixing of several Korean ropes below the ice balcony on the summit pyramid was doubtless very valuable. Neither of the two parties, however, can have done a calculation of the time involved, or, if they did, it was unrealistic. For the whole arrangement to have worked with the presence of only one Korean tent at Camp 4 at 8,000 metres, the three Austrians would have needed, on a single day, first to attach the fixed ropes, second to reach the summit, and third – on top of all that – to descend to Camp 3!

That this is hardly possible is obvious to anyone, even to those who are not familiar with K2. Nobody has ever tried such a thing.

Some light into the darkness of what happened up there is thrown now by the Koreans' expedition report, which has been written in minute detail: it not only documents movements on the mountain, but also the walkie-talkie discussions that took place with Base Camp.

Kim Byung-Joon, the leader, did not take decisions lightly. When the Austrian summit team (via Chang Bong-Wan) radioed down from the Abruzzi Ridge to ask whether they might have a hundred metres of rope and whether they could borrow the Korean tent for their summit attack, he reflected long and hard. For the request placed him in quite a dilemma: if he refused help, he feared for the good name of Korea; yet if he granted it, he saw risks developing which could threaten the Korean success. This did not affect the concession of rope – the Koreans had 800 metres of that up there! But the tent: even though it was undoubtedly a help to both parties if the Austrians carried it, Kim Byung-Joon feared that they might even take it up as far as 8,300 metres or use it too long in the event of bad weather; or they might – exhausted perhaps after their summit attack (made possible by this arrangement) – claim the help of the Korean assault team.

Kim, for this reason, wanted a safety guarantee: and only after Hannes Wieser had given him express reassurance that the Austrians would make use of the tent on the Shoulder for no more than one night did he declare himself in agreement. The cession of the ropes, however, was without condition.*

While the Austrian expedition was busy clearing up in anticipation of an imminent departure and at the same time three of their number attacked the summit, the Koreans had divided their team into an assault group and several support groups, who supplied the camps on the spur with all essentials, as well as restocking Camp 3 which was feared destroyed by the 'teapot avalanche'. Given this situation and taking into account the

---

* *K2 1986 Expedition Report* by Kim Byung-Joon (see Bibliography).

above-mentioned report of the Koreans, it appears to me totally incomprehensible that Willi Bauer (in his book) should subsequently express indignation that the Koreans had not carried another tent up to the Shoulder for themselves! Did Bauer not speak to Wieser?

Doubtless, by now, everybody has his own view of events.

THE LOST DAY

The 'mountain on top of the mountain'.
The summit pyramid of K2, rising from the Shoulder.
Both are in the Death Zone.

Reflections: By whatever manner a person arrives at such a critical height – whether it be fast or slowly – it is to a certain extent a matter of choice. It may also depend on the weather, the weight he is carrying, and other circumstances – on his style obviously, too … But once there, he has not much time: three days at most – with two nights in between; a third night would be cutting it fine. He would still be able to descend then, but any movement towards the summit would automatically involve a fourth day – and that's definitely too long. He would hardly be likely to achieve very much anyway.

Nevertheless, the fact that within such three-day periods at high altitude there have been mountaineers who have managed to venture twice towards the summit into the region above 8,000 metres – from Noel Odell on Everest, via Fritz Wiessner to Willi Bauer and Alfred Imitzer on K2 – proves that with exceptionally good acclimatization, even this is possible. Naturally not everybody can allow himself three days, and most would hope to make it in just two, but, really, somebody for whom these three days are too much should not even go up there in the first place. Oxygen can obviously change these basic timings, but it is over-valued and is no *carte blanche*. Basically, one should spend as little time as possible in the Death Zone and lose no day unnecessarily – not waste even an hour.

On the five 'big' eight-thousanders – Everest, K2, Kangchenjunga, Lhotse, Makalu – there is (apart from a couple of extraordinary feats performed under special circumstances) nothing that can be done in

less than about two days; the third, the reserve day, you should hope
not to use. Even if resting can relax you, can restore your strength, a
real recuperation is no longer possible. The dangers of altitude are
ever-present: embolism, oedema, the weather. That perfect
physical shape and full acclimatization are prerequisites goes
without saying.

And something else, too, which is not easy to define: a 'com-
patibility with the universe', balance, harmony ... you feel it on
certain special days ...

The China Wind is blowing! Its whisper along the snow rim,
through the undulating formations which air turbulence has created
almost everywhere on the surface of the Shoulder, sounds like a
reassuring voice ... 'Luck will go with you' – it says – 'Tomorrow
you will go to the top.'

Yes, we've calmed down again. They've possibly reckoned with a
bivouac up there. That must be it, otherwise they would have
already turned back. After all, the weather is beautiful!

Out in the distance, far away, Nanga Parbat has appeared,
immediately to the side of the SSW Ridge of K2. Considerably
closer, in the same direction, just beyond the Baltoro glacier, soars
the Matterhorn-shape of Masherbrum, 7,821 metres high.

Julie and I have now reached Alan and Mrowka again. They have
set up their tent on a moderate incline below a somewhat steeper
slope – just within calling distance of the plateau above, at the edge
of which the Korean tent can be seen standing. But I want to get up
there – if the China Wind blows up more strongly, the Korean tent
will offer a sort of windbreak for our small shelter. I wish Alan had
set himself up there as well: it would make it easier for a common
start tomorrow; well, we can always shout! Was it Mrowka who
chose this place, I wonder? She always has firm ideas about things.
Perhaps she ruled out settling on the plateau because of the huge ice
balcony which hangs above it from the summit face? Or did Alan
want to be closer to the exit route through the Ring Wall? All he will
say in response to my question is a laconic 'I like it better here ...'

And Mrowka? While she is tightening the guys of the British
two-man tent, her keen eyes repeatedly turn towards the summit.
She is small and delicate like an ant, busy like an ant ... yes, and as
obstinate, too (that's something we have in common). This time the
mercurial, energetic 'Ant' – in 1984 we often used to rock-and-roll
together in our 'glacier disco' at 5,000 metres – is absolutely set on

reaching the summit. Her expression is cheerful enough – but it masks strong determination. The summit of Nanga Parbat escaped her by only a few metres. She has no intention of letting that happen a second time!

Briefly we discuss arrangements for tomorrow with Alan, then we plod up the slope to the Korean tent.

While everybody on the Shoulder is preparing for a summit attack, 3,000 metres further down in the K2 Base Camp Alan's friend Jim Curran – the British cameraman – is enduring considerable heartache over the way things are going on the mountain. 'Four days up and two down,' Alan had told him; a feasible estimate, if somewhat optimistic for a mountaineer who is carting everything he needs for a summit attack on his own shoulders up the full length of the Abruzzi Ridge. This was on 29 July – and in the evening of the same day Alan had started out with Mrowka. Since then, Jim has been trying in his mind to follow Alan's ascent; it is true there is a Korean radio link between the Abruzzi Spur and Base Camp, but because of language difficulties Jim seems unable to get in touch with his friend or to leave messages for him.

He is, however, in contact with the Poles; their leader Janusz Majer has put Jim personally in charge of the walkie-talkie connection between Base Camp and the SSW Ridge. Julie and I don't know yet that the Poles' summit assault on their 'Magic Line' is in full swing (Reinhold Messner's route, but different in the upper section). There has been no news of its progress, but Alan must have been aware of Jim's unexpected commission: '... to act as Base Camp Manager, and more important, maintain radio contact each evening with their team ... Weather forecasts each evening could be picked up from Radio Pakistan. We also arranged to open up the radio at eight each morning in case any message was necessary' is how he was later to outline his role in his book *K2, Triumph and Tragedy*. Radio Pakistan may or may not have proved helpful as regards the weather outlook, but Jim himself was a careful observer, as his notes describing these days reveal; but whether his conjectures were on target, whether or not his worries well founded – no doubt they carried the usual uncertainty inherent in all weather forecasting – none of us were in a position to judge because up where we were we heard nothing from him. How much Jim agonized only appears from his tape-recordings. So, for instance, 2 August seems to him to have been 'a perfect summit day' for Alan, yet at the same time Jim has the greatest misgivings for the day after that, should Alan be late ... 'I very much fear that the weather may be deteriorating and by tomorrow be bad again', he confides to his recorder with his next breath. The 2nd was the day we reached the Shoulder. Around us the China Wind was blowing, the fine weather wind ...

Had we had any worries (then or later), any concern over the weather, we could easily have asked the Koreans for a walkie-talkie connection to Base Camp. Jim's silent reservations were no help to anybody on the Shoulder.

Not far from the gently rounded rim of the plateau Julie and I have trodden down a patch of snow to make a platform for our *parapluie* in the wind-shadow of the Korean tent. By ramming our ski-sticks deeply into the snow (we won't be needing them any more, higher up), we anchor the little French wonder. Its intense red shines cheekily in the sun. The snow piton we brought up from Camp 3 serves as another anchor, and then, near the ground, we connect our 'umbrella' to the massive dark blue dome of the Koreans at two points. How high are we? It's difficult to say, given the strongly differing figures quoted for altitudes on this mountain – around the 8,000-metre level at any rate. Judging by the scenery, we are not far from where Walter Bonatti's bivouac site must have been. In 1954 he spent an icy night in a snow scoop with the Hunza Mahdi, after the two of them (together with Eric Abram) had carried up oxygen destined for the summit assault of Lino Lacedelli and Achille Compagnoni. Their tiny shelter was somewhat higher than this, further up on a rocky step.

We've plunged our two ice-axes in the snow of the narrow space between the two tents, and attached to them our crampons and karabiners. Julie crawls into the tent, and I pass to her the short yellow mats (we have halved a normal one) which insulate against cold and humidity, then the rope, the rucksacks ... Astonished, I suddenly notice that one of the Koreans is starting to descend. The two Hunza lads are already off. What's the matter? Has a new walkie-talkie directive of Kim's arrived from Base Camp? With the Koreans, so it seems to me, all goes according to plan. And now? The Korean waves to me as he leaves the tent.

'No summit?' I ask him. 'Not possible. Three climbers in this tent. No space ...' is his answer. Was there a note of regret? He says it with a smile and shrugs his shoulders. Then he plods down along the wide white curve towards Camp 3.

So then, there are three Koreans in this tent – and they 'attack' tomorrow. Curlyhead is among them: I noticed that earlier.

Julie calls for snow! She pushes the empty plastic bag out through the entrance and I hurry to fill it with wind-pressed chunks … thirstiness is a faithful companion in the cold dry air of high altitude. But until the tea is ready, I still have time on my hands. While she is brewing, I can tighten the guylines, arrange one more anchor (it's blowing, in fluctuating waves, this China Wind); some kind of step in the slope in front of the entrance wouldn't be a bad idea either …

Occasionally I look up to the ice cliffs of the great balcony. Like ants, the three are attached below it. Yes, they are definitely fixing some ropes there …

Don't lose too much time! Go on …! I silently bid them. They must surely have looked down and seen what is happening here. One of them must have counted heads?

Possibly they are planning a bivouac, further up, there where Wanda and her companions passed the night … 'Tea is ready!' Julie's hand with the steaming mug appears in the entrance and then she too emerges. 'What's the matter up there?' she asks, looking up with a frown. But I cannot give her a satisfactory answer … Beside us, in the Korean tent, things have gone silent. The quiet before the summit storm.

Julie goes on cooking: soup with mushrooms. With it, we have *Bresaola* – air-dried meat – and crispbread; we cannot complain of lack of appetite. Next thing is to fill the drinking bottles – at least one for the night! Without porters, we have of course no Thermos bottles – they are heavy as well as being liable to break too easily; we'll have to leave cooking our tea for the summit assault until tomorrow morning – at least we can partially anticipate the time-consuming process of melting the snow. In the English aluminium bottles liquid stays hot for a long time, if you take them into your sleeping bag – and everyone loves hot-water bottles. On Nanga Parbat, I had –

Hallo – things are moving up there at last! They are no longer fixing, they're climbing on! Slowly, it's true – but gaining height … Announcing this to Julie, I crawl into the tent beside her. She smiles: for both of us it is as if 'a stone fell from our hearts' – the Austrians have gone beyond the crucial passage now; even the fragile French umbrella seems to draw breath, in the Sinkiang breeze …

I snuggle into the sleeping bag, continuing to spin my thread of thoughts: ... well then, on Nanga Parbat in 1982 I took a real rubber hot-water bottle up to the high camps – the contents of which I usually drank during the night, even if the taste wasn't that special. I rarely remind Julie of this expedition as she leaps into a fighting mood whenever she thinks of Pierre Mazeaud, the leader – he wouldn't allow her to go above 5,000 metres and even tried to imply she was lazy. Since then we have been to 8,000 metres three times – to err is human! 'I need more snow!' I am put out like a cat from my warm place ... (Never a moment's peace! Not that I complain ...)

And up there, how is it going now? Slowly my gaze sweeps over the wall. Neither beyond the compact rock barrier in the first third of the 600-metre high summit wall (which you can only overcome by climbing through the narrow, icy Bottleneck) nor on the difficult and terribly exposed traverse which follows, overshadowed by the giant ice balcony, is there anyone to be seen. Instead the three tiny figures are working their way in slow motion up close to the left edge of the ice overhang. It is less difficult there, just snow, but enormously steep ... I know that from our first attempt at this monstrous feature, a month ago. Its sheared end alone, with its dangerous lustre, beckoning and terrifying at one and the same time, must be 150 metres high. What is a human against such dimensions?

Willi, Hannes and Alfred could now be about 8,300 metres. Why do they keep going directly upwards, hugging the scalloped edge of the balcony?

Julie and I traversed the steep snowfield there a bit lower down, at the end of the difficulties, before we turned back in order to avoid the risk of a bivouac ...

I collect chunks of snow, then crawl back with my bag through the sleeve entrance. It's still a tight fit – I haven't yet acquired the sleek lines of a Frenchman – but at least it's downhill, like the entrance of the Korean tent next door, which makes it somewhat easier; Julie passes me the last mug of tea from the previous brew. It's tepid. While drinking, I reflect ... even if they follow the edge of the overhang, from the top of the ice balcony, that heads summit-wards as well! Soon they will be at 8,400 metres; yes, they can still make it to the top today. They should be up there by evening, they will certainly experience a beautiful sunset – tomorrow they can sleep it off down here. I don't begrudge them the 'first Austrian ascent', which means so much to Willi; Julie and I are an international rope, but we are here neither for Britain nor Austria, we simply climb for ourselves, it is our dream mountain, we are climbing beyond any classifications …

What should we take with us tomorrow? I sip the last dregs of tea, at the same time gathering with one hand a couple of the things which we shall need; some I hand to Julie – now and then a word drops in between; we have done this so often, it is second nature to us. This time, we will go with the minimum of weight: there is the light, pink Japanese summit rucksack for me, and Julie can take the grey hip-bag, which will hold a full drinking bottle along with something else – there is the very light Husch cooker … the alu-mug we can put in only after cooking tomorrow morning … we'll only take one of our two head-torches, together with a spare battery … the sunflower-coloured windsuits – they weigh next to nothing – the new long down jackets we're already wearing: it is all top-quality British equipment which Julie got this spring specially for K2. Further: gloves and spares, two titanium ice screws, two titanium pitons. Is it worth taking a rather heavy jumar for the sake of five or six fixed ropes? One, perhaps. Our two little bears? Hmm … isn't it better for them to wait here? (Hey! – here Julie interferes! She wants to take them …) A lighter: yes, we must have that. Better, take two. But everything has its weight … even the tiniest … a spoon, for instance, would be a luxury; the two full drinking bottles are heavy enough. Every litre of water weighs a kilo. (An absolute *must*.) We'll leave those till tomorrow morning, but one thing goes into the rucksack right away: the space blanket for bivouacking. Essential too … because you never know. We shall still do a countdown later on, check through everything once more – at this moment Julie's camera comes to mind, but she has that of course; the little recorder she will certainly leave here … otherwise I shall do my best to dissuade her from taking it.

'Would you mind having a look to see how they're getting on?' Julie's voice betrays a slight unease. Well, it is to be hoped they do – get on, I mean. I squeeze out of the door …

Great God! They've turned round!

They're coming down, rather fast …

'Julie!' I call into the tent, 'I am very worried – the Austrians are retreating – in a bit of a hurry …' No summit. No bivouac. Descent.

Heavy silence. 'No accident,' I add. That much I can see. Nevertheless, the question hangs in the air like a menace: where do they intend going?

*   *   *

'I only hope they don't want to stay here ...' Julie says at length in a low voice. If they do, it will be chaos – there's no room!

They could still make it down to Camp 3, I think to myself, it's only afternoon. No problem, timewise. But will they want to? That is a different question! Without the summit? There is another solution: Willi, the strongest, stays here – at a pinch the Koreans might take one of them in. That way the 'first Austrian' on K2 could be assured.

The other two would have to go down to Camp 3 and try again a day later. And would they still want to do that? I am not convinced – one of them appeared to me rather slow today during the ascent. Soon we will know all!

'Get the stove going, Julie!' They will be thirsty for sure ...

'It's going already!' Of course it is. Idiot. The altitude ... I am nervous. My curiosity to know what brought about their failure up there combines with worry about the space problem: to be squashed together before a summit assault is a real *Krampf* – physical condition is bound to suffer, sleeplessness ... anything is possible. The three Koreans, it's true, have a bottle of oxygen between them for the night ... Silently I crawl back into the tent for a while.

Do I hear footsteps in the snow? The Austrians are coming – puffing and snorting, and at a good speed, like Alpine zebras making for the waterhole. Here they are ... Willi Bauer, the stocky, red-haired, iron-hard born endurer; Hannes Wieser, cheerful daredevil; and Alfred Imitzer, consciously deliberate, the expedition leader.

It's impossible to tell with Willi how much he has been through, he seems as indestructible as ever. Expressions on the faces of the other two reflect what a hard day they have had. All three are totally dehydrated.

'Our next tea is just ready,' says Julie. 'They're lucky!' I call Alfred over. The other two squeeze in with the Koreans for a drink.

Something puzzles me a little: whereas Willi says they fixed ropes and in so doing made themselves too late, Alfred openly declares that he ordered a retreat from the summit attack because of deep and unsafe snow towards the top of the balcony – he wouldn't have wanted to take the responsibility of going any further. Alfred has a giant thirst. He is certainly a giant of a man – I realize that as I watch him greedily sipping his drink: his legs are outside, down the snowslope, even though he sits inside the tent. We are tightly pressed together in our small, flexing shelter. We can just manage to hold the steaming teapot between the three of us. While Alfred tells us more of their summit push, I wonder gloomily what his intentions might be now, and those of the other two ...

We are not left in doubt for long. Soon, from next door, from the Koreans' tent, excited Asian voices can be heard ... It's like a tidal wave, gaining in strength, getting louder and louder. Now and again I catch the pacifying voice of Willi Bauer ... but it is soon blotted out by the angry babble. It doesn't take much imagination to guess the reason for this hubbub: it's not a tea-break the Austrians are after. They plan on staying overnight.

You don't have to understand Korean to gather that the 'amicable settlement', as Willi was later to call it, is a somewhat exaggerated way of describing what happened next – he must have been speaking from a very individual point of view. The way the Koreans saw it has since been described by Peter Gillman, quoting Chang Bong-Wan, the leader of the assault team:

> ... But the Koreans' leader, Chang Bong-Wan, confirms Kurt's account. 'After failing to reach the summit the Austrian team asked if they could sleep in our tent,' he says. 'We refused their request as we had to try to reach the summit the following day. But they repeated their request. They begged us. There was no way to escape so two members of the Austrian team slept in our tent. It was very overcrowded ...*

Unfortunately there are enormous discrepancies in the different descriptions of events, according to perspective. At stake in the argument were: the winning or losing of an important day; the possible saving of effort and struggle; how to find a solution, a way out of the cramped situation – and, of course, the summit. It was not an emergency situation: if it had been, everybody would have accepted it without question.

When, later, after endless terrible days I arrived at the foot of the mountain, clinging grimly to my last iota of life, I never dreamed that I would need to speak about the argument on the Shoulder. I kept quiet about it. Everything that had happened up there bore down on me too heavily.

* *Clouds from Both Sides* by Julie Tullis (with final chapter by Peter Gillman).

But there was the 3rd of August: the lost day. It was more than just Julie's and my planned summit day. It was a fact: *seven people idled the day away on the Shoulder of K2 in beautiful weather*. That could not pass unnoticed, it was inconceivable …

All around the world mountaineers racked their brains about it. And not only them. The most absurd explanations emerged – one even went so far as to make out that the strongest man up there in those days of the summit climb, namely Alan Rouse, was a fantasist with no ability to gauge the situation, and someone sadly out of shape into the bargain. Elsewhere, it was said that we all frittered away a day up there cooking tea because we were deluded by a sort of euphoric summit fever. Even when the real reasons slowly seeped through and became known, experts (so-called) preferred to air their own theories and to consider only the consequences, not the whole fatal chain of events that led up to them. However, the worst were – as they are always – those who instead of thinking and searching for the root causes, preferred to hide behind facile judgements and their own subjective views, people who were unwilling and incapable of putting themselves into similar situations. There are always those who could have 'told you so' (they exist in their thousands!); there are also others who, using respect for the dead as an excuse, want to draw the final line under every human tragedy – something only time can do. The voices of the dead do not demand reverential silence, but rather an appreciation of what happened to prevent it doing so again.

This *3 August* – just a day. How much depends on a single day? On an eight-thousander … perhaps everything.

The evening before we were already plumb in the middle of a critical turning point – perhaps it would prove the most critical one of all:

Camp 4, on the Shoulder of K2 (from diary notes):
'What about that tent you left up here?' Willi calls over. 'Unfindable,' I answer shortly. Should somebody have another look, I wonder? This space problem will not magic itself away – even by tomorrow! But at 8,000 metres decisions seem hard to take …

'We could all three sit in here overnight, even if it is narrow,' says Alfred, still sipping his tea. But it's already unbearably cramped: Julie and I – legs hugged to our chests – are not able to reach anything we want, cannot finish packing for the summit, to say nothing about cooking in the morning. And Alfred – his legs are still outside! He really is a giant! This tent, the smallest in Camp 4, is so meticulously worked out that the groundsheet even has a lateral pocket, extending outside, in which the two inhabitants have to stick their legs if they lie down. Otherwise they won't fit in. Through the vapours of hot tea and breath, I notice Julie's startled expression …

'There's no way,' she murmurs.

I take courage: 'Alfred – it won't work; with the best will in the world it won't. I'm sorry you haven't made it to the top today – that's a pity – but we aren't here for the first time, like you. This is our third expedition to this mountain. Tomorrow is our summit day. We cannot accommodate you – We have to be fresh tomorrow.' Give up everything?

We've finally got the right day and the right weather! And in Alan and Mrowka have another strong rope to climb with – what the Koreans will do, we don't know, but anyway they will be using oxygen – it promises to be the best possible constellation. No, we will not simply sacrifice our planned summit day. Who knows how long the China Wind will keep blowing? I see Julie's worried face, which gives way more and more to an expression of determination. 'Alfred – you have to sort it out with the Koreans, we are not party to your agreement,' she says. However it came about, this problem has to be solved between those two teams. It is still not too late to go down lower. The question keeps coming back: was there a misunderstanding? Confusion in settling the details? Whatever it was, we are now all in the soup. 'Perhaps you might manage to squash in with the others – or take turns to be in the Korean tent? There's still time to establish an extra bivouac.' I can't resist adding, 'How on earth did you think it was going to work up here with the space?' 'We believed that after the summit we could still get down to Camp 3,' Alfred admits hesitantly. Is that the rabbit in the cabbages? But if that *is* the case …

Alfred continues: 'Yes, I can see that ideally we ought to descend to Camp 3, but it was really hard work up there, you know. Tomorrow we will take a rest day here, then have another go at the summit.' A second summit attack? Hats off to his sublime obstinacy, but it is no comfort to Julie and me, and robs me of my last patience. 'Alfred, if you have failed today, and intend resting tomorrow anyway, you don't need to obstruct the summit attempts of everybody else! You'd do better to have your rest day lower down, in Camp 3; if you get yourself together, you can still make it – one or two of you at least should go down ...'

Alfred reflects. 'Yes', he replies, and takes a long pause – 'but perhaps it will still work the other way.'

'Tell him we'll dig a snow hole *and* cook him tea,' Julie chips in again. A solution! A snow hole! British mountaineers have lived for weeks on Everest in snow holes. There's no black magic to making them – we could all help. Put a sleeping bag inside and take turns in it ... not the greatest of all pleasures, perhaps, but tomorrow all three can make up for their lack of sleep in the empty tents.

In vain: it seems that 'snow hole with tea' is nobody's dream of luxury up here. 'Just for this one night,' Julie persists – tomorrow we are prepared for that ourselves ... Walter Bonatti 'survived' worse.

Alfred doesn't answer. Can he still squeeze in with the others? A three-man tent with five people – then a sixth? It seems almost impossible. Why in all heaven weren't two tents carried up here? I explode silently. With only one, everything has to run like clock-work – otherwise, it simply will not function. And with all due respect for the installation of some Korean ropes ... a lost day is too high a price to pay. The discussion in the angry red, bending *parapluie* has not yet deteriorated into a scrap between French fighting cocks – this is not possible between Alfred and me – but what is the way out? Julie is at a loss, at the end of her proverbial helpfulness: she would even concede Michel's gift to the three Austrians – but not before our own summit attempt; no solution for tonight. We are at a dead end.

It's getting later and later – and it goes on, with pauses, here and in the other tent. Every preparation for tomorrow has ground to a halt. Slowly, I feel a fury growing within me: something has to happen soon! Otherwise, totally uninvolved people will end up footing the bill for a non-existent tent. Wherever the blame lies – either Julie and I or Alan and Mrowka will have to pay with tomorrow's summit. Adieu to our common ascent? No! Alan is one of the best British climbers – and Julie sets so much store on that, we must undertake the dangerous adventure with him – he is lucky that his small tent is situated further down the slope, so that he will not be drawn into this fracas ...

Gone six o'clock already; for some while on the Shoulder of K2 we have been dipped in the cold shadow of the summit pyramid. How long has this tug-of-war been going on? One hour, two? ... an eternity.

*   *   *

All of a sudden, it takes an unexpected turn. 'Yes – someone should go down – but there ought to be at least two of us,' says Alfred. 'We can always come back after a rest day in Camp 3; I'll go and see what the others say …' He squeezes out awkwardly. 'Can you let Alfred have five minutes of oxygen?' I yell loudly into the voices of the neighbouring tent. 'He needs a boost!' But what will the Koreans make of that? They will wonder what for … 'No – they need the oxygen for the night and the summit,' Willi calls back at once. 'Only five minutes,' I insist. 'He's thinking of going down to Camp 3 with one of you – and that will give him the necessary impetus – otherwise, it means even more of you will have to squash in together. Or we have to dig a snow hole …'

Then, everything happens with the speed of lightning: in a few moments the fateful decision is taken. The Koreans refuse to take a third person under any circumstances; Willi and Hannes don't want to give up their places; Alfred – the one left over – unwilling to descend alone to Camp 3, stands forlornly with his sleeping bag in front of the Korean tent. Suddenly, we catch the name 'Rouse' … 'Try with Rouse …' Only a few words.

It wasn't loud, but Julie heard it. As if bitten by a tarantula, she shoots up and shoves her way out through the tent entrance: 'there is no way you should do that,' she yells, trembling with protest. 'Alan needs his night's sleep. How can he go to the summit tomorrow, otherwise?' Julie has a strong sense of justice, she is terribly upset – not so much that our plans for a common ascent are being run into the ground, but more than that, by the way it is happening. 'You are not leaving him any choice!' she shouts, still shaking with anger. But Alfred, his sleeping bag under his arm, is already making his silent way down to Alan's tent.

What can a fair-minded person do if somebody suddenly appears outside his door with a sleeping bag at around 8,000 metres? I am shocked. Sympathetic as I am to Alfred's plight, I make no secret of the way I feel about the proposed solution – but it makes no difference. Instead of letting us dig a snow hole together or going down to Camp 3, without a second thought the Austrians are prepared to condemn the person spearheading the summit assault on the second highest mountain in the world to a miserable night in a narrow tent. Is there no respect any more for other people's plans, I ask myself, distraught. In that moment, I wanted nothing more than to go down – to be shot of the whole thing. And if Julie and I had not already spent three years trying to climb this mountain, I would certainly have done so.

My distress was not so much directed towards Alfred, who at least had shown a measure of understanding in the end; but the fact that nobody else was prepared to consider a solution that was acceptable to the others I couldn't understand! It seems to me that great altitude temporarily damages people's judgement.

One thing is beyond question: caught in the machinations of fate at 8,000 metres, things are very different from on an Alpine peak: the sluggishness of decision-taking, temporary forgetfulness, an inclination to immobility, sometimes also a certain tunnel vision, and a quickness to temper – these are all effects of altitude which can strike everyone (and I don't want to exempt myself). From a comfortable sofa, such situations can only be judged with difficulty ...

The argument on the Shoulder definitely tipped the balance. Later on, only the uninfluenceable forces of nature raised their voices; the 3rd of August was the last day on which we were not yet within their power; it was the last day on which somebody could reach the summit of K2 and still get down in good order.

With the decision of the Austrians not to descend to Camp 3, the dice had fallen again: without knowing it, all three of them – Alfred as well (he was the last) – were caught in the merciless machinery of altitude, time and storm, from which there was virtually no escape. And along with Alfred, Alan and Mrowka had also been pulled into the invisible cogwheels. The next to go would be Julie and me. Although not necessarily! At that time, there was still a chance for things to have gone differently for us ...

But the following night and morning brought us, too, to a fateful juncture.

Night. Unease tortures me. What shall we do? My thoughts go backwards and forwards, round in circles; they persecute me. What shall we do? The spontaneous creation of a team of strong experienced people, brought together by coincidence (or predestination?) seems to have broken down. This time when even the weather was on our side; when 3 August, the day planned for the summit assault, finally seemed to be the right one – to suffer such a blow is doubly bitter. Alan Rouse, the British ace, and the indomitable Mrowka are hardly likely to start after a miserable night crammed together in such a tight space. The Koreans may overcome it better, thanks to their oxygen – nevertheless, the overcrowding can't have done them much good either. Julie and I are no longer directly involved – but we have suffered nervous stress as a result of it, too. One thing is sure: the failure of the Austrian summit attack has thrown us out of kilter.

Don't let yourself get involved! I remember now my talk with Julie in Base Camp. Still, we couldn't help getting involved …

And now? What shall we do now? Something keeps resurfacing in the endless circle of thoughts – an inner voice, like an inner conviction, telling me: You have to go tomorrow! That is Julie's and your day! Maintain it, whatever else happens – don't delay!

It is as if it were a categoric imperative.

Then there is another voice, which murmurs to similar purpose: The Koreans are good guys, you get on with them … no matter whether in Base Camp or on the mountain. They radiate friendliness and helpfulness, they treat you like a 'father', and you for your part often find yourself advising them as if they were sons. You feel closer to them than to the speed-merchants, who may sometimes have a better chance of getting to the top, but what does the mountain itself really mean to them?

Go with the Koreans tomorrow! It whispers, this voice.

At the same moment a third voice interrupts, forcefully, like the command of a general: You do not know the Koreans: in a mountaineering sense, they are an unknown quantity. It's a gamble!

A fourth, gentle, voice: Kurt, if you two were really on your own, you would certainly try tomorrow. Go tomorrow, as if you were alone … (There it is again – it's the same voice that came before …)

But now a fifth voice joins in the debate – a voice devoid of all emotion, rational only – which says: If now, after three years, this is at last *the opportunity* that you have been waiting for, be sure and weigh all the factors carefully – you must be sensible about this. At this height, you only have one shot and that must be a 'hit' – to waste energy on a doubtful attack is the last thing you can allow yourself. Almost certainly, you won't get a second go on the following day – and even if you do, it will have less chance of success. Sound strategy is decisive on the mountain, as ever in life! Even here, where no war is waged – because the confrontation of man with great altitude and the mountain is on quite a different plane – sometimes the language of battle describes the situation of a summit attempt better than anything else; and here, too, there is truly life itself in play.

(Certainly no summit in the Himalayas has ever been 'defeated'; all the 'summit conquerors' are just humans who by virtue of intelligence, strength or sheer luck have won a special game – which for many of them, however, includes something unexplainable, a sense of their innermost being.)

So, the rational voice – what does it tell me? That I don't really know the Koreans, but if they start early – and that is their intention (4.30 one of them said; better six o'clock, I suggested, because of the morning cold) – then it might still be good to go together. We could collaborate in trail-breaking, and should they give up, we might still continue alone. Most of our high-altitude climbing to date Julie and I have done on our own, just the two of us. However, if the snow is as Alfred reported – heavy and deep – two people on their own could not manage the trail-breaking to the summit. Ergo: we *have* to start *with* the Koreans. That means, be ready in time.

What will Julie think about that? She is quiet – I don't wake her.

For a while I'm satisfied; I doze a bit and sleep. Then I can't help it, I have to let her know: I submit my proposal.

The answer is not very encouraging: 'If you really think we should ...' No eager echo there to my Korean plan. 'I would prefer we go with Alan, but my fear is he'll be knackered in the morning – almost certainly after a night like this. It's a real shame,' she grumbles. 'I fear it, too,' I agree.

For a while there is silence, then Julie remarks: 'If Alan stays here – and we went a day later – it makes a much stronger team.' Is her countryman the deciding factor for her?

Something inside me bristles against this going-later variation; there is no exact reason for it, just that we ought not let this day slip by: tomorrow – our day! 'Julie – something tells me not to lose tomorrow ...'

Again there is a silence. Both of us know too well how much can hinge on a single day on the great peaks of the Himalayas – summit luck, delusion, fulfilment of years of hope ... even your life – the loss of a day at such altitude can be fatal.

'If we start with the Koreans early, we could see how it works out – then continue, or go back,' Julie concedes thoughtfully. Of course: that does not rule out the day after that. But there is a problem: they are going with oxygen and we without. Our speed could be totally different ... Perhaps it will all run like clockwork – but what if their apparatus breaks down, or they run out of oxygen? I remember bad experiences with masks on Makalu – if we get stuck with the

Koreans somewhere in the midst of it all, the chance may well be gone. Not everybody is a Compagnoni or a Lacedelli, able in such a case simply to continue 'without'.*

'Well,' Julie breaks into my silence with some hesitation, 'if you think we should attempt it with the Koreans – let's give it a try...'

She is not enthusiastic, but she would go; she has obviously decided – I still have to. But has she really? Dear God, let Alan get enough sleep! So then, I go on grinding the mill of my thoughts ...

There are two unknown factors in the calculation for tomorrow: Alan on the one hand; and the Koreans on the other – and on top of that, there is the uncertainty of their starting times. When can they really hope to get going with all the overcrowding in their tent?

Also, there is a lot of snow up there ...

After tomorrow, we'll know all about that; the situation will be clear, unambiguous ... that's if the weather holds, of course. It's a great temptation to wait –

In the end I tire of thinking: ... why are things building up against our ascent on the planned day – is it some sort of providence, perhaps? Should we not go? Will the Koreans fail tomorrow, and we with them? Once more the voice in me says no!

It will be best to keep one eye on Alan's tent and one on the Koreans at our side, then make a spot decision in the morning ...

Be ready, at any rate!

No better solution comes to me. Finally I fall asleep.

Sunshine on the tent! Light seeps through the fabric and I hear sounds of movement outside, coming from the Korean tent. Seized by a sense of duty, I start brewing up. Julie is still completely muffled inside her sleeping bag; I cannot see her face.

By the time the morning tea is ready, I wake her. We sip from the steaming mugs in silence. That really does you good! Hot liquid slipping down your dry throat; you breathe deeply, inhale the vapours, cough your lungs free ... Julie looks at me and her dark eyes hold a question – but she says nothing.

---

* When Kim Chang-Sun – as Kim Byung-Joon reports in his book – checked his oxygen gear at six o'clock, he discovered a hissing, which he was unable to stop. Breathing two litres of oxygen per minute (which is remarkably little for ascending) he should have been able to reckon on his bottle lasting eleven and a half hours, but the pressure gauge told him he only had nine more hours. In spite of that, he started – intending to switch off the oxygen during his stops on the way. By twelve o'clock he was already at 8,400 metres; then – at 14.00 hours – the pernicious hissing finally stopped. Kim Chang-Sun continued towards the summit ... (another Lacedelli?)

Naturally, I have been keeping a careful eye through the entrance to see what's happening, especially down towards Alan's tent – but there's no sign of life there yet. It's probably as we feared.

'Let's get ready, Julie,' I say.

She does not answer. Slowly we prepare for a start. The weather – it does not surprise me – is still good. There are sounds of activity 'next door', of course, but it takes little imagination to figure that it must be quite a stew in there, with five people in a tent only designed for three. Five people means five sleeping bags, a heap of boots, to say nothing of the cooking and the preparation of oxygen gear. It will take them quite a while yet to be ready.

In fact, it turned out to be considerably more than 'quite a while' – it went on longer and longer. I kept shouting across and getting some sort of reassurance: Yes, soon they would be ready, soon they would go. But nothing of the sort happened. It was totally puzzling – what should I do? I didn't – couldn't – know that one of the three Koreans, Kim Chang-Sun, was feeling unwell. Another reason, in an overcrowded tent, not to get started.

At any rate, no matter what caused the delay, the effect on me was that I began to waver; it certainly did nothing to boost my confidence, and time continued to tick by unmercifully …

It goes without saying that 'an early start' no longer came into it. Moreover, Julie showed no enthusiasm; it had become totally clear in the meantime that Alan was not going to make an attempt today. We saw him – just for a few moments, but enough to get the message. 'He's definitely not going,' Julie assured me.

It was seven o'clock when we gave up the day for lost.

There is no doubt about it: the Koreans had a very delayed start; but as to the exact time the summit team finally got away, there are differences of opinion. Peter Gillman, in *Clouds from Both Sides*, maintains that Chang Bong-Wan declared to him that they left at 6 A.M.; according to my recollection, this is way short of the real time. I had the impression it was nearer eight (see the interview I gave to *Climber* magazine in their Issue XXV, December 1986) … and certainly no earlier than 7.30 A.M. The camp had already been in full sunshine for a long time when the last of the three Koreans made his departure. Before that, we organized his oxygen regulator to deliver three litres a minute, rather than the two he'd had it set for. Is it possible that a watch was wrong, or that a glance at the dial was perpetuated in memory over several actions, thus effectively 'freezing' time? At such a height, all sorts of things are possible. It's more likely, however, to have been an error in translation: Dennis Kemp, who recently returned from Korea, told me that a member of the summit team had been most emphatic to him that they were *preparing for their departure at six o'clock*. It would have been quite understandable, too, at that stage of the proceedings, for the Korean assault mountaineers to have been hesitant in admitting over the radio to their leader just how late they were in getting away. (They all held him in such enormous respect.) Indisputably they reached the summit at 16.15 – and if they really had left at six, that means they were climbing for ten and a quarter hours – longer than it took most of us to reach the summit, without oxygen, the following day! As each of them only had one bottle of oxygen for going to the top, it's worth considering, too, how long that lasted.

From a practical point of view, it is rather unimportant the precise time the Koreans made their start: Julie and I did not follow them – and for a number of reasons.

However much, and whatever has been written about the 3rd of August – and it is a colourful kaleidoscope of opinion – none of the authors has solved the enigma, the real 'why' of the *lost day* ... which passed now to no real purpose as far as most of us on the Shoulder were concerned. The Austrians' 'rest day' undeniably turned into one for everybody except the Koreans, who went to the top. Even Peter Gillman has no explanation and concludes drily: 'Whatever the reason, the loss of that day was to prove disastrous.'

Out of the clamour of voices in the night, it was the low one, the voice of my deepest instincts, to which I should have listened.

The day – 3 August – went by initially with no remarkable events. When, from inside the tent, I heard some of the others remarking that the Koreans were steadily gaining height, I disappeared into my sleeping bag with very mixed emotions. Should we have started despite everything? Never mind the delay? Was that low voice right which had urged me, 'Go today. Behave as if you were on your own'? Still I could hear it. But it was too late now to change anything. Even as I tried to console myself with the thought that we could not have made the same progress as the oxygen boys, for us it was simply too late. There was no getting away from the certainty that we had lost our summit day.

Soon afterwards, Julie spoke to Alan. He confirmed that he had passed a dreadful night: there was so little space that he hardly closed an eye; he wanted to make up for lost sleep now, during the day, and was planning on an early start tomorrow. Julie suggested he move his tent up nearer to ours – we could keep in better contact then in the morning. Accordingly, he and Mrowka carried all their things up the slope to our plateau and erected Alan's small two-man tent in the snow a few metres beyond the Korean dome. I had more or less calmed down about the side-effects that the Austrians' failed summit push would have on our own plans: tomorrow we would all go to the top – we'd be a big and strong group – and yesterday's fight would be forgotten. So I told myself. Nevertheless, I saw clearly what a muddled kind of mountaineering this was. Travelling *en masse* along the same route, as we were doing this summer, was not at all to Julie's and my taste. It seemed just too obvious that chaos would be the inevitable result. We would take care in future, never to let the same thing happen to us again ...

In our opinion, it was not simply that there were a lot of people on the mountain – after all, there had been quite a crowd of mountaineers in the one expedition when we climbed K2's North Spur. It was more the different atmosphere that prevailed, a different spirit. It seemed as if a different wind were blowing ... Could the reason be found in the great variety of people and styles? In the colourful patchwork strewn over the mountains' ridges and faces extending towards the summit – which confuses the good spirits of the Himalayas and causes them to flee? Twilight of the gods? Twilight of mere mortals? Something is out of balance. It's not only to be found on K2 ... and the real cause cannot be attributed to any single individual.

I was longing for Tashigang. And for the loneliness of the glaciers and valleys to the north of here.

What do you do on a 'rest day' at 8,000 metres? Not much. You sleep, you cook. It occurred to Julie and me that the way things were now, our porters would arrive in Base Camp on 5 August for the return march before we could be back down. It wasn't something that worried us too much: we only needed a few men and the liaison officer would surely hold them back a day for us.

The change of plan did however bring another problem: on a rest day in particular, a day of inactivity, everybody uses substantially more gas and provisions than on a climbing day. Julie and I had done a careful calculation at the foot of the mountain – as we always did – to include contingency provisions, but now I was reluctant to start using something destined for the climb or descent. It crossed my mind that three days ago, before Hannes knew how things would turn out, I had given him a cooker and a gas cylinder. By now the Austrians had no more headaches on that score: they were sitting pretty on the Korean reserves*, which would not now be needed as the Koreans had stuck to their plans.

And thanks to their valuable assistance in fixing some of the Korean ropes during their initial summit attempt, the Austrians were first in line to 'inherit' them. So I took heart and explained to Hannes that because of the loss of the day, I could do with having the gas cylinder back. He at once understood – and a moment later gave us an Epigas stove. It was Korean, he said, not camping Gaz – but we certainly didn't mind that. So our calculations, including spares, were back in balance again. They even came with a free gift: a packet of crispbread and a sachet of strange powder. This latter intrigued me greatly – it smelt of fish – what kind of delicacy might it be? Fish soup, perhaps, or some Asian 'energy powder'? With pleasurable anticipation we got the stove going: I really love fish soup! But the culinary delight was a delusion – the 'ocean brew' tasted foul! One sip – and we threw the rest away, making tea as fast as possible! Perhaps, in my eagerness, I had failed to dilute it sufficiently; perhaps it was not fish soup at all! Korean 'hieroglyphs' – who can read them? At any rate, afterwards I told Julie the famous story of Anderl Heckmair's sardines. They almost cost him the first ascent of the Eiger North Face. And we drank yet more tea.

Gradually, the bad atmosphere lifted. We were full of hope and looking forward to the following day. Out of the blue Julie confessed that she was happy now we had not gone that morning: she had no wish to reach the summit before Alan. She didn't want it to look as if the British ace was losing his edge. That would not be very good form on her part, she thought.

At a certain point I noticed that the freshening wind was no longer blowing from the Chinese side. It came now from Pakistan. At first I was worried – then I calmed down; we could not change it anyway. All we could do was hope that fate would grant us another day for the summit tomorrow.

---

* The Koreans had stocked their camp on the Shoulder with all essential provisions and gas for five days. However, as far as oxygen was concerned, only four of the five cylinders originally provided arrived in the camp – three of which were reserved for the summit ascent (one for each climber); the fourth was to share between them at night.

Huge clouds had built up around, and the wind was moving the tent, inside which we were lying. The sun shone on the bright fabric, and we let our thoughts carry us where they would. Now and then we spoke of our plans and dreams: the most important was that we carried on, along the path we had come together. We were both content simply to exist, that the other was there. For a long while we'd had so little solitude, had not had a day like this of inner peace on a mountain; even the wind swaying the tent was like a familiar voice. Nobody wanted anything of us; we could simply relax here undisturbed, each for the other.

In the afternoon Alan told us that he believed the Poles who were climbing the SSW Ridge might reach the summit today or tomorrow. The Koreans, too, were very close to it now. He did not say anything about the weather – obviously there was no call for alarm. Wind from Pakistan, with clouds, is not infrequently encountered by would-be summiteers in the Karakoram. The China Wind is the exception, not the rule.

There may have been signs of a change in the weather that we missed by being inside the tent. I am not sure whether there was anything to notice or not; certainly there was nothing to prevent four other groups of mountaineers in or near our vicinity from preparing an assault above 8,000 metres the following morning – and to set out, just as we did: around noon on 4 August Yugoslav climbers reached the summit of 8,035-metre Gasherbrum II, as well as that of Broad Peak (8,060 metres); the soloist Tomo Cesen began his seventeen-hour climb to K2 Shoulder (his route a first ascent); and the Americans on the North Spur of our mountain went to 8,100 metres before they – there were only two climbers – had to give up the exhausting struggle of trail-breaking in deep snow. They escaped the deadly high-altitude storm whereas we were caught by the change of weather when within reach of the summit. And while the Koreans on 3 August were still heading upwards, the mountaineers of a French expedition hugged one another on top of the 8,068-metre Hidden Peak.

The 4th of August had now been established as 'our day', having taken over the role from the day before. It seems an irony of fate that even the Austrians could have had 3 August as their summit day, if only they had brought up one of their own tents from below House's Chimney. On 4 August now, at any rate, it *had* to work for them – if they eventually got off the Shoulder by midday on the fifth, they would then have passed four full days in the Death Zone.

Neither for them nor us, however, did the disastrous consequences of the lost day owe their origins to the *length of stay* in the Death Zone up to this time – we all endured one day's prolongation without any physical problems – but to the simple fact that the delay brought us into the storm's own fateful and unalterable 'timetable'.

At four o'clock in the afternoon a feeling of relief runs through the camp – the Koreans are about to stand on top of the mountain. We all enjoy their success with them, with Kim, and with the others in Base Camp and on the Abruzzi Spur as well. They've deserved it!

At 16.15, K2 is theirs. Julie and I think warmly of our curly-haired friend; at this moment not even Kim would object if we were sitting near our barrel, clinking foaming mugs together ...

If and when? But the weather on this late afternoon does not look bad. Sometimes in the Karakoram, a tug-of-war takes place between the various factors that influence the weather from the Chinese side and from the plains of Pakistan – out there will be monsoon now, which does not exist here, yet in some way its pressure is felt here, now and then. We shall see that tomorrow morning! It's windy ...

We've rolled up like hedgehogs to conserve energy; we concentrate on tomorrow, completely focus our minds on it. All is ready. We have spent almost the whole day in the tent together.

Then, out of the blue, we hear about the Poles. It can only be them! Somebody else has appeared on the summit: the SSW Ridge is climbed! Incredible – everything is running like clockwork today ...

Then, suddenly, someone observes drily: 'They are coming down ...'

Coming down?

Here?

Normally I can keep a rein on my temper, and in my case I'm a fairly phlegmatic soul – people say I'm something of a stoic, even if they also say I speak my mind too much, which isn't easy for everyone to take. Agostino often remarks, 'Kurt, you are terrible ... really terrible – but we like you!' I believe in still trying to find the reason why, even if a giraffe is looking in the window. But occasionally I don't understand something, can't accept it because it seems just so totally impossible ... and then, heaven help me, I blow up! Even among friends. This is one of those times.

'Polnische Wirtschaft! What kind of mess is this? How on earth do

they think they can come down here? Nothing was agreed. The K2 Hilton is already overbooked …!' I am swearing. I no longer understand the world at all! And with all respects to our mountain friends from Warsaw and Krakow and wherever else … what *is* happening here?

It strikes Julie the same way. She grumbles, 'How can climbers come over the top of a mountain to other camps without having made any provision for their accommodation or support?'

It cannot be! They know we're going to the summit! They must be desperate! I calm Julie, so far as I succeed in calming myself. Mrowka, I'm sure, would have a walkie-talkie – amongst other things – if this had been pre-arranged. She would surely have known about it … it can't have been planned ….

But there's no getting away from the fact that chaos reigns up here on this mountain, and has done for the last two days. If it were a lower peak – you could go along with it – but here, on the mountain of mountains….

Somehow it will have to be resolved, one way or another … there will be thirteen people sitting here at 8,000 metres tonight … We won't be in clover, that's for sure.

But the most terrible event of this night – it far exceeded everything else – had not yet happened. It was Wojciech's death.

It was an event so grievous, the question 'why' was not asked at the time … thus I can only relate what came out later.

The Poles reached the summit by six o'clock in the evening, not too late to embark on the descent. Willi told us about it as we lay in the tent; he had been keeping an eye on the situation up there and later fixed his head-torch onto the Korean tent, so that all the people descending could find the camp. But even before it got dark, when he could still see quite well, Willi had a sudden impression he had spotted somebody falling from below the top.

Whatever it was Willi saw remains unclear; but later, shortly before midnight (around 23.30), one of the Poles did fall – in the region of the Bottleneck. It was Wojciech Wroz, an experienced mountaineer who had already been twice to over 8,000 metres on K2 – on the North-West and on the North-East ridges. Julie and I knew the gritty-looking Pole with the sharp-cut features from our occasional perambulations around Base Camp, which sometimes ended sipping vodka in the cheerful circle of those who 'only' have the wintry Tatra Mountains (and industrial chimneys) to train on, but who (along with the Yugoslavs) are nowadays considered to be the hardest Himalayan mountaineers in the world.

The assault team, which besides Wojciech comprised Przemyslaw Piasecki and the Czech climber Petr Bozik, all extremely tired after several very high bivouacs, were struggling down on the Abruzzi side of the summit pyramid, fighting not only the effects of altitude but latterly also those of darkness – and they did not know this face at all. Nevertheless they had opted to come down this way as it was easier than returning along their Magic Line.

Two of the Koreans, also now descending, were rather slow (one of them finally attached himself to a piton and bivouacked) and they, too, were present in the Bottleneck at the fatal moment. All of those involved were exhausted, and apart from the possible failure to pass on a warning, altitude alone can be blamed for what occurred.

It is not totally clear, however, what did happen, even today: on the extremely steep terrain which was provided with fixed ropes, some of them old, some newly installed, there was one unbelayed and dangerous gap in the line. According to reports, the Korean who descended first wanted to 'bridge' this gap with a length of rope, and in the course of so doing left the end of another rope hanging, which he had shortened for the purpose … From there to the next belay was easy.

On the other hand, when Julie and I climbed up the next morning, we found at the foot of an almost vertical corner (the steepest section of the Bottleneck) not a gap in the fixed ropes but a new, free-hanging blue and white rope which led directly to the steep snowslope below. This rope had no restraining end-knot. It was lethal – and not only at night. We immediately tied a knot in it, one so thick it could not possibly slide through the karabiner of any climber coming down from above, and a hand-loop as well. When descending, this would be the very last of the sequence of ropes.

At this time, we were still under the impression that Wojciech had sustained his fall below the summit – as Willi believed he had seen. But Wojciech certainly got as far as the Bottleneck. His two companions, Petr and Przemyslaw, who after abseiling in the darkness had waited for their companion below the ropes at about 8,100 metres, heard a sudden dull sound as if somebody had fallen … Did the unsuspecting Wojciech hurtle into the depths, just when he felt himself safe on a rope, because in the darkness and in his state of extreme tiredness, he did not notice the missing end-knot?

Here, in this place? Or further up? Did the piece of rope above have a knot, was it perhaps too small, or iced over, or was Wojciech himself simply not fully aware of what was happening? In that moment it was unimportant to the others which it was – Wojciech had fallen, disappeared, was dead – there is no chance if you fall up there. When all hope for his safety had gone, the survivors descended to Camp 4, where they arrived at two o'clock in the morning.

Thus, during the night between 3 and 4 August, there were finally *eleven* people in the Shoulder Camp. As the bivouacking Korean only came down at daybreak, Alfred was able to squeeze into his place in the Korean dome. And Alan Rouse? After the cramped night he had passed before, he was not willing to endure another like it. His solution was a snow hole. He invited Petr and Przemyslaw, who were in shock from the loss of their companion, to use his tent (that made three in there, with Mrowka) – and he himself bivouacked, half inside, half on the outside of his small shelter of fabric, in a snow-niche – uncomfortable, but at least he had air to breathe, even if it was cold.

It is an interesting fact that this did not affect him adversely. On the contrary: Alan proved to be the strongest on the summit day. He broke trail, leading most of the way to the top. Only perhaps a hundred metres short of the summit did Willi relieve him and take over the lead.

It is also worth remarking that Mrowka (who six days later still had energy enough for a descent) experienced a noticeable drop in performance during the following day after another night in the cramped tent.

In Camp 4, after the nights of overcrowding (ten to eleven people) several times there was somebody who suffered deterioration as a result of being packed tightly into a confined space: Alan Rouse and Kim Chang-Sun after the first night; Mrowka and Hannes Wieser after the second. (Despite Willi Bauer's assertion that Hannes gave up his climb on account of damp mittens, from the way he was moving for the hundred metres he did manage, it was patently clear that he could never have reached the summit even with dry ones … Julie and I predicted his turning back before it happened. This is to cast no aspersions; very few mountaineers have accomplished more than one summit assault within such a short time.) Kim Chang-Sun, after feeling unwell in the morning after his bad night, was nevertheless the strongest Korean on the summit climb, as Alan

1. 'I have two passions: the mountains and martial arts.' Julie in meditation.

2. Julie reaching the storm-battered surface of the Shoulder at our first attempt in July; the summit of our 'mountain of mountains' seems so close – but is still some 800 metres higher. (The dangerous Bottleneck below the ice balcony and the highest ice cliff, the 'Shark's Fin', are clearly visible.)

was on ours – and Mrowka, too, was still in good shape days afterwards. Were lack of sleep and tight confinement, or the lack of oxygen inside an overcrowded tent, reasons for the temporary wretchedness?

Condition is certainly no linear constant, it is all too easily influenced. The French theory that the physical shape of a mountaineer in the Himalayas decreases continuously during the course of weeks while his acclimatization is increasing steadily is from a practical point of view rather odd to say the least. (A medical friend with a sense of humour said to me: 'It's right enough if somebody has diarrhoea.') According to such calculations, we ought all to have been flat on our backs on the Shoulder from the word go, because all of us had already spent many weeks on K2.

'Despite their bad shape, X, Y and Z did reach the summit of K2!' asserted the author of the mathematically inspired French report – you are tempted to add, 'and, moreover, without oxygen.'

That this, as well as the fact that we endured many more days at high altitude afterwards, is clear evidence against the above *courbe de forme*, must have escaped the selective vision of the ardent theorist. He obviously did not want to see it: in reality, physical shape is a very individual and serpentine curve, dependent on many factors – not only on time.

The 3rd of August, the lost day, passed into the 4th with no marked separation; this passage was marked by a continuous sequence of events which were in some way all linked together – apart from Wojciech's death, which rose lonely above them all. There were now two walkie-talkie sets in Camp 4, a Polish and a Korean one, but it was the events which dominated the brief 'air time': as far as the next day's seven aspirants to the summit were concerned, there was no direct communication with Base Camp, nor any message received from below.

The mood here is subdued and tense at the same time. The last chance, the last effort … everybody reflects on what that entails, but everybody knows he will try it. You feel the immense might of the big mountain … You are scared of it, but you cannot leave it. And at the same time, you trust it.

3. Exhausted but happy, our two Basque friends are back from the summit. Renato went to meet them (from the left: Mari Abrego, Renato Casarotto, Josema Casimiro).

4. Nothing ventured, nothing gained! Our companions from Quota 8,000 had fantastic weather for their final ascent; even so, the dangerous traverse at 8,200 metres below the ice balcony must have felt like some sort of Russian roulette.

5. Establishing a safe number of well-equipped camps is a strenuous job; Kurt carrying some 25 kilos on the glacier, and (6) at 6,500 metres, tackling Bill House's Chimney. (7) Photographer Massimo in a deeper and somewhat unexpected 'reconnaisance' of the Godwin-Austen Glacier.

THE SUMMIT – OUR
DREAMS COME TRUE

… A tiny figure, and a whole sky of ice above …

The 'sky' has fissures, clefts – iridescent and glistening up there, silent in the light of the sun. And though you ask yourself how it can be possible that these thousands of tons of cantilevered ice don't come tumbling down, at the same time, you will them most urgently to cling together.

If this were not so, if they were not supporting one another, the giant 'balcony', this monster, would not be poised up there. But what if the mysterious forces should suddenly relent? Then, an enormous cloud of ice-dust would thunder down the steep slopes and ribs of K2, down the Abruzzi Ridge, gathering such momentum that it would not stop, but surge on, up Broad Peak on the other side of the valley.

Instead, the ice continues to hang there, as silent as sky above a tiny, hunched human figure, who approaches it on all fours – while the frozen forces remain quiet.

If you look at K2 from the valley, on your way perhaps to the Windy Gap, it is impossible from that distance to comprehend the dimensions of this icy projection. The mountain appears as a marvellously faceted and pure white crystal, but having – as the result of a whim of some giant – half a 'glass apple' stuck into its side just below the top (an apple complete with teeth-marks around the edge!). The whole summit pyramid, from down there, appears remote, floating, unconnected to the crystalline strength of its massive base: its multiplicity of lines, a tissue of buttresses and spires, seem to have grown together into one single heavenward swoop. The whole huge structure, about 2,000 metres high, rises out of the glacier surface from a height of about 5,300 metres, the busy upward thrust of its many lines calming finally in the wide expanses of snow spread over the gently curving summit slopes like a smooth white cloth.

From the middle – as if on an altar – rises the main summit pediment. To stand before such harmony, such a conjunction of power and beauty, releases strange emotions, impossible to describe. This mountain radiates a force, coupled to remoteness, a greatness which in its simplicity overwhelms you completely.

When you're leaning into the wall below the 'glass apple', you have approached this highest sphere – and your eyes search and check it at close quarters. The image of an altar is reinforced, a mysterious altar housing equally mysterious offerings – and you stand in awe.

Or you might call it – fear. It is fear.

Nobody can escape this feeling when he climbs to the highest point of K2. The small, bent human figure creeping on all fours is Alan Rouse. A little lower is another shape: Mrowka. Further down still: Alfred. It is seven o'clock in the morning on 4 August. Julie and I have started too; below us we soon make out Hannes, and a little after him Willi coming up as last man. But Hannes meanwhile has turned back.

It is not long before Julie and I find ourselves last in the line. We are the only two to climb roped – it's safer, but it takes more time. However, we were only about an hour behind Alan when we started out, and we don't expect to increase that by very much on the way to the top.

How lucky we are with the weather! Dazzling brightness all around, glaring sunshine …

Step by step, we draw inexorably closer to the Ice Monster, feeling much as a mouse must feel, trying to crawl silently between the paws of a sleeping cat.

The only comfort to be drawn as we pass below the giant serac is that the fatal collapses seem to occur only irregularly and at considerable intervals. We don't like to think about it – nobody does – but to a certain extent, it is just a question of luck whether you are underneath it or not when it goes. We are all painfully aware of the danger, and hurry past the spot. It is one of those rare, unavoidable situations, where the risk is obvious and you accept it with your eyes open.

Not far above Camp 4 we saw traces of one such break-off, hundreds of half-melted blocks were piled under the balcony, covering a wide section of the slope.

Faced with the choice, whether to go up through the dangerous Bottleneck just below the ice balcony, or to tackle the difficult and time-consuming climb further left, through the vertical rock formation, most people would opt for the Bottleneck – because time is such a decisive factor in a summit assault. At an altitude like this, and with regard to the difficulty and steepness of K2, you cannot count on being able to gain as much as a hundred metres of height in an hour (something which presents no problem on Broad Peak or Gasherbrum II). Here, from a final high camp at about 8,000 metres, you may need from eight to ten to fourteen hours even to reach the summit of K2: the extraordinary variation depending on snow conditions, your own physical condition, the degree of acclimatization you have achieved, the weight of your load, the possibility of sharing the chore of trail-breaking, the quality of sleep the night before the summit, how much time you've already spent at 8,000 metres, the existence of or the necessary application of fixed belay points (and in critical places of fixed ropes as well), on whether it is an 'oxygen-free' ascent or you're climbing with the help of mask and respirators. Heat, cold and storm will also be major influences. Thus, with so many unknown, or only partly known factors, it is nearly impossible to gauge in advance how long it will take to climb the summit pyramid of K2. Sometimes it will not be possible to reach the top at all. Therefore, this variable time scale cannot even be considered as a rough guide.

The 'mountain on top of the mountain' remains sphinx-like, an enigma beyond human understanding.

On this same day – 4 August – at eleven o'clock in the morning, Yugoslav mountaineers on nearby Broad Peak are approaching the summit. In the sky long veils of thin cloud have appeared, and just below the 8,000-metre level, puffier formations are building up. Only the summit block of K2 – the 'mountain on top of a mountain' – stands free in the sunshine. Half an hour later, the high veils have dissolved and the sky is blue with some large patches of transparent cloud. The fluffy layer, however, has settled itself around the Shoulder of K2 and become more dense …

Tomo Cesen, making a solo bid on K2, turns back in the fog from a height of about 7,800 metres. Later, light snow begins to fall there. The Koreans, as well as Petr and Przemyslaw, start their descent. The second group of Poles on their Magic Line has also been swallowed up in the 'grey soup' and opted to retreat in miserable weather.

The climbers on Broad Peak, however, reach the summit at about 11.30. Visibility above the sea of clouds is still good. At noon, their compatriots further east stand on top of another eight-thousander, Gasherbrum II. And even in the early afternoon, Willi Bauer photographs Al Rouse, who is still in the lead, against a cloudless, cobalt sky. Dressed completely in red, his dynamic figure can be seen below the last seracs, close to the summit. He is steadily breaking trail.

So the weather appears totally different on this day, according to your perspective. This is not unusual for an 8,000-metre peak: Julie and I witnessed similar conditions more than once on Nanga Parbat … and when I stepped onto the summit of Dhaulagiri with my Swiss companions on 13 May 1960, far below us, 2,000 metres down, a storm was raging; the roll of its thunder crept up to us from a great distance.

But – back to K2!

'Julie, it's only midday! This time, we'll make it!' I am in high spirits as we near the end of the traverse.

'Yes – this time we will … ' she replies in a low voice, and smiles. We are happy. Behind us, the bizarre ice formations of the hanging glacier glisten in the sunshine. Once past them, and with your ear no longer cocked nervously for sounds from above, once the huge sheets of ice, taller than houses, the blue-green daggers and splinters and cogs no longer threaten your head – well, then they are beautiful!

The weather is fine and we still have half the day in front of us. All the same, we don't want to be on the summit any later than 4 P.M. With the worst difficulties now behind us – the Bottleneck and the traverse – K2 will be ours! At last! Our spirits run high …

Here is the last fixed rope! Alan Rouse or the Koreans must have put it across the flank, since Alfred, Willi and Hannes, when they climbed up the day before yesterday, chose to go straight up along the ice balcony, before getting stuck in deep snow over there, somewhere.

The last fixed rope … it isn't really necessary here, I think. This ascending traverse is not difficult. Still, the snow is deep in places and it certainly provides a fantastic trail-marker in case of a storm, when visibility is poor. I know only too well how you are more than grateful for every little assistance provided at 8,000 metres! Nobody can be sure, up here, that his memory is not playing him tricks – especially when, in swirling winds and racing cloud, it all looks so different that you can't recognize a thing. These are hazards of the Death Zone. Once, long ago, during the first ascent of Shartse (7,502 metres), anticipating a stormy retreat, I marked the whole route with pieces of clothing: strips cut from my second pair of trousers (sacrificed especially), my spare yellow socks – one of the socks on a prominent boss of rock, the other further up … the route was very complicated. We did not need them to save our lives then – Hermann Warth's and mine – but we might have done … if we had suddenly disappeared into cloud.

8,300 metres! From the last piton, above a giant isolated boulder on the left edge of the steep snowslope, I belay Julie as she climbs to join me. We are now on the rocky rib, which Fritz Wiessner followed with Pasang Dawa Lama in 1939 during his attempt on what was still, then, a virgin summit. Pasang was one of the best Sherpas of all time. Both men climbed without oxygen and knew they were within reach of their goal. There was no doubt they could have made it, and Wiessner was prepared to spend the night out, but suddenly Pasang, usually so imperturbable, became paralysed with terror. He dared not continue for fear of evil spirits, which come out at dusk. Only 230 metres of height separated them from the summit.

So, you never know, up here, what to expect. This is the third time that Julie and I have penetrated the final sanctuary of K2. Four years now this mountain has held us in its spell … invaded our dreams. We had almost given up hope of ever climbing it. Now the sun is shining; we feel great – better than ever before at this height on K2. The past weeks of relaxation at Base Camp have paid off. Above us, the mountain still towers into the sky, but is not as steep as the section below the ice balcony. A large, wide ridge stretches ahead, scoured and fluted by the tempests, its surface marked with hundreds of horizontal runnels carved by the elements; it is a white desert with thrusting dunes of ice and snow, and here and there isolated seracs. High up, just below the summit, outlined clearly against the blue of the sky, there stands the remarkable, shimmering ice cliff which Julie and I call the 'Shark's Fin'. Below it, a lonely red figure moves higher through the steep world of snow – slowly but inexorably gaining ground, undeterred it seems by anything: Alan Rouse. He is maybe a hundred or a hundred and fifty metres above us. The others have been swallowed by the enormous landscape, have disappeared somewhere between the dark pulpits of rock and the dazzling undulations.

The indefatigable figure, plugging higher and higher, seems the very symbol of hope ... almost blurred by the blinding whiteness, and framed by the sinister, nearly black sky whose deep, velvety darkness threatens to engulf everything. The world of humans is so far away.

All of us up here are held within the power of the mountain. We feel it acutely. We cannot know how this will turn out, where this path is leading us – up here. But already we feel joy: this time we are so early that by any human reckoning the summit we have dreamed about for so long will really be ours, unbelievable as that seems. With the joy comes the sensation, however, the menace, that up here human judgement hardly counts for a thing.

Your companion is the only being up here that, amazingly, still derives from a far distant earthly life – she and your thoughts, and both of you are linked together like floating thoughts, linked by the rope ... two islands in space.

And Pasang Dawa Lama's sleeping demons? Where are they: will they wake? Something urges us to hurry, an uneasiness which overshadows the pleasure, the joy at our good progress. Soon it will be one o'clock. How time is racing!

We still have some 300 metres to overcome before we reach the summit.

Should we leave my pack here – with the stove, bivvy gear, jumar clamp? Hang it on the last piton? Every kilo carried multiplies at this height. Surely, we will have no trouble getting back this far, whatever happens? I consult Julie. She nods, pushing up her dark ski goggles to reveal her face. Her eyes are shining – with the excitement, I suppose, of being at last so close to our goal. 'Yes – one sip from the bottle, and then press on,' she says between the deep breaths, which, up here, accompany every move. Sure, a little drink and let's go! Spare gloves, a plastic bag with Ovaltine, the head-torch – we stuff them all into the pockets of our down jackets. I take along the two titanium ice-screws as well – you never know! The teabottle we drain and leave behind, but decide to hang on to our second one, which we pack in Julie's hip-bag.

Somehow we overlook the space blanket – a pocket-sized pack of foil fabric, weighing next to nothing; it gets left in the rucksack. Now we have to move as lightly and speedily as possible. Not that it is late, but ... K2 is high, incredibly high. We feel that distinctly when we look back down at the puffy sea of cloud, into which the other eight-thousanders have now also sunk: Broad Peak, the Gasherbrums – all gone. A mingled sense of excitement and fear grips us now; I know no word for that!

Higher, and yet higher ... Leaving our rucksack at that last piton means we have to get back that far today, no matter what.

It is almost half past one when we set off again; the sun is still shining, but the light seems a little weaker now. This might well be our last fine day. Again I tell myself: Kurt, we're doing fine, feeling fine – never been this good, this high! We're bound to make it this time!

Still, I feel a slight unease. But it passes.

Moving on a short rope over the rocks and snow of the rib, we reach a rocky outcrop, a vertical wall about ten metres high, rust-coloured streaked with sulphur yellow, and overhanging. The ground at the bottom – it seems absurd – is totally flat, and sheltered, large enough indeed for a small tent. To one side, on the lefthand edge, is a yawning drop – K2's South Face. Somewhere around here a month ago Kukuczka and Piotrowski struggled out after completing the Face, having had to abandon nearly all their gear because of the extreme difficulties encountered near the top. Certainly this must have been the spot where the Barrards had their bivouac – Maurice and Liliane, with Michel and Wanda.

We pass to the side of the rusty rock formation and continue between slabs of snow. Above us, a final rocky shoulder has appeared, from where we will traverse right onto the steep, wide vaulting that leads to the summit. For a while I catch sight of the half-hidden figures of Willi, Alfred and Mrowka moving behind a snow-barrier at the same height as the rocky shoulder – then they vanish again. Perhaps they have sat down for a rest.

Only Alan is visible now, further up, climbing over a steep snow wall. He has slowed down a lot ... it doesn't look too easy up there! Glancing up a little later, I notice Alfred and Willi right on his heels, but they have tackled the obstacle at a different spot, and not without difficulty. The strain of climbing for so many hours at such altitude shows in their every movement. They seem to be in slow motion. Everything now is bathed in a milky light. With blue shadows. But, good God! What about Mrowka? Where is she?

This terrain is unbelievably tough going. The snow has been all churned up: there are sinuous braids and ribbons of a marzipan-like consistency and slabs chiselled into fluid, fluted shapes by the wind, then fused to the bonehard surfaces beneath by the sheer force of moving currents of ice-cold air. There are shields fashioned in different thicknesses from crystal powder and often fallen across each other chaotically, like the ruins of a huge, collapsed slate roof. Most will hold your weight, but not all – you step between them or through them, and they shatter into fragments, or slide away …

'Careful, Julie!'

'I know … Don't worry!' Even with crampons we need to pay the utmost attention here.

After skirting a chest-high barrier of snow with an overhanging rim, we put the treacherous wind-ploughed landscape behind us … only to find ourselves sinking at every step in deep, loose snow. Gasping for breath, I reluctantly track back towards the rounded spine of the ridge. The distance between us and the three figures above has widened, but they, too, are barely moving, hanging up there like marionettes on the slope beneath the final seracs. We must get on! There is obviously another struggle waiting for us up there! The time it takes to gain altitude increases dramatically in this last section below the summit – for everyone.

'Julie, how are you feeling?'

She smiles at me, 'Don't worry!'

'No headache? Not at all?' I need to know. After all, we are approaching an invisible barrier, which it is only possible to cross on certain days of your life, the very best days. The exaggeratedly slow movements of everyone up here is proof of how far we have already penetrated into the forbidden zone.

Julie's answer dispels my anxiety. 'No, Kurt. No headache – *kein Kopfweh* at all!' She nods her head for emphasis. 'Go on, keep going. No time to lose!'

Up! 8,400 metres … it will soon be three o'clock.

Soon after that we discover Mrowka.

She is leaning, immobile, into the steep slope above the small rocky shoulder. 'She's asleep!' says Julie, amazed. I don't trust my eyes. Can she really be sleeping here?

Before, earlier in the day, at the end of the traverse where the last fixed rope was, Mrowka had dozed off with her head on her arms. It is obviously not 'her day'. Willi took a picture of her in that position towards the edge of the ice balcony, in sunshine and with the clouds below. (Alfred is in the picture, too – you can recognize him by his rucksack.) Worried about her, Willi told Mrowka she ought to go down. But she was a long way from giving up. So Willi and Alfred continued in Alan's tracks with Mrowka following on her own.

I tentatively approach the huddled figure on the snow slope. She really is asleep! Her forehead, framed by dark blonde hair, is resting on her right arm. She has her hand in the sling of her ice-axe, which is anchored deeply in the snow to belay her. But what, I wonder, would happen were she to wake up suddenly?

'Mrowka – do you want a sweet?' I ask anxiously, clutching on to the back of her yellow anorak. She reacts with alarm, looking up full of surprise: 'No ... Up ... I have to go up!' That is what she wants.

I am startled, shocked. It's not the Mrowka I recognize. The good and helpful 'Ant' seems to be obsessed. There is no way of slowing down this bundle of energy – even if the lack of oxygen has put her in a strange state of mind – as is quickly demonstrated ...

To Julie's consternation, Mrowka suddenly climbs up between us. At any moment she could stumble, grab at the rope and pull me down. Why not follow us, Julie suggests, adding, 'You can always go ahead when we get to the summit.' But Mrowka only increases her speed and retorts drily, 'I don't want to climb behind an old man ... '

I cannot believe my ears. Is she bewitched? Don't take any notice, Kurt, I say to myself. Let her get in front! I stop and immediately Mrowka steams ahead. With much concern, I watch the hasty, uncontrolled movements of the Polish woman above us, as she swings hammer and ice-axe into the unsafe and uneven surface of the snowslab, working her way upwards. She is in a state halfway between sleep and waking. I am irritated, with a feeling of impotence: there is really nothing I can do about it. If nothing else, it urges her every fibre upwards. She is fighting for her summit. For her, turning back is out of the question, however much for the best it might be. Seconds later, a terrified Julie shouts from below, urging me to overtake her. If Mrowka should fall, she could tangle in our rope and sweep us all off the face. I try it, but it's completely out of the question to overtake by breaking a different trail. Every time I get close, Mrowka speeds up. Gasping for breath, I give up.

'Basta!' I yell down to Julie – I'm fed up. We have to take the risk ... just as we would with any ice tower above us. But then I change my mind: keep a safe distance! It is the only thing we can do.

How much valuable time and energy has been wasted on this unexpected intermezzo? Hopefully it won't be long before Mrowka meets Alan. Perhaps she will listen to her partner.

'Let's have a rest and a drink,' I say to Julie. We need a breather, anyway.

Mrowka now climbs above us and to our right. We are out of her fall-line, thank God. The sky above has meanwhile paled. Clouds are welling up from below. It is happening very slowly, but it's still worrying. When I look out to the Baltoro, I see the outline of Masherbrum, and below it an ocean of peaks, but a soft, hazy greyness has spread over the whole landscape.

The weather is slowly worsening, that much is evident. It reminds me of my summit climb of Gasherbrum II. Then, seven years ago, the weather was almost exactly like this when I reached the highest point with my companions – worse, even, if anything: the sky grew steadily darker and the sun penetrated the leaden curtain with a sinister light. In the end, darkness lay over everything like a burden – *Götterdämmerung* on the Karakoram mountains – but nothing happened. Just a delicate veil of fog of an almost transparent greyness, which slowly grew denser, swaddling the enormous pyramid of K2 so that it rose, like a wraith, above all the other peaks. A mist like chiffon … eerie and of ominous beauty … but that was all. It stayed like that and we came down safely.

The atmosphere around the summit slope, as the weather slowly starts to turn. Kurt and Julie, two tiny figures at about 8,450 metres, have stopped to take a short break for refreshment.

212 THE ENDLESS KNOT

4 August 1979 … and 1986. Is history repeating itself? The date is the same, just seven years later … Nobody knows – it could just as easily be different. We are too high to escape, that much is sure. In the event of a real breakdown in the weather, we are doomed – even if we turn back now …

I cling to my memories of Gasherbrum, try to calm down, while the mantle of greyness slowly, very slowly, increases. Another ingredient of danger? I guess we have to take the risk, the unavoidable sort of risk with any high climb* like this, but I still have the feeling it will turn out as it did on Gasherbrum.

I wonder what Julie feels about it?

'Julie … '

But she does not reply. She is staring up, fascinated. 'Look, there!' She points. On the soft skyline of the summit, at the dark edge of snow behind the serac immediately above our heads, is a figure! Now another! They are half-hidden by the edge, but now one raises his arms in triumph – the summit! That's got to be it, just beyond them. They are almost there!

It's an effort to hold back my excitement, to force myself to be calm, realistic. The summit seems quite close for us too, but appearances can be deceptive – we might still have another 200 metres of climbing to get there, and that's a lot up here …

'Yes, let's rest and drink something.' It does us good!

We empty the bottle. We are standing next to each other and have no idea that at this very moment Willi is taking a photograph of us from above, albeit unintentionally: we appear as two small figures further down the summit slope, behind his friend Alfred who is taking the final steps to the subsidiary summit. It is 3.15 P.M. Looking up a little later, I spot somebody else. That's three of them have made it. Onwards!

Like a giant suitcase, a projecting bulge of snow bars the way ahead. Mrowka went to the right here, which meant burrowing in deep snow for several steps. I prefer to put a titanium screw deep into a corner on the lefthand side, where I have found some good ice. Belayed by Julie, I climb obliquely to the edge above, then work my way along a steep hard rib on all fours, using the front points of

---

* One thing confirmed by the subsequent course of events was that nothing would have changed for us, even had we turned around. We were as equally trapped as Hannes Wieser on the Shoulder, who did not even tackle the summit climb; as Mrowka, who turned back just below the summit; as Alan Rouse, Willi Bauer and Alfred Imitzer, who got to the top. There was no difference: it was not a question of hours. We were all too late by one whole day.

my crampons and my ice-axe. It soon widens out. At a small crevasse, I set up a good belay and bring up Julie, who removes the titanium screw on the way. Above us, in the bluish-grey mixed light, we see a succession of steep convex snowslopes, a three-pointed serac – which hides the summit from our view – and on the right, higher, but still so close you think you can touch it, a gleaming white shape – the mighty 'shark's fin' of ice. That, we know, is not far from the top.

It is four o'clock. That was to have been our limit for the summit – but we are so near now, so near.

Suddenly Willi Bauer appears. He and Alfred are on their way down.

'Are you sure you still want to go up?' he asks me.

The question takes me by surprise. 'It shouldn't take us more than an hour at most,' I answer. What is he talking about?

'You're wrong,' says Willi. 'It took us four hours!'

'Come off it, Willi!' I object, reproachfully, and for a moment feel a sense of panic, wondering how such a thing could be possible. He must have misunderstood me.

'It took us four hours,' Willi continues, 'from down there.' And points in the direction of the ice traverse.

Ah, well. That's an entirely different thing!

Nevertheless I am quite concerned, because I suddenly remember our rucksack is down there – with the stove and the bivouac gear. It takes far less energy to descend, but we'll need at least an hour to get back there from the summit. What shall we do if we cannot make it down in time?

At this moment Agostino and Joska come into my mind, our two friends who in 1983 found shelter near the summit and escaped with only minor frostbite.

'Are there any crevasses where you can bivouac?' I ask Willi. He nods: 'Yes, sure – and of course you'll reach the summit.' He follows after Alfred, who has by now climbed down the snow barrier.

A whirl of thoughts buzzes round my brain. It is close enough, the summit, but what bothers me now is not so much weather as time.

Willi, with his vague reply, was not a lot of help. But up here time is like a rubber band: you are so engrossed with what you're doing, paying attention to do everything correctly and precisely, all your concentration focused on the snow and ice, every step taken in this landscape dedicated to the climb – that you forget all about time. It is as if the whole dimension ceases to exist up here.

Heads down, we continue – every step requiring several breaths. 8,500 metres … What's that – suddenly – as if something magic touched me? Aghast, I stop and look up: a weaving play of light and shadow, eddying, whirling, dancing above the last dark curves of snow … Is this the prelude to a storm? A coquettish tease before all the forces of heaven start to roar?

Is it about to start? And we, will we be in it then, right in the heart of it? Or is it just the fluttering of the pale, silky folds of this mantle of mist which enshroud us and will eventually dissolve …?

An inner wrangle between my faith in 'our' mountain and instinctive fear brings the lunatic response: Up! While it's still possible – let's go up! Even so, I would be prepared to turn round. If the occasion demanded it, if Julie wanted to …

'Should we go on, or not? The summit is so close – there it is! But we can still turn around.' I notice Julie's tense expression. She has also seen the dancing veils.

'I'm feeling very fit!' she says.

'It can't be more than an hour … '

'If you think so – let's go on!' she replies decisively. Go! Go! We know everything is at stake. Once in a lifetime! Today! We are going into this thing with our eyes open, totally aware of what we're doing.

The dancing veils disappear. The air does not move at all. That's not the way a storm announces itself. The transparent greyness over the landscape indicates rather a gradual worsening of the weather. Will we manage to avoid a bivouac? We must be above 8,500 metres …

Here's Mrowka again! She swings her ice-axe, thrusting it into the steep snowslope, a look of wild determination on her face. Without doubt she is driven by an unremitting will to get to the summit, but she has to rest every few steps now, stopping, sinking her head on her arm on the slope. I shudder, imagining her spending an icy night up here. It is obvious she should turn back, but how to convince her of that? If she will listen to anybody, it will only be to Alan, her partner. Where in all heavens is he? Julie has already remarked earlier that we would never be able to support an exhausted Mrowka to the summit and, more to the point, get her safely down again – a descent that without doubt would be partly in the dark. After all these years, we have a sense of what we can manage between us, the two of us, but we couldn't do it with three!

At last Alan appears on the curved outline of snow above us, his slim silhouette against the grey of the sky. Alan Rouse, who has acted as saviour more than once in the chaotic situation on this mountain!

'Are there any crevasses we could bivouac in up there?' I ask him. A good bivouac site could be a matter of life and death. 'Yes, you'll find somewhere,' he tells us. 'And please, Alan … ' Julie implores, 'take care of Mrowka. She won't listen to us. But we think she ought to go down.' She indicates to where Mrowka is leaning into the snowslope, resting. Will Alan succeed in talking her into giving up? 'Whatever you agree, both of you,' Julie says, as Alan, very surprised, reaches his companion, 'stay with her.'

Not long afterwards we see the pair descending; it was a black day for one of Poland's best mountaineers. Even back in Camp 4, she still cried for her summit.

We are alone … the snow around us, the ribbed surface, hundreds of lines. The Shark's Fin is now directly above us and very close. A thin transparent haze muffles everything. We climb towards the summit. The dice are cast …

It really isn't that far now! With every step, I feel it more strongly: we're not going to need a bivouac up here! But I notice a wind-carved niche, directly below the huge, icy triangle and make a mental note, just in case. Tension is increasing. Our way ahead is suddenly blocked by a large, almost vertical ice barrier, about three metres high. We can't even see what lies ahead. Have we really got to climb that? There looked a much easier way on the other side of the big triangle, but I am loth to go back. The titanium ice-screw grinds as I turn it into the hard wall with my ice-axe. I chip some handholds with the pick (any energy saved is a help) – then, curious to see what waits on the other side, I push myself up. Glancing down at Julie, as she belays me, her eyes I see are big and questioning, her face full of excitement. I cut another two hand-holds in the ice, then pull myself over the edge …

There is the smooth line of snow leading up to the summit with, below it, a moderate slope, a shallow depression. At once all seems ridiculously easy. 'We're almost there!' I shout down. 'We can leave the titanium screw in place for the way back.'

Over there, not much higher, the mountain ends. K2. Taking up the rope, I belay Julie. Our K2. A shine seems to come over her face as she raises her head above the edge and looks over. Just a few minutes more …

I see she has brought the screw with her anyway. I spot another possibility for a bivouac, and glance along at the hole at the beginning of the depression almost with a smile. It is much brighter up here. A friendly place compared with the dark steepness of the enormous mountain flanks. But we won't sit here in a bivouac. Not without some irony I think about time: we have actually arrived here much earlier than we thought when we were so nervous about coming on.

One more crevasse, then we follow the smooth line of snow, gently leading us higher …

The joy! The happiness! We cling to one another. For this one moment of eternity, K2 – beautiful K2 – is ours.

'Julie – the peak we most desired!' I feel my voice trembling as I look into the big, dark eyes under the yellow hood – eyes which can radiate so much power – the familiar glance and the little smile. 'Our very special mountain,' she whispers. It is, it is – our own and very special mountain.

Thousands of peaks lie at our feet, but we see none of them. They don't matter. Just to be here, together. Minutes in the snow, in the highest snows of K2 …

It is just after 5.30 P.M. I notice as I glance at my watch. On the curved, rounded crest of snow, in the grey haze which surrounds us – now clearer, now darker, are propped some bulky yellow Korean oxygen bottles, and fixed between them, the large red-white-red Austrian flag (which used to fly in Base Camp); and, barely moving in the still air, a little triangular pennant from the *Naturfreunde*, and a British flag, smaller than a pocket handkerchief, which Alan must have placed there. I detach it and hand it to Julie … 'For you,' I tell her, 'Alan won't mind if we take it down … ' Hesitating, she holds it in her hand for a moment, then stuffs it into the pocket of her down jacket … 'You can have it later – or Alan, if he wants it … ' She doesn't seem to attach much importance to the flag, the summit of our dream mountain means more, much more.

At the same time, the all-enveloping mantle of grey prevents us from seeing very far: a small, but prominent, subsidiary summit of rock and ice over on the opposite side must mark where the Magic Line comes up. Below us, to the north, we can see an elongated bank of rock through the silky fog: it is a secondary top – just a step, really, but the highest on the North Face. A thought flashes through my mind, leads me down for a moment to where we turned back in 1983 – and a feeling of satisfaction rises inside me …

But the fog is darkening and a cool wind sweeps over the summit. It is like a warning. Quickly we shoot off some pictures, but Julie says, 'It's high time we left … ' Anxiety flickers in her eyes. It's past six already. We really have to go!

THE FALL

Night on the Hanging Glacier

We'll be able to move more quickly if I do the leading. My route finding is better and I have no qualms about Julie following on behind. She is in very good shape. I wouldn't dream of letting her come down second otherwise. There should be no problem about making it back to the top camp on the Shoulder without a bivouac, but unfortunately we'll not reach the rucksack we left hanging at the end of the fixed ropes before dark; it's still 300 metres further down. Good thing we have a head-torch.

'I'll go ahead, then – if that's OK?' I glance back at Julie, see her nod of agreement; she blinks at me from under hoar-covered hair.

'All right, but go! No time to waste!' Her voice follows me as I leave the summit. She's right. Every minute counts. I must hurry. There is still some light: we can see well enough. And only a light wind. But how long have we got before it's quite dark? Everything will become twice as hard then, every step a problem.

Don't rush, don't go any faster than is safe, a voice inside me keeps saying.

That's the subsidiary summit behind us. In the grey mist, I make for the icy silhouette of the Shark's Fin. Suddenly, I remember that somewhere around here, there was a small crevasse. Accordingly, I detour a little to the right to be sure of avoiding it before going on towards the Fin. In the snow, I can see our tracks from the way up. I pause for a second and take another look round – and freeze. Oh, my God! At the other end of the rope, Julie in her haste has omitted to make the detour. She is coming directly at me in a straight line, and just in front of her – almost invisible – is the dark smudge of a depression. The crevasse!

'Stop! For God's sake, stop!' I yell just in time to bring her to a standstill.

I hadn't seen the crevasse from above, either; it was only my memory that warned me.

'Go back up, and follow my steps round,' I instruct her. But why hadn't I said anything before? I should have warned her. Can that be an effect of the extreme altitude? The thin air up here leads to all sorts of short circuits, even when you think you are behaving perfectly reasonably. If you don't do things the minute you think of them, you are apt to forget, or what is even worse, to think you have done them just because they occurred to you – thought becoming reality. No less disastrous, you may take the very thought of an action as sufficient to render the deed itself unnecessary ... 'Not now,' you tell yourself, 'later maybe.' Dangerous delusions!

I am quite sure that the two of us have not reached that state yet, but so narrowly avoiding the crevasse has set alarm bells ringing in my mind. Don't break your neck. It doesn't matter how slow and cautious you are. The descent is always the most dangerous part ...

Julie stopped the moment I shouted. Now, carefully, she retraces several steps, reaches my tracks and follows them. I let out a deep, long-held breath – I don't dare to think of what might have happened if one of us had fallen into a crevasse up here at 8,600 metres ... Onwards!

Almost immediately, I reach the top of the short vertical step, make a stance, and belay Julie down. We are now at the same height as the Shark's Fin.

'Put the screw in at the bottom,' I call down to her as she descends.

Yes, even though it costs valuable time, it's worth putting in an ice-screw! Not that I think I will fall – but safety is worth those few minutes.

'Come on!' Julie's voice floats up to me, and I lower myself down while she takes in the rope. Only a few words are exchanged as I join her, and already she is removing the screw. Not for the first time, I notice the determination in her face. Yes! We still want to get down to that camp: we need to move as fast as possible, but at the same time we must do so with the utmost caution – we have to make the most of the last of the daylight to get over the seracs.

Onwards!

We move together now. My feeling is that, going down, we would do better to cross the lower ice and snow step at the place where Mrowka came up, rather than where we tackled it. Already we are just above the steep section where the two tracks divide. It is obvious from the trampled surface which way the others have gone. Again, going ahead alone, I sneak carefully down until I reach a small horizontal crevasse which lurks below me in the twilight, and I wait there, belaying Julie with my ice-axe rammed deeply into the snow. I am relieved – because Julie, having appeared at the edge above me, tackles the steep obstacle with surprising agility. Now she is with me.

'Take care. There's that little crevasse. Remember?'

With the reminder, I am anxious in some way to make good my sin of omission further up.

'Yeah. Sure!' she says, a bit breathlessly. Was that a smile?

Of course, we both knew the crevasse! On the way up it was where we went to the left and Mrowka to the right …

'Let's keep going. Down!'

I wonder if Mrowka and Alan have already reached camp? Meanwhile the daylight has faded more and more so that I can just make out nearby snow formations, but not much more than that. Peering into the depths I can faintly recognize by its dark silhouette the highest of the rock shoulders. That's where we have to get to. That's the way.

We'll be at about 8,400 metres when we reach there and not very far from our rucksack. We should be able to manage that even when we have to move more slowly once it's dark. We'll need that head-torch pretty soon now.

Shall I get it out ready? I ask myself.

No. Let's not waste time. We can still see enough.

I grope my way over the slightly curved slope, stepping sideways, step after step, time and again thrusting in the ice-axe, my gaze resolutely directed downhill.

Here are those damned snow shields – irregular wind-pressed slabs. Don't take it too fast, Kurt. Take great care. Really, we can hardly see a thing now.

'Take care!' I call up to Julie. 'Great care. Go slow here … '

But I know that she is prudent. Again I ask myself whether we should get the torch out now. It's in her down jacket. She put it in the pocket when we dumped our rucksack at midday. The surface of the snow here is very irregular – and what are these here – still tracks? The slope is not steep on this section and I know we are in the right direction, but never mind, let's get the torch out.

'Stop. We'll do it … '

'Oh, Kuuuurt!!' The yell splits the darkness, loud, terrified, desperate. In the same moment, I spin round and ram the ice-axe with all my force into the slope, hurling myself on top of it. The rope! The rope! Here it is! Already, Julie, a dark bundle, hurtles by at incredible speed …

Hang on, you *must* hang on, Kurt.

Terrified, I wait for the shock. Though it's hopeless, I still pray for that one in a thousand chance of being able to hold this unexpected fall.

Kurt, my head tells me, you haven't a hope. This is the end: you'll both fall 3,000 metres down K2.

With vicious suddenness, the shock comes on to the rope, and for a fraction of a second I succeed in holding it. Then I'm catapulted out and flung with incredible force down the mountainside, powerless, weightless, like a feather in an erupting volcano.

I am helpless … helpless … The speed is terrifying … An overwhelming fear of impact grips me … this endless tumbling … head-over, head-under, down, down … The slope! The slope! I clutch at it frantically, get a grip and hang on with all the force of desperation. Again, the shock: a giant fist rips me once more from the surface and flings me into the air. The tumbling goes on …

Stopped! The giant fist has crushed me into the snow. In a sitting position, back to the wall, I am stuck upright in the snow, buried knee-deep, legs trapped in deep, heavy snow. The rope is still in one hand, but my axe gripped in the other is buried deep under the snow. Words fail to come …

Julie? What's happened to Julie?

'Kurt!' Through a haze, the words float down the slope.

'Get your ice-axe in. Belay yourself!' I howl up into the darkness. My whole body is trembling uncontrollably.

At the same time, I press myself even deeper into the snow. By some miracle I have come to rest in a natural, safe belay position. Miraculously, too, Julie has stopped several metres higher up. I can just see her indistinct form on the slope above. Did she brake her fall?

'I can't get my ice-axe out … I'm lying on top of it.'

If she's on top of her axe, then probably she did manage to brake. But why can't she pull it out? I have trouble understanding the whole thing properly – can't even grasp that we're still both alive, that we are not lying smashed at the foot of the mountain. It is truly a miracle.

'I'm trying to get my axe out now, but I'm in an awkward

position. Watch out!' The voice from above sounds muffled.

Attention, Kurt!

What does she mean, in a bad position? Is she lying obliquely in the snow? Or with her head downhill, perhaps?

Whooshhh …

The sound of sliding – eventually, Julie bumps into me with full force. Thanks to my bomb-proof position in the heavy, deep snow, I resist the impact. Once more it went well!

'Julie, are you all right?'

'Yes. Fine,' she replies matter-of-factly. 'But my ice-axe is still up there.' Only a deep sigh betrays the relief she feels to find herself still alive.

Ice-axe still up there? Uh-uh! But the main thing is she hasn't hurt herself. I climb up and get it.

What will happen now? It is almost totally dark. Nearby I recognize the indistinct outline of a crevasse in the gentle curve of the hanging glacier on which we have landed. We are at the beginning of the giant balcony in the upper half of the summit pyramid. The fall has thrown us off route and night is almost upon us. The best thing would be to bivouac over there. It ought not to be that cold as it is overcast and there's no wind. Perhaps this crevasse will make a good bivouac site? If we wait a couple of hours, we might be able to continue the descent … but I doubt it. Although I can vaguely see the outline of the highest rock shoulder away off to one side, to get over there to rejoin the route in the middle of the night may not be that simple. We have to be content that we are still alive, thank God! After that, we can cope with all the rest. The weather certainly is not good, but neither is it really bad. We are in cloud – for a free bivouac that is better than an icy, star-clear night. But we're high. Very, very high. At a guess 8,400 metres – perhaps slightly less than that.

'Julie, we have to bivouac. Let's go over to that crevasse.'

We stamp through deep snow across the moderately inclined slope. By the time we reach the crevasse on the hanging glacier, it is almost pitch dark, yet it is still possible to pick out the main features: the icy trench looks an ideal place to bivouac, being perhaps two metres wide and with a ramp inside that leads down as if into a den. I feel how close we are to the edge of the giant balcony. Uncomfortably close. The snow here is hard and reliable. A good belaying place – Julie rams her ice-axe into it. The ramp then ought also to be of good hard snow: all the storms should have tamped a good, thick crystalline layer over everything, the same as is very often found on the wind-exposed sections of the summit pyramid. The crevasse is certainly chockful of snow. Nevertheless – perhaps just because everything does seem so perfect at first sight – I cannot suppress slight mistrust. And Pasang's evil demons come to mind – those demons who spring to life at night.

Haven't we just survived this fall by some enormous stroke of luck? Escaped certain death? All of a sudden, this miraculous shelter seems to me more like a trap.

'Julie, I have to check it out before we can go in. Please, get the flashlight, then belay me.'

Yes … that's it, before we move into it, I must examine it carefully, probe all round with the ice-axe; I ought definitely to be well belayed for that. Julie rummages for the torch in the pocket of her jacket. Both of us lived for days in a crevasse like this on the North Spur of K2. The expedition set up a whole camp inside it. It offered a really safe refuge in the dangerous flank of the spur, while the avalanches kept sliding down over our heads. On Tirich West, too, in the Hindu Kush, Dietmar Proske and I occupied a similar crevasse-bivouac on the north face of that 7,000-metre peak. But such shelters are not always so benign.

Julie finds the torch. 'I'll need to turn the battery round,' she says with a sigh and fumbles with the casing. Perhaps our eyes have got used to the darkness, or is light coming off the snow itself? Whatever the explanation, there is a strange shimmer all round us, even in this cloud. It's not pitch-black, anyway. That's something. We can recognize shapes, and the task Julie is doing now, she has done a hundred times before. She always carries the battery back-to-front as a precaution against the torch being accidentally switched on and draining all the power; now she has it the other way round. Already I am beginning to regret that for reasons of weight we decided not to bring two torches with us.

With resignation in her voice Julie announces, 'It doesn't work!'

She tries the switch several times without success, opens the casing again, and fiddles some more with the battery. I feel a hot fury welling up inside me. Perhaps the nervous tension of the past few hours has finally proved too much.

Bloody hell! I think. That's all we need! Night! At 8,400 metres! We've had a fall; we're sitting on the highest balcony of the world;

we're longing for any kind of shelter, and now ... *this.*

Julie has put the battery in again, closes the case and switches on. Nothing.

A wave of utter frustration overcomes me, robbing me suddenly of good sense. I tear the lamp from Julie's hands and hurl it into the night ... Even as I do so, I am bitterly shaken by my outburst.

'Hell!' I mumble into my beard, shocked at the consequences of my sudden temper. This must be the altitude. Julie doesn't say a word, but it is obvious that we should have kept trying longer. Now, we're very definitely without any light. In the darkness in front of me yawns the black mouth of the crevasse. Inside, there is a sinister silence. Nevertheless I have to try it.

'Belay me!' I chew into my icy beard, then crawl slowly and carefully down the ramp, probing as I go. I'm in a square tunnel between the walls of the crevasse: the floor is quite firm, but much too steep yet for a bivouac. My optimism rises. Again I probe. The snow seems solid and carries me well. If only I could see something! It's still steep. For a moment, I stop and a sense of misgiving rises once more. Hadn't I better back out?

'Julie, belay me carefully.'

On my belly now, hand anchored on the ice-axe, I edge feet-first a little further into the tunnel, sliding along ... Now it's more even. This would be all right, but I want to make one final check. Then I notice: as far as my feet have reached, the ground is still firm, but testing sideways with my boot has revealed an open hole where the hard snow ramp fails to meet the edge of the wall. For God's sake! We can't stay here – there's nothing but air below this ramp!

'Julie! Julie! Pull!'

Immediately the rope tightens, but in the meantime a huge chunk of the ramp has broken away and clatters into the void. There is no anchorage left for my feet any more.

Panting heavily, and with a frantic surge of energy, I slither upwards, back over my ice-axe, looking for some kind of hold to enable me to get a bit higher still. I succeed and force in the axe again in front of me.

'Julie! Pull as hard as you can!' I yell, panic in my voice. 'It's a bridge and it's crumbling away!'

My breathing is desperate. I can hear the broken pieces echoing down into the crevasse. Somehow, I manage to stick my left crampon into something; but my right foot is still hanging in space. For a moment I don't dare move ... Damned, damned trap! Didn't I just know it? If any more of this stuff breaks away, I'll go down with it … Scared, I think of the way Renato died … Carefully, I wriggle a tiny bit more and succeed in bringing my foot up out of the hole and back on to the crumbling ramp, but I don't dare trust any weight to it. I can only pull up on my hands.

I scream: 'Julie!'

I'm finished. That's it. I can't do any more. Heart hammering, I'm wedged obliquely in a fragile equilibrium, sustained solely by the ice-axe, one crampon-tooth – and Julie. I try to collect my wits, muster some strength, tank up my lungs with oxygen. Heaven knows there is little enough of that up here. Then I have another try.

'Up again, Julie! Pull as hard as you can!'

Panting like a steam engine, I inch higher until at last I have found holds for the crampon-points of both feet, but my energy is totally spent.

'Stop pulling. Just hold me.' Mouth agape, I force out the words.

I rest my face in the snow of the ramp. All around me it's pitch-black. I can't make out a thing, but I can sense, below me, the pitiless emptiness of space, invisible, ever-present. I cling to the sides of my icy coffin. Exhaustion grips me, as do the long black arms of the chasm. Pasang's demons are on the loose! I am suddenly filled with indescribable panic, unlike anything I have experienced in my whole life before. Will I ever get out of here, escape this icy crypt?

'What's the matter?' A voice from outside.

'I need to breathe,' I reply feebly. It's like a paralysis, like being under the influence of a spell.

At this very moment, and for no apparent reason, the whole edge collapses under my right foot. It cracks, breaks off and crashes into the depths. Terror strikes harder. Utter panic. There is no doubt about the spirits! My hand tightens like a claw around the ice-axe. No, no! You won't get me! 'Up!' I yell, and immediately feel the pull. For a moment practically my whole weight comes on to the rope. I jam a fist between the left wall and the snow, just enough so that with the other hand I can pull out the axe and thrust it in a little bit higher. 'Pull!' I *will* get out of here.

I can hear Julie's heavy breathing above me now. I dimly see her dark, hunched shape as she pulls at the rope with all her might. At last the demons are losing their grip. My teeth are clenched tight with effort. Push. I work myself higher. Again and again, gasping for breath like a fish out of water, I press the axe into the surface. I have hardly any strength left at all, but God, Yes! I am getting out! God, Julie, you held me!

'Don't panic. You won't die here.' Her dark silhouette looms over me. Her voice is very quiet, like an oracle.

No, I shall not die here. I am out! Lying outside with my face in the snow. Julie, you've saved my life.

'Thank you,' I gasp with my last breath. 'That was very close.'

Where will we stay?

I have an overwhelming desire to get away from the crevasse, even if there is safe snow around it. The terror is still in my bones. Where can we stay? Dig a snow hole somewhere on the face? That's the only option left. A little higher than we are is a steep section of snow with a hard crust. I start swinging the ice-axe, hollowing out a half circle, a place for two, tight together … It's absurd! Our bivouac gear is hanging only a hundred metres lower in the small rucksack at that last piton. Everything seems to be running against us now.

Without a head-torch there is no way we can reach it. It's much further over, out on the spur. We'll have to wait till first light to find a way back from our hanging glacier, from the balcony, to the route. We are both working hard at the hole. We don't feel cold. An old bivouac rule says, the longer you prepare the bivouac, the shorter you need to spend in it.

Clang! The ice-axe hits hard ice. We try further up, further down, further everywhere – there's a hard wall below the snow. Bloody hell! So much for a snow hole.

We have to be satisfied with an open niche. At least I manage with the axe carefully to hollow a small hole behind the hard crust without breaking it. One of us – Julie – will have room to kneel or sit inside.

The ground is level in front of the hole and there is no wind, so the other can just crouch there, half sheltered by the curve of the niche. A Spartan luxury: some sweets and a small plastic bag with Ovaltine powder. All we have to sit on is the rope (for one of us), and Julie's hip-bag (for the other). We're wearing our long down jackets, the yellow anoraks and our overtrousers, but we miss the warm down trousers which are down at ABC – not me so much, I'm fairly impervious to cold, but Julie. Otherwise, we're well enough protected here with our mittens and overgaiters. As it happens, neither of us sustains frostbite on our feet up here. Nor do I on my hands – not then. But the tip of Julie's nose suffers and possibly two fingers on one hand.

However, it is a terrible misfortune that we haven't been able to reach our bivouac material. What's more – and this error was surely to do with high-altitude absentmindedness – we've even left the foil space blanket, which weighs hardly anything, down in our rucksack at the last piton. I can't believe it. Desperately I search again and again through all my pockets … but in vain; we really have left it behind in the rucksack.

It is a long, long night. Luckily the weather does not break, but towards morning it grows very cold and windy. We've tried, as best we could, to keep each other warm by hugging and rubbing each other and moving from time to time, but we're relieved when finally the thin light of dawn breaks through the veils of cloud, glad that the long night is over, and we are still alive and still possessed of sufficient strength for the complicated descent. Thank God the weather did not break down totally. Thankfully, we welcome even patches of sunlight as we start to search out our way down.

DOWN TO 8,000 METRES
The illusion of safety

Where *is* the camp? The refuge at the end of our space odyssey? We have to find it!

The descent from the top of the ice balcony has cost us many hours of the utmost effort and concentration. It was the last act in our fight for survival on the summit pyramid – or so we thought. Now we are somewhere around 8,000 metres, and can't see a thing. A short while ago – but who knows, maybe it was as much as an hour since – I could still make out the Bottleneck and the ice overhang above us, and that gave me a clue to the direction we should follow; now we are caught in a grey soup and in real danger of passing clean by the camp without noticing it! We can't allow that to happen! I am uneasily aware that the descent has sapped almost all our reserves – and we felt so amazingly well this morning! For quite a while now Julie has been calling for a rest, but I've resisted, allowing us only time to catch our breath – just half a minute or so when we reach the end of the rope, Julie on a belay stance and me climbing down to join her from above. We move on all fours, facing into the slope.

We're in a real stew of clouds: filthy grey masses moving slowly, banks of fog, flurries of snow crystals that seem as lost as we are and are now roaming from one place to another. It's all white, or grey, or oppressively dark, according to the density of this icy cotton wool. The steepness of the slope and how well I can remember it from the way up are the only indications of where we are. A short while ago I mistook a rock for a tent, and the disillusion was almost unbearable. Still the shock shook me up and remobilized all my senses. We *will* find the right way. I'm known for my sixth sense when climbing at night or in fog – and not without reason; I would have been dead long since without it.

I see Julie's vague outline, filmy, grey, watch her slow movements. She knows as well as I do that it must have been somewhere around here that the Barrards – Liliane and Maurice – lost their way. 'Let's continue to zigzag,' I shout. 'We *must* find the plateau.' I say it as much to keep contact between us as anything else, although of course we do have to locate the small level section on which Camp 4 is situated. 'Yes, we have to find it,' she agrees. 'But the slope here is still too steep … ' I notice the look of seriousness in her dark eyes between the frosted strands of hair. It's so gloomy now, dark twilight, that we have had to take off our goggles. She's right, the slope *is* too steep. A horrible thought flashes through my mind: we could miss the plateau completely and stray onto the China side, ending up among those giant cornices! They overhang enormous drops. Maybe that's where Maurice disappeared after he lost Liliane. Julie and I are on our rope: whatever happens, we're together: it is either our life or death.

It has to be our life. Let's give it another try to the right. Only by maintaining our downhill zigzag will we find this camp. 'To the right, now!' I call, praying in my heart that it is the right decision, and nurturing the absurd, crazy hope for a gust of wind to part the clouds – to open them if only for a few seconds.

Zigzagging, we make our way down, but we hardly seem to get any lower. We're wasting our last energies, yet it's our only chance. It's the only way not to miss the camp in this grey and white desert. Our anxiety increases … how much longer? We're tired … we have come through so much … will this mountain ever let us go? Surely, it would have taken us earlier if that is what it had wanted? We have been at its mercy ever since our fall.

The slope is easing off! Julie, by God, it's getting flatter! That has to be the plateau! Or couldn't it just as well be the top of a giant cornice? I can't see the curving mounds of ice debris, the rounded chunks, half-melted and then refrozen, glued together by the icy night winds and continually replenished from the giant hanging glacier on the summit wall above. The shards and fragments fall 200 metres before coming to rest on the easier angle … Where, then, is this zone that should mark the upper edge of the plateau? It was such a feature, I remember, on the way up. Where on earth are we? Is this a cornice after all? Maybe everything has been covered by impacted snow, freighted in by the wind? Is or isn't this the start of the plateau?

It shoots through my mind that they should be able to hear us from the camp. If we are where I think we are, all we need to do is yell.

'Ha-a-ll-o-o-o!'

I holler into the fog, and with a glance to Julie, add, 'They should hear that!' She looks at me in astonishment. 'Are you calling for help?' 'No, just so that we don't miss the camp.' That's if there's anyone around here. There follows an anxious wait – and silence.

'Can I sit down now?' I hear my companion say. 'Of course.' I continue to listen out into the clouds. Then I call again. I'm beside myself with agitation. Is this day going to end in another bivouac? Again, no answer. Only clouds … and silence … and the low noise of the wind over the surface of the snow. 'We have to go on,' I tell Julie. Disappointment. Hopelessness. But then, a resurfacing of hope. Julie pulls herself together and gets up.

Suddenly I hear a yell through the fog. There *is* an answer! The next moment both of us are shouting back at the tops of our voices. Relief surges through us – it's as if a great weight of fear has lifted from us. The camp …!

No more bivouacs! We hear the voice again. It sounds like Willi. From its direction, I know we must be at the beginning of the plateau. Immediately afterwards, I come upon the first mound of ice chunks – so, then, this *is* the zone I remembered! Now the angle diminishes. We are standing on a gentle snowslope, which – as I know – leads to the camp we set up at the lower end of the plateau.

With all that has since been written about the tragedy, I cannot forbear to comment at least once – and it has to be here – on the many distortions that have emanated from a number of quarters concerning the whole course of events. I have to do it for Julie's sake and mine: we who fought our way down from the top of the mountain to the highest camp completely on our own, by our own efforts and relying solely on one another. It's not true, as several writers have said, that Julie crawled the last part of the way into camp; it is also not true – as Willi reported – that her nose and cheeks were black with frostbite and that shreds of flesh were hanging from one hand, that she was *unable* to stand and had to be dragged by him to the tents. The considerable discrepancies which recur again and again between our two accounts could, in my opinion, indicate that Willi was the victim of hallucinations, that he experienced visions and thoughts which bore no relation to reality. Nobody who reaches 8,000 metres can be sure of being immune against that. But when other writers, who were below the cloud layer at the time, grotesquely misrepresent the time Julie and I arrived on the summit, saying it was 7 P.M., I'm lost for words. That goes, too, for the last 'speech' accorded to Renato Casarotto on the rim of the crevasse – when in reality, he was unconscious and almost dead. It seems to me that artistic licence has been stretched to breaking point many, many times in the reports of what happened on K2.

'I definitely want to rest now,' says Julie, letting herself down onto the snow. Both of us are incredibly relieved to discover that the camp is so close.

Just for a moment, a breath of wind tears a spinning hole in the fog, a circle within which I can make out the coloured shapes of tents. They also appear to be turning. A second later they are gone. Keep the direction in mind, Kurt. Hang on to it. Which way? There? Straight down, that's where it must have been. But we could do with another opening like that to be sure. I crouch on the snow next to Julie, put my arm around her shoulder. Tiredness and relief show in her face. We've made it. Made it down safely from the 'mountain on top of a mountain'. K2 is 'ours'. But it was a narrow escape this time. I think of the fall and the bivouac. I see the stamp of frostbite on the tip of Julie's nose, discoloured, brownish – but, thank God, we are alive and K2 is ours. We will never come here again. The final full stop has been added to our long association with this mountain – even if K2 will always be bound to us and we to it. We pushed to the very limits, but despite everything, I feel content that we got there. We are free to go another way now …

It opens up again: I see the camp, the three coloured tents, see Willi standing there. We have to go across to them before it all closes in again. But Julie still wants to rest, sit a little longer. Can I pull her? Over there is tea, warmth and recuperation. There is the end of the terrible odyssey. I stand up. 'Come on, I'll pull you,' I tell her, taking her hand. Then I start yanking her down the slope. It's easier than expected, because she is wearing her shiny yellow nylon trousers and the snow, despite its corrugations, is pretty regular and angled slightly downhill. Julie puts out her other hand to steady herself during the slide, lifting her cramponed feet a little to keep clear of the surface. I remember there is a small crevasse somewhere here on the plateau – please God don't let us fall into it! I keep my eyes skinned. Gasping, I tug Julie towards the camp. After a while, I stop. 'Wouldn't you like to get up?' I pant, asking myself

1. The 'teapot' avalanche started off a chain reaction, sweeping away the Austrian Camps 3 and 4. However, the evidence of Mandi's teapot (2), found at the foot of the mountain, indicated what had happened.

3. K2 seen from Windy Gap, showing the tent positions before the final tragedy. Half circles indicate the destroyed Austrian camps. Their last undamaged camp (indicated by the full black circle) at the time of the summit attempt stood at 6,500 metres (more than 2,000 metres below the top). The empty circles show the subsequent positions of the Korean tent, which was spared by the avalanche. It was carried by the Austrians from 7,350 metres to 8,000 metres on the Shoulder of K2, becoming the key factor in the tragedy.

4. Russian roulette? The avalanche which buried Al Pennington and John Smolich was impossible to predict. Tons of snow slid down the steep flank below the Negrotto Saddle.

whether she just fancies this way of moving, or whether now that our ordeal is over, she has suddenly been smitten with fatigue. Surely she would rather walk into camp under her own steam – especially since we managed so well all day coming down those really horrible slopes to the plateau? Wouldn't she?

'I can't see very well ... I'd rather stay on the ground.' Her answer catches me by surprise. Is there something wrong? She had no problems with her eyes before now. Is it the effort? Or the start of snowblindness?

'OK,' I tell her and lean forward to start pulling again. From somewhere I hear Willi's voice, but I know now where the camp is, even if for the moment it is lost in fog once more.

'My glove! My glove!' Julie cries out. She must have lost it while supporting herself in the snow. Hopeless trying to find anything now! 'We're almost there, hang on a moment!' I gasp. In front of me I recognize the tents, emerging from the fog, and Willi, who has started towards us from the Korean tent. I pull Julie up from the ground and we approach Willi together. We hug one another: we are returning to a different world, from a different world.

'Please make some tea for Julie,' I ask Willi. It is obvious to me that there is not enough space for both of us in their tent. And I'm glad there is somebody to take care of her. Now that we're here, I realize that I have given everything, all my strength and mind, to make it possible. Now I am tired to death and all I want is to sleep. The Austrians take Julie in, and I lie down in our small tent and soon drift away. I don't remember seeing Alan or Mrowka, but they must be here. Nobody can go down with the visibility at zero like this.

As Willi told me later in Innsbruck, Julie soon recovered her strength after some hot tea. Knowing she was safe must certainly have helped. The worst was over. That's what everybody thought. Julie's feet were not frostbitten, Willi discovered, but she had sustained an injury as well as frostbite on one hand. In Willi's opinion, there was no doubt at that point that she would manage the descent. Her eye problem was giving her headaches, though. 'When we gave her drinks, she kept missing the cup,' Willi later recalled. Hannes and Alfred began talking about getting a helicopter to pick her up from the lower part of the mountain, but Willi knew that helicopters could only operate up to 6,000 metres, and only then under perfect conditions. Julie did not take the idea of 'rescue' seriously, although she would not have turned her nose up at a

1

2

`6:35:37:15`

3

4

7

8

9

Key

C4 = assault camp;
P = Plateau at *c.* 8,000 metres;
BN = Bottleneck;
T = Traverse;
R = Rucksack depot;
S = highest small rocky shoulder at *c.* 8,400 metres;
M = Mrowka's highest point, and meeting with Alan;
SF = the 'Shark's Fin';
B = Kurt and Julie's bivouac from 4 to 5 August.

helicopter flight – anywhere! She told Willi that General Mirza had promised her a ride in a helicopter if she reached the summit of K2. I remember we were in Base Camp when he made the offer and I saw her delight at the prospect: sooner or later she would get her flight! Julie had never been in a helicopter and it was another adventure she looked forward to – some time – with no less excitement than a trip in Concorde, even if, in the end, it proved only a sightseeing trip over London!

Willi has since assured me, several times, that on that first day nobody had any doubts but that Julie – who had now recovered – would cope with the descent. She stayed in the neighbouring tent with the Austrians all the rest of that day. Like me, she was making up for lost sleep – as I was told at one stage when I woke up and asked for her.

As I had observed in earlier years, there is often quite a variation in the weather on K2: it may be almost calm on the lower Abruzzi Ridge, while higher up storm clouds sweep horizontally across the rocky ridges; the Shoulder can be stuck in dense cloud while the summit has different weather entirely.

Its great height places the top of K2 almost at the cruising level of jet planes. Passengers on flights from Islamabad to Peking often observe a remarkable pyramid floating in the sky above an ocean of cloud – the summit structure of K2; sometimes the highest tips of the Gasherbrums and the sharp roof and dorsal scales of Broad Peak will be there as well – when below everywhere is experiencing filthy (or at least unpleasant) weather.

On 4 August, the bad weather began to develop in layers during the course of the day. But the force of the gathering storm failed to strike the upper reaches of the mountain. Julie and I could never have survived the bivouac in the open niche at 8,400 metres otherwise.

Below 8,000 metres, however, by five o'clock in the afternoon of 4 August, swaths of snow had swept the whole south face of K2. It grew increasingly dark and the clouds muffling the upper part of the mountain soon reached right down to the glacier as well. Then it started to rain, very steadily, before finally turning to snowfall. Petr and Przemyslaw, the two survivors of the Magic Line party which had gone over the top of K2 and now were struggling slowly down the Abruzzi Ridge, noticed that the snowfall was not so heavy higher up.

5. A cross and memorial plates at the cairn for Art Gilkey near the Base camp. The 'black summer' of 1986 claimed thirteen victims on the mountain – more than all the past years put together.

6. Discussion about the events: near Kurt is Janusz Majer, leader of the Polish expedition to the 'Magic Line'; Jerzy (Jurek) Kukuczka, looking thoughtful, stands behind them.

7. The 'mountain on top of the mountain' – the summit pyramid of K2 (400 mm tele-photo lens, from the Shaksgam valley). The Bottleneck and Ice Traverse below the sheer wall of the huge balcony are amongst the most dangerous sections of the whole route. Liliane and Maurice Barrard were last seen here, and Wojciech Wroz (8) fell to his death. Maurice Barrard (9) fell under the spell of the mountain in 1979 when he got close to the summit via the SSW ridge.

At noon on 5 August – according to Jim Curran – you could even see a tiny bit of blue sky from Base Camp, but it was obvious how strong the wind was because of the swirls of cloud drifting away from K2. However, by half past one in the afternoon, the weather was worse than ever. Full of concern, Jim confided to his tape recorder: ' ... expect the worst. There are actually twelve people on K2 at the moment, all at or above 7,000 metres and the weather up there must be horrendous.'*

It was not until 8 August, two days after Petr and Przemyslaw, that the last climbers from the Magic Line route – leader Janusz Majer and the two Polish girls Krystyna Palmowska and Anna Czerwinska – made it back into Base Camp. The retreat down the difficult route had been a hard struggle for them. It was lucky there were fixed ropes.

Even if a rescue operation had been suggested for the seven of us

* *K2, Triumph and Tragedy.*

The three tents of Camp 4 at *c.* 8,000 metres.

marooned on the Shoulder, there was no chance at all of anybody getting there from Base Camp so long as the storm was raging. It wouldn't matter how many people were in the party, in those circumstances, nobody would have made it. Besides, all those left in Base Camp were either exhausted, or had frostbite or other troubles. Of the Austrians, only Michael Messner was still around; the others had already set off for Islamabad some days before, bearing (in good faith) the exciting news that three Austrians had been to the summit of K2.

The Koreans, during their descent down the Abruzzi Ridge, left everything in their tents necessary for an emergency, and Julie and I had our own depots, too. But the big question for all of us on the Shoulder was: how could we actually get down onto the Ridge without killing ourselves on the way?

Jim, in Base Camp, observes the weather day after day and keeps hoping. But the chances for those high up decrease rapidly. No human can survive indefinitely in the Death Zone, even when fully acclimatized and given sufficient to drink. And they must by now have exhausted their Gaz supplies. What about oxygen? There wouldn't be any of that either. For a stay of such length, a whole truck-load of bottles would have been necessary. Could anybody still be alive?

The 8th of August and Jim Curran is desperate: he is firmly convinced by now that Al, Julie, Kurt, Mrowka and the three Austrians are probably all dead. Yet he doesn't give up hope entirely.

On 9 August, together with Michael Messner, he goes up to the Advanced Base Camp, but doesn't discover anything. He spends the night in our small dark green tent, the only one still there, where all night long the wind rattles the swaying shelter, beating torn guylines against the roof.

The roaring of the storm continues on into 10 August, although the weather looks better. Jim goes back to Base Camp.

On 11 August, the news that everyone has died is sent out to the world.

But let us return to 5 August – to that island at 8,000 metres, lost in the storm …

BLIZZARD AT 8,000 METRES
The Agony of the Five Days

Night. I hear the hissing of the wind, the repeated crackle of snow crystals against the fabric of the tent. I lie awake listening to the gusts: so long as the sound doesn't change, just keeps recurring like this, it is drifting snow. The wind picks it up from one place on the mountain and deposits it somewhere else! You can tell from the intervals that the snow is not coming down now, just being shunted around. That's not too much to worry about – even if our little tent is facing the wrong way now that the wind has changed direction. When Julie and I put it up, the wind was blowing in from China, so we erected our fragile-looking shelter in the lee of the Korean tent, close enough to gain protection from the massive Asiatic dome. But that was on 2 August, since when the wind has turned a full 180 degrees, coming now from Pakistan. So we catch the full force of it! There's nothing we can do about it: the anchorage points have long since disappeared deep beneath the snow and are frozen into the ground. We'll go down tomorrow morning if … Full of worry, I keep my ear cocked to the wind noise, but it's still only drifting snow …

In any high camp, you can tell at once when the real snowfall starts. The sound is steady and much softer. Avalanche danger and a forced and speedy retreat are usually the attendant consequences.

It's high time we got away from here. We *must* get away tomorrow. We lost one day – and still made it to the summit. But now 5 August is almost over. It's more than enough.

What about the visibility, though? That's a big problem: since the disastrous collapse of the serac barrier when the 'teapot avalanche' broke off below the Shoulder of K2, only a very narrow passage remains which was the way we came up here. If only there had been enough bamboo wands to mark it, we could have descended it even in fog, but they ran out at the end of the big slope above Camp 3 at

7,700 metres. Alan Rouse and I would have needed another ten to fifteen sticks to finish the job.

The weather was glorious when we came up – and most of the others probably thought we were being fanatically over-cautious to have used the sticks at all. Now we are marooned in this fog, and if only we had a line of markers, we could find our way down. Make one mistake here, and you are likely to fall over the edge of the seracs …

Nevertheless, we will have to try it. God, I hope we don't get a snowstorm as well. If that happens, then there's no way out – we really are in a trap. The risk of losing our way in the swirling mass of a blizzard is enormous; we probably wouldn't even find our tents again. It would be certain death. So, what do we do in such a case? Wait and hope?

I wonder how things are with Julie in the next tent?

Frightened, I listen in the darkness to the sound of the snow crystals. Still only drifting snow. I fall asleep again.

What's that at the front of the tent? 'Open up!' I hear Julie's thin voice. Dozily, I grumble into my beard. She could have come back earlier! I open the entrance sleeve and Julie crawls awkwardly inside. 'It's a job to get in,' she pants. No wonder, with all this packed snow! The entrance is small and very low, just above the floor of the tent. Not much good in rapidly growing snowdrifts! I remember thinking that down at intermediate camp at 7,000 metres.

'Why do you only come now, in the middle of the night?' I grumble.

'Willi was taking care of my fingers. He gave me his silk gloves.' I hear Julie's voice in the dark. Well … she will need them. At least she has recovered over there, drinking tea … and caught up on her lost sleep … and at least she's here now! We snuggle up in the down bags and sleep.

A ferocious rattling of the tent wakes us. What a storm … it has to be a blizzard. Hell, no! I feel a knot in my throat. We really are in it this time. Getting down's going to be a real swine now.

Our little tent buckles under the force of the wind as the atmosphere sucks and seethes outside; a dull thundering comes from the direction of the summit pyramid.

The wind is gusting at 100 kilometres an hour, pushing waves of blown snow against the tent. It builds up higher and higher outside, pressing into the fabric. Will the masses of snow smother our small shelter completely, as happened one night on Nanga Parbat? At least then we had a solid tent.

Instinctively I pull Julie close, hug her in a tight embrace. We survived then – that was 7,400 metres – but here we are at 8,000, considerably higher. Julie doesn't say a word, presses herself to me. I know her thoughts are running along the same lines.

Slowly the morning comes up, but here in the tent it stays gloomy. I feel really sorry for having been so grumpy last night – somehow I want to say something nice … 'We made it to the top of K2, Julie. We survived the fall and the bivouac. We'll come through this, too. K2 is ours – doesn't that make you happy?'

No reply. Her silence oppresses me.

'I don't know …' Julie finally says hesitatingly, in a low voice. And after a pause, 'I can't see very well …' My God! What does that mean – she doesn't see very well?

I'm shocked. I suddenly remember she said the same thing yesterday, when I pulled her over the snowslope. Quite out of the blue – and I thought then it was just tiredness. Something similar happened to me on Everest. But now?

'Do you have any pain?'

She shakes her head. 'No, no pain,' she answers softly. I look into her face; her eyes, large, seem darker than usual. But this is probably due to the dim light in here.

Her lips are cold. It scares me, but I don't let her see that. Something is wrong, I know it. I have never known her as low as this … It's certainly not snowblindness. Surely she will be a lot better tomorrow? If only we weren't up here, in this storm trap! One thing is clear: this is another reason why we can't leave yet. 'We'll wait here till tomorrow – then you'll be feeling better and we can go down.' I force myself to appear calm. A descent in this storm would be madness, anyway.

But something must be done to buck Julie up. Tea! Liquid! I hurry to get the stove going. How much can Julie still see? I mustn't let her know how worried I am. How can I find out how bad she is? An idea comes to me. 'Pass me the knife,' I say, 'for the snow …' (I'll cut some chunks from outside the entrance, for cooking.) Anxiously, I watch out of the corner of my eye. She hands me the knife. I let out a deep breath. It was lying around in the tent, near the side, but she must have seen something – she couldn't have known so precisely where it was, otherwise. Could she?

Tea's ready. Sipping it is a real pick-me-up, for both of us. Julie leans against me. Despite the blizzard, still raging away outside, it is not cold in here. The rising walls of snow at least keep us insulated. Finally, we even take off our down jackets; we stretch out and, still in our sleeping bags, push our feet into the strange lateral pocket, and wait. After a while we doze off.

I had taken a close look earlier at the fingers on Julie's right hand: they're a little brownish as is the tip of her nose. Frostbite, but not third degree. Two are not too good, but the third is only slightly damaged. I'm convinced this should not present any insuperable handicap. She is worried it might mean she will be unable to hold her sword … not that she complains, but I know how much her martial arts mean to her.

I try to reassure her – but we always knew such a thing could happen one day. The snowstorm keeps howling …

'Bloody hell!' I swear involuntarily in English. The tent! It is slowly bending forward. Masses of snow have accumulated on the uphill side and are pressing heavily into the dome. The flexible poles of the *parapluie* no longer seem strong enough to withstand the pressure, and in two places they're bending like snakes. I'm worried: how much longer can this French contraption bear the strain? There is only one solution: relieve the weight!

To do that, I have to get out. There is too much snow over the tent to clear it merely by punching energetically from the inside!

Indeed, in many storms over the years I have been out to free a tent from its burden of snow usually without taking the trouble to struggle into boots and overpants – I have enough spare socks, even up here! But the problem this time, as I soon learn, is not just limited to the weak struts: I can't even get out through the entrance! The opening, with its short nylon tube just above floor level, seems to have been designed with gentian-filled Alpine meadows in mind, not deep snow. Despite having pitched the tent with the entrance facing downhill, so much snow is weighing down the tube that I can't push my way through it. 'To hell with this umbrella!' I swear, gasping after my unsuccessful struggle. Here we are, trapped like two mice under a cheese-cover. Not quite as bad as that, perhaps, because in the last resort we could always cut a hole and step out – but that would be a drastic solution, and not to be advised in this weather! Right now, I have some choice words for our French 'wonder tent', this funny umbrella with a floor in it. Instead of furiously clouting the walls, as I'm now obliged to, I would prefer to be stepping into the ring with the inventor. *Merde! Merde!* I pant, not without reason.

At this moment I hear Alan Rouse's voice outside. He seems to be talking to Willi.

'Al will help us,' says Julie. We yell to him to ask if he can free the entrance.

'Of course!' Ever helpful, Al digs away like a dachshund into the deep snow. I cannot see him, but hear his laboured breathing through the thin fabric. It's very hard work: he's using just his hands as there's no shovel in this camp.

'I have to stop,' pants Alan. 'I've dug a great pit, and I'm not there yet!' I can believe it. Now Willi gives it a try, first with his hands, then with the ice-axe. One false stroke rips a hole in the tent, but at least the 'pit' has now reached the sleeve entrance. 'You'd better do the rest yourself!' Willi puffs like a hippopotamus, he's had enough. 'And hurry up,' he adds, 'or it will close in on you again!' I hear him crawling into the nearby tent with his companions. Alan, too, must have returned to his shelter. I cannot hear him any more.

What now? Get into my boots? That will take far too long! My thick, woollen socks will be OK. I've got spares. In a few minutes I can be back inside … clear the entrance, find a prop for the sagging poles – an ice-axe or a ski-stick – there's sure to be something I can improvise, then nip back.

And Julie? Can she help from inside? 'All right!' she replies and we discuss what each of us should do. She seems full of energy again, positive. I look at her anxiously, but with more confidence now, as she sits, half upright in the sleeping bag, waiting for me to go. Julie, good Julie, I think … we will make it! Then I start getting out …

Lying on my back, I push feet-first into the narrow entrance which, as I have already realized, slopes uphill. I wriggle like a worm, then once my legs are outside, turn over onto my belly and continue squirming up through the snow, my head still inside the tent. Gasping for breath, I finally arrive outside and stand upright on the slope, facing the tent and the funnel-shaped hollow our companions have made at the entrance. At the same moment, the storm catches me. There is snow in the air, swirling everywhere. Through the gloom, I can make out the silhouette of the Korean tent, shaking in the racing blasts; of our own squashed red dome, only the top is visible …

This is one hell of a storm! Snowflakes whip my face. God, mountains of snow are piling up out here! and it's bloody cold after being inside! But I'll warm up in a minute. I work like a beaver. The tent is buried so deeply, God knows where the guylines are. I cannot find a ski-stick! On the side nearest the mountain, the flat slope of the plateau has built up into a huge wave, level with the top of the tent. I burrow away as fast as I can at the downhill end in a bid to clear the entrance completely, but it is the work of Sisyphus and all the time I notice that the tent keeps leaning more and more towards the funnel.

Should I use the ice-axe to prop it up from the inside?

Dodgy.

And how long will it be before the entrance is blocked once more by drifting snow? By the look of things, not long. I am increasingly aware that nothing will keep this tent standing very much longer. The icy cold seeps into my body from all sides. I never intended to stay out here so long … 'Try and lift the tent!' Julie's voice calls from inside. Lift the tent? What for? But, with resignation, I grab it and heave upwards. Is she having much luck inside? I notice Julie working on the struts to the left of the entrance. 'I think we can make it!' Her voice sounds as positive as ever, full of hope … Oh, brave Julie! I admire you …

But a moment later the tent tilts crazily forward once more. Such a nonsense, to have been in such a hurry just now! Mad to have come out without boots … I should have taken the time to put them on. Let's get back in! Come on – fast! Can I still get in?

And who will dig us out again in half an hour?

And what if the tent collapses? Everything inside me resists having to tell Julie that we are left with only one possibilty.

'I can't fix it.' Julie's disappointed voice comes from inside. Poor Julie. There's nothing that can be done about it.

'We're going to have to abandon the tent, Julie. It means splitting up!' The words sound strangled. There's no way we can get into another tent together.

It's horrible, but we have no other choice. This icy cold! I am shivering all over.

'Quick, give me my sleeping bag,' I beg her. 'Will you go to Alan and I to the Austrians?'

Julie, make up your mind fast in there – I'm shivering as if I've got malaria and I can't spend another minute here!

'No, let me go to the Austrians, you go with Alan.' The sleeping bag comes out through the entrance …

'Willi! Quick! Our tent has had it – please take Julie in with you,' I scream at the dark dome. 'Can you help out? Now, immediately?'

Stinging flurries. Fractions of seconds pass – an eternity – Willi's massive bulk pushes through the entrance. 'Yes of course,' he says.

Now Julie's hand has appeared … 'Please help me out!' I hear her calling. Already Willi passes me to give her a hand through the narrow passage. 'Julie!' I yell through the storm. 'I'm freezing. Willi is here to help you. I have to run … see you later!' Trembling, and dusted all over with powder snow, my feet numb in the woollen socks, wooden, without any sensation at all, I am running through the deep snow to Alan's tent, sleeping bag in hand.

'Please, let me in!' I gasp … but Alan has already opened the entrance. Looking back, I see Willi still outside our tent, bending forwards …

No, Julie. We could not have saved that tent. We had to part. Crawling in with Alan and Mrowka, I feel thankfulness, warmth and yet at the same time an infinite bitterness rising in my heart.

I am leaning against the snow wall, which I can feel through the tent, cold and solid. By my side are Alan's legs. He is asleep, with his head at the entrance. With me in the back of the tent, half-sitting, is Mrowka; she is quiet and withdrawn, staring into space, railing silently perhaps against the fate that denied her the summit of K2. She was nearer the top than last year on Nanga Parbat. She seems not to be here at all.

Alan took touching care of me when I arrived, helping me into my sleeping bag – once I removed all my clothes. Everything was covered with powder snow. The only thing I have left to wear is my down jacket – apart from that I am lying naked in my sleeping bag, in this frightfully cramped space. We threw my wet things into the space between the tent and the flysheet, where they will surely freeze bone-hard in no time at all. All my other clothes are inside the *parapluie*, along with my boots. In our unplanned flight, there was no way of getting hold of them. Hot tea, prepared by Alan, revives my spirits and goes some way to soothing my bitterness about the whole miserable situation. I know Julie is being looked after in the neighbouring tent, even if there is no way of calling to her over the storm. It would mean going outside and shouting. When things ease off a bit, we'll be able to make contact from in here. I can't go out again without shoes and socks. Are Julie's eyes any better, I wonder?

I find it painfully sad that the two of us, who've always taken all our decisions together and who've come through so much, cannot now do a thing for each other – divided as we are by a few ridiculous feet of snow and these roaring masses of air. We still have our thoughts – but they don't help us much. I wonder if she will come over?

In the meantime Alan and Willi have made a shouted agreement that we will all descend together at the first possible opportunity – as fast as we can go. But in such a heavy storm, the risk of getting lost and then losing the tents as well is so immense that it is better to wait a day.

'Jesus Christ! So much snow …' grumbles Alan, rising with difficulty and squeezing out through the entrance into the open. He is fully dressed. It is not the first time that his powerful, long arms flail like windmill-blades through the piles of white powder, trying to keep at least the downhill side of the tent and the entrance clear. To the leeward, the banks of snow keep rebuilding themselves with alarming speed. Alan has already given up on the side nearest the mountain; there the snow drift is packed solid into a massive, rigid wall. But the sturdy little two-man tent bears the pressure well. I have nothing but admiration for this young British mountaineer: for his alert mind and seemingly endless energy, and for the fairness and helpfulness, which he, more than anyone else, has demonstrated on this climb. Four days ago he gave shelter to Alfred Imitzer and just three days ago gave up his place to exhausted climbers from the Magic Line. Where does he get so much strength? Of the Austrians, Willi is the one in best shape. He, too, is quite helpful now.

If only we can get out of this trap. That lost day: I don't want to think about it, but it remains like a bitter taste on my tongue. By now we could be descending the Abruzzi Ridge, be well down – maybe even as far as our tent at the foot of the mountain. I lean my head against the snow wall and listen to the storm.

What has been happening outside our confined world on the Shoulder, where we huddle like prisoners longing for release from the elements? Where every day we have hoped and believed it would be our last one up here?

The Yugoslavs, who stood on the summits of their two eight-thousanders around noon on 4 August, have meanwhile made it back down. The American contenders on the north side of the mountain have accepted that given all the deep snow, there was no point in pushing further and turned back from around 8,100 metres, retreating in worsening weather down their fixed ropes on the North Spur. They reached their Base Camp safely. The Koreans, too, made it down the fixed ropes on the Abruzzi on 4 August; but the Poles on the Magic Line have been fighting for days against bad weather and are still not down. Petr and Przemyslaw only left Camp 4 at 10.30 on 4 August, when the cloud layer was intensifying, but now they are safely off the mountain.

The rest of us are stranded high above.

On 5 August Jim finally called Camp 4 – but too late. Petr and Przemyslaw took their walkie-talkie down with them, as did the Koreans.

Our group, stormbound on the Shoulder, was now without radio communication. Seven people stuck in the clouds, unable to receive a message from Base Camp of any possible improvement in visibility. It was of no help to us then, that on the morning of the 7 August, Jim described a moment of hope: '... K2 is clear up to the Shoulder and the pinnacle behind which Camp 4 lies is also visible, so the whole of the Abruzzi and the whole of the descent is out of cloud ...' and ' ... it's certainly not as windy as last night and anyone up there will, I imagine, be hot-footing it down. The big question is, *is* there anyone up there?'*

All this was totally unknown to us. We were aware during the night of 6 to 7 August that the storm was easing and planned to make a break for it, but there was no visibility on the following morning. With only the one line of escape, the risk of getting lost in thick fog or cloud on the Shoulder was great, especially when we did not know how far down the cloud extended: none of us could know that below the Shoulder the weather was clear! Thus, for want of information, the chance slipped by. A walkie-talkie at that moment could doubtless have saved lives.

'Let's hope our gas will last!' Breathlessly, Alan struggles at the entrance once more. He is very worried we may run out – his original calculation has been thrown out by all the loss of time. 'I still have another full cylinder,' I try to calm him. 'The one we kept for the summit push.' The unused Husch cartridge is in the pocket of my down jacket, and there's a nearly-full Epigas stove in our tent

* *K2, Triumph and Tragedy*, p. 141.

as well. Does he want to get that? Alan shakes his head. He doesn't feel like it right now. So bang goes my chance of having my boots and other clothes brought over at the same time! There are no worries yet about gas in the neighbouring tent, because of the provisions left by the Koreans. And all of us think: the storm cannot last forever. There is not much food left anywhere, but what really counts up here, is being able to drink.

I wonder how Julie is faring? I wish I had my boots …

An attempt to get them picked up by Mrowka also fails; by the time she is outside, taking a turn at freeing the tent, she forgets all about it. Anyway, it's blowing a gale.

Night. All quiet. Quiet? Is the weather getting better? I hear voices outside. Willi. Are we going down? But after a while, the voices stop – so I guess we won't. If the weather is really improving, we'll wait for daylight I'm sure. Alan crawls in from outside. 'Looks a bit better. We can go down tomorrow.' That's it, then. Off in the morning!

This was the night, Willi told me later, when Julie said, 'It's quiet outside, we could go down.' But later still, in the Innsbruck hospital, his memory of the event changed … Julie's words, he then said, were, 'It's quiet outside, *you* could go down.' She had not included herself apparently.

At any rate, I remember that I wasn't unhappy about delaying our start until morning; I still had no way of contacting Julie. (I was told once that she was sleeping – nothing else.) And all my necessary gear, including boots, was still in the abandoned tent.

I am lying in a rigid, cramped position in the furthermost corner of the tent. My neck hurts. This narrow squeeze is a torture. In my sleeping bag, I'm warm enough and it really doesn't matter that I have no clothes on. But the pressure of snow against the side of my head is really bad. Aching, I seek to ease my position. This immediately involves the other two – whether they like it or not. We are an exhausted tangle of limbs. Moaning … laboured breathing … then, again, silence. Why are the nights so dreadful? Why is the crampedness a hundred times worse at night than during the day?

From outside comes the low shuffle of the wind and now and then a hard pattering as crystals of snow strike the vault of the tent. It is daytime again. I guess it must already be quite late in the morning of

7 August. All grey outside, but a little brighter. So far, nobody has mentioned anything about going down. I feel worry and disappointment; obviously the weather has worsened again. No visibility! At least the storm is no longer roaring.

Do people think it's likely to clear up soon?

I'm still a prisoner in my sleeping bag, and leadenly tired after the nightly ordeal in a confined space. The intermittent crackling of the snow crystals, the whistle of the wind lull me back into my doze …

Wasn't that Julie's voice? 'Hey, Kurt, Julie's calling you!' Alan shakes my arm. 'I think she's coming over.' I rise abruptly, unable to believe it. I am beside myself with joy. She's coming over – and if she can do that, she *must* be able to see!

'Julie!' I yell at the top of my voice.

'Oh, Kurt!' I hear the faint reply from the direction of the Korean tent. Then comes the sound of approaching steps. A moment later she bumps against the tent on the downhill side, beside Mrowka. 'No, Julie! The entrance is here, to the left!' And I tell her, 'It's great, you are coming …' In a rush I realize how worried I have been for her, how much I missed her! I am so happy she is here, and feeling better. 'I just wanted to say hello,' she says and stoops over the high snowdrift which has accumulated at the entrance. 'How are you?'

I cannot see her; there is only a small opening left now – even the flysheet extension is half-filled with powder snow. I am stuck in the rear of the tent, with my feet to the entrance, legs half-wedged under Alan's body.

'Don't worry, I'm fine!' I lean forward as far as I can. 'But I want to see you. Can you bend down?'

The edge of her hair appears …

'I still cannot see you – I want to see your face!' I insist. Can't she crouch lower? 'Look, you must see my hands!' I stretch my arms towards the entrance, towards her …

'Here I am … yes, I'm OK. But how are you? Are you all right with the Austrians?'

The fringe of hair lowers; it is like a tissue, a web, grey and brown in the fog, familiar but still so far away …

It reminds me of something, a crystal pattern, something I have seen in the past, a long time ago … yes, I remember … it was on the Chinese side of K2, on the northern glacier … we were happy then … K2 above us, dream mountain for us then … On a flat spot in the loam at the edge of the glacier, a garden of ice crystals had grown

overnight – long, thin, needles, a web of them, twinkling, shimmering – and all vanishing as the day warmed up … They left a magic
imprint on the ground: the crystals themselves disappeared every
morning, yet still they were there! The image was so bewitching
that we were suddenly caught by its beauty and clutched each
other's hands as if under a spell: there it was … gone, but still
existing. And the next night would bring it back to the beginning.

… the endless knot …

'Kurt, I am feeling rather strange … ' Julie's voice floats in as if
from a far distance, through the web of hair and ice crystals: it is as
if she is speaking close by, but from somewhere else as well. What
does she mean, feeling strange?

She came over on her own … under her own steam …

She must drink … drink, drink, drink … And tomorrow we will
all go down. It's not going to work today … not any more … As soon
as I have my boots, I'll go across and see her. I tell her that, and
urge, 'Be strong, Julie! I'm thinking of you!'

Can I lift her spirits? I lean forward – as far as possible – but still I
cannot get close enough to see her face. And now Julie's hair
disappears, too. 'Bye, bye!' she says, and as she takes the first steps
back, adds, 'I don't have your boots …'

A strange answer. But while I listen to her steps receding, I think:
at least she can see again! She must be seeing all right to find her
way over here alone. She retreats back into the Austrian tent. I'll go
and visit her later; but first, I have to get those boots!

More than anything, I want to free myself from the back of this
tent, pressed hard into the mountainside – why don't I turn round,
get my head to the entrance – especially now I know that Julie might
come over again?

It turns into rather a major undertaking: after about an hour of
multiple disentangling and squirming, finally, I find myself lying
with my head in the corner of the fly-sheet extension directly
opposite Alan. His face is right in front of mine: sharp featured – the
straight nose, the open clear-eyed look – sometimes a bit absent and
dreamy, but always positive. Mrowka has decided to remain in her
original position, on the downhill side, her head to the rear of the
tent – like a marmot in its hole.

I offer to free the tent if anyone can fetch my things from 'over
there'. Alan agrees, but then falls asleep. Alarm rises in me at the
impotence of my position: I have no way out – quite literally.

'Alan,' I say, 'let me borrow your overtrousers and boots – just to visit Julie?' Then I can dig everything I need out of our tent, too. He mumbles his agreement, but then says, not to worry, he'll get my stuff later ... today or tomorrow ... before we go down, anyway.

Something is wrong with Alan. He's no longer the same pillar of strength ...

It is afternoon. The wind is blowing intermittently. They should be able to hear me now, over there. I sit up and yell at the top of my voice, making it clear that I want to come over for a few minutes. The reply is disappointing: no space! Absolutely no space! Besides – Julie is sleeping ... I am depressed. Slowly it gets dark. I will go over tomorrow ...

The morning of 8 August. Another night over, slightly less cramped this way round. Alan is awake. I will ask him once more for my stuff. I can hear the wind – on and off, pauses between – it is not too strong.

Is that Willi's voice?

Yes, he's shouting something. I call back: should I go over?

'Kurt!' Willi calls. 'Julie died last night ...'

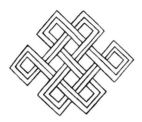

'If I could choose a place to die, it would be in the mountains. When we were falling in the avalanche on Broad Peak, I knew that I would not mind dying that way. There have been a number of other occasions in the mountains, when just to sit still and drift into an eternal sleep would have been an easy and pleasant thing to do, but hopefully the circle of nature will not close for me too soon. I have a lot to live for ...'

(Julie's thoughts after the death of our Basque companion, Juanjo, from a discussion in 1985 at the foot of Everest, and later included in her book *Clouds from Both Sides*.)

... It was like a hammer blow, and so totally unexpected. Alan, at my side, tried to comfort me. I heard his words without grasping their meaning – but in the end I was forced to believe it.

Everything was different from that moment, totally changed – the days, the light, the darkness, everything. The rope binding the two of us had been severed – by the storm, by something ...

Only gradually did I come to realize that the bond still existed.

8 August: Camp 4, last days of the storm:

... flashes of light, thoughts ... adrift between this world and beyond, the present interrupted by dreams of the past ... Reality is all these – the now, the then, together; up here, down there ...

Julie once said that perhaps the best way to die would be to fall asleep, high in the mountains. Is that, then, how it was? Did she know when the time arrived? How could she have died so suddenly? We should never have split up ... that was the real end. Was it destined to be? I don't think so. But now it has happened, it is irrevocable. For ever.

It's a strange thing: since she died, something has taken hold of me, a force that isolates me from everything else, yet at the same time binds me to the earth. Whatever it is – it has unbelievable strength: the now and the then, united; the up and the below.

But as soon as I find myself no longer able to make the distinction between Then and Now, Up and Below, I won't be able to go down. For the moment, still, I can.

What if the blizzard persists many more days? Here, at 8,000 metres?

Notes from my diary:

When the gas in Rouse's tent had finished and my boots were still lying in the *parapluie*, I managed to talk Mrowka into fetching the lilac rucksack and the stove, too, from over there. Unfortunately, she again forgot the boots. But we had gas once more, three teabags, a few sweets, two and a half slices of crispbread (which we divided scrupulously, like treasure), having had nothing to eat for days. The three teabags offered only a little taste as we could no longer afford to boil water – but in our state of near apathy, they stimulated some interest, were an unexpected luxury. Unfortunately, we 'lost' two of them pretty soon – once it was Alan, and once Mrowka, who forgot to remove the teabag from the pot while urinating! (How we managed to do all these things in the restricted space is a mystery to me, but we had no choice. Outside the storm still raged. Now that I have time to reflect, I realize Mrowka must have been twice to the other tent – this must be so, because at the very last I got my boots. The exact time sequence of all the days we spent in that tomb has not stayed clear in my mind.)

Since Julie's visit on the second day, I have lain with my head to the entrance. This way I could easily reach the snow, and taking turns with Alan, operate the stove – for as long as the gas lasted. He and Mrowka freed the tent several times from the drifted snow, and Willi helped twice, too. But in the end, there was so little air in the tent that the flame floated like a ghostly halo above the burner and almost immediately vanished into the gloomy darkness before we managed to set the small pot of snow onto the stove. Only after many tries, and having forced an air-hole through the snow by the entrance (which was an awful exertion), did we succeed in melting water again.

Worst of all were the nights: the hipbones of your neighbour pressing into your muscles, until pain forced you to find a different position; but then, because of the crush, very little change was possible. As everyone had the same problem, the result was an interminable carousel, which only slowed to a halt in the morning (God knows why). Once, during our tangled nocturnal contortions, I realized gas was leaking from somewhere. Terrified, I hunted for the stove, and eventually found it underneath me and turned it off. I do not know how much we lost on that occasion, but I do know the gas had run out by the last day – or was it the day before? In the end, nobody had strength enough, nor will, to clear the entrance – the snow slowly poured in as if filling a hourglass. It would do so, steadily, I supposed, until our time ran out. Meanwhile, we simply grabbed handfuls of the stuff, and ate it.

9 August, twelfth day on K2:
…As I wake up, I notice that I have been asleep with my hand in the snow. All feeling has gone from several fingertips – they're frost-bitten. I register the fact …

Kurt, I tell myself, you know you shouldn't fall asleep with your hands in the snow. Still, it's happened now … No other frostbite apart from that. Nothing like that has ever happened to you before. Is that how it's going to be from now on?

Sooner or later, I won't have any strength left.

There's nothing to do, but wait.

The wind decides.

… The end of my middle finger has swollen into a huge, blueish blister … I guess that's had it. Not nice, to die off piecemeal, like this. Is that really how it will be? Outside, the storm is still roaring – there's not a hope of making a break for it.

I remember once asking somebody if an eight-thousander was worth a bit of frostbite. Oh, yes, he replied, this one was! That was at the foot of K2, and Julie was at my side. It was a beautiful day, the sun shining and the light flashing between the ice towers …

When I breathe I feel some sort of resistance, a blockage some-where below the right shoulder-blade. Is it the lung? Slight dis-comfort, a resistance – I don't know how else to describe it. Is that a sign that the end is coming?

How much longer?

How much longer will this storm last? Alan is going downhill. Last night was bad, he was thrashing about, agitated, like a chained animal. He would lunge suddenly, delirious, quarrelling with destiny. I tried in vain to calm him. Good, kind Alan, Alan who took my arm and sought to comfort me when Julie died, is fading away. His face is drawn with the fatigue of these last days; really, he is not here any more. He begs continuously for water, which we no longer have. I put a piece of slush to his lips, which he sucks at greedily. Alan – the question beats dully in my brain – Alan, how long can you hold out? Up here, if you lose the power of walking, you are doomed – even if the storm should end.

Mrowka, still huddled in the corner, is immobile; she seems to have drifted into a sort of hibernation.

Again I notice that slight resistance when I breathe – apart from that, and providing it isn't an indication of something really bad, I feel I could hold out for another day … but not much longer. I chew slush – only liquid and an end to the storm can save us now …

I am surprised that I am so calm about it. But it would not help to get agitated. It is all so simple: everything depends on how long the storm lasts. Meanwhile, I have to eat more snow, let it melt slowly in my mouth … I know I must have water, even if my stomach feels absolutely horrible. I push another piece of slush between Alan's lips. He slurps, sucks … his eyes are red, a network of little veins … they weren't like that yesterday. He looks up into the vault of the tent … 'Jesus Christ!' he murmurs. And again, 'Jesus Christ!'

Outside, the storm continues. Snow crystals rattle intermittently against the tent. In the background, you can hear the dull, sinister, steady roar of the air masses as they part around the bulk of K2: an eternal, distant sound. I close my eyes …

Fields in sunshine … green barley swaying on the terraces … virgin forest all around with the fabulous silhouettes of giant trees … the village with its smooth roofs of bamboo matting … Tashigang – a Tibetan song – the song of the sun … 'la tela khor rhe – e nyima che shar' … and so it turns and turns – the great sun is rising … thus Drugpa Aba, head of the family, 'father of Drugpa', welcomes every new day, and the light of the sun, this wonderful light, penetrates everything, penetrates the ears of barley and the shining leaves … it is a shining green, a wonderful light … It is the Light.

… Night. The constricting torture of our prison. Bow to fate – but hang on. Exhaustion – but keep hanging on! Dreams: sunshine, meadows, dear ones at home, life … what is reality?

10 August, thirteenth day on K2:
Pallid dawn: inside the tent the bent shapes of bodies in sleeping bags; exhaustion. Another night over. Outside, the air still roars, but at least it's no longer dark – be thankful for that. Even this cramped hell can be accepted more easily once you can see around you. It seems a little brighter than usual. Is life giving us one more chance? Is there still hope? The snow crystals continue to rattle relentlessly against the little patch of fabric above our heads – the only bit that has not been covered by the snow which has engulfed us. Up there, removed from us in some way, is the storm; inside our

tomb, we're no longer part of it. But is it brighter? Has it stopped snowing? Is there a break in the deadly clouds which have held us prisoner for so long, like blind men in a labyrinth; which have granted us only the sanctuary of this icy vault, this place of lingering death? Hardly one of us can last another day …

If you no longer have strength left for the descent, all that remains are the last dreams …

Sun – that is sunlight, isn't it, on the tent fabric? Dear God! I dig through the powder inside the doorway, stretch my arms, reaching up to the surface – there, there, through a tiny hole in the snow, blue sky looks in! There is the blue of the sky – scarred by the racing crystals of snow whipped by the storm across it – the blue of the sky bringing us one last hope of getting out of here alive!

… It *is* real.

FLIGHT FROM THE DEATH ZONE

There's movement, voices calling from tent to tent. The sun has awakened the camp from its deadly torpor. But Alan is delirious, mumbling for water – and there is none. And who knows what the position is in the other tent? All I can hear is Willi's voice. Go down: yes, it is our only, our last chance. It is impossible to tell how long we shall be able to see the way down, how long the clearing will last. And although we have sun at last, the storm is still blowing; it may take hours before we manage to get away: we are in a complete daze after our long incarceration at 8,000 metres. The flame of life flickers only in the innermost core of our souls.

Decision time: the situation is extreme. Whoever stays here any longer will die.

Mrowka prepares for the descent; in the oppressively cramped quarters, only one of us can move at a time. To give her as much room as possible, I press tightly against Alan, immobile in his corner. As she struggles into her boots, I notice that one of Mrowka's big toes is completely frostbitten – it's dark blue. But that shouldn't stop her making it down – and apart from this, little 'Ant' has weathered these last terrible days well. That is probably in part thanks to the warm water with which Alan kept plying her, so long as we still had gas. He and I mostly made do with cold water and slush. But Alan, who sacrificed all his energies in keeping others going during the days of the summit assault, has finally reached the limit of his incredible endurance. The terrible certainty already hangs in the air: in his condition, he will not make it down alive. Even if he will never know that …

The prospect of having to leave him up here is a ghastly one. While Mrowka, with painfully slow movements, puts on her gear, I gesture towards Alan: what shall we do about him? He is moaning in his sleep. I know, it's a pointless question. Mrowka turns her eyes away. 'Life is down there,' she says in a low whisper. A little while ago we tried unsuccessfully to sit him up. He sank back and wanted water. It is his only wish. Yes, life is down there. And water is down there, too. But it is impossible for us to carry Alan. There is no way we could do it – it would be too much.

The storm still rattles away at the tent. It must be icy cold outside. I need my boots! Mrowka knows it, but I remind her once more as she crawls out, 'Mrowka, don't forget my boots: they are over there in the tent, with the blue rucksack.' She mustn't forget! Do you need the rucksack?' she asks. 'No, I've got Julie's' …' 'So I can have it, for my sleeping bag?' 'Yes, of course …'

I am lying with my face on my boots. I must have fallen asleep. I remember Mrowka giving them to me. Now she is off, somewhere outside. I have to get dressed! The storm is howling … but there's still sunshine. How long will it last? It must be nearly noon.

Up! Get dressed! I raise my head, look around. Where are my trousers? Oh yes, I remember, here, the light down pants, they're folded up on my chest, tucked into my down jacket to keep dry. I'm still completely naked in my sleeping bag except for the jacket, just as I have been all these days since I took shelter in Alan's tent and had to get rid of all my snow-sodden clothes. Crazy, that … but it was the only way to avoid soaking my sleeping bag, too. I still have Julie's lilac rucksack from our summit bid, the yellow windsuit, a single glove, one mitten, and one orange overgaiter … everything else has disappeared in the chaos of snow in the half-collapsed tent. Three pairs of gloves? Yes, once upon a time – but now I have to fix myself up with whatever's left. It's enough. Alan groans next to me, 'Water!' It tears my heart. God, if only I could give him what he wants. Fulfil this one wish. Maybe I can find a drop somewhere – perhaps over in the other tent? Alan sinks back into his shadow world …

Slowly, stopping repeatedly to draw breath – one, two moves, pause – I get dressed. This inner boot is wet, I notice; it was under my head on the ground – breathe! – no, there doesn't seem to be any frostbite on this foot – not yet, at any rate – pause again for breath. That was lucky. Neither one of them frostbitten – breathe! – the second inner boot is dry. Put on the harness. What a good job I put all the stuff into the rucksack after coming back from the summit.

Breathe! Well, not everything – sadly – I've only got the one glove and one mitten – but at least my feet are OK…

So, the harness is on. That gives me security for abseiling down the fixed ropes on the Abruzzi. Pause for breath … I will take Julie's and my rope down, too. It may be no use to anyone, but who knows …

Thank you, Mrowka, for getting this rucksack for me. I would not have dared to go over for it barefoot. Why on earth didn't I take the trouble to put my boots on before freeing the entrance of our tent? Because I had done it so often in socks before, I suppose. If only the entrance of that bloody tent hadn't been so narrow and the poles so flimsy – we would never have needed to split up …

But what can I change? Nothing, any more.

Mrowka has come back; she is outside the tent, wanting her sleeping bag. I have already stuffed my own damp, icy bag into Julie's rucksack. Better than nothing, for a bivouac. I hand Mrowka hers out. Alan murmurs in his sleep. I still don't know what to do … yet at the same time, I know I have no choice. Except to stay up here and to die. Wouldn't it have been better to have remained with Julie in our tent forever? We should never have separated … So, she died alone, and nobody told me … Bitterness overwhelms me: could it have changed anything if I had been with her? Maybe – yes. Certainly, for her. Now here I am, but at the same time, distant from all this, faraway, forcing myself with great difficulty to make one action follow the next, everything in slow motion, requiring all my concentration … I take the utmost care not to forget anything – because at heights like this you pay so dearly for every single mistake.

Perhaps I can still find a few drops of water for Alan. I squeeze outside, to be immediately struck by the icy blast of the wind: enormously strong gusts, chasing scudding clouds, lower than we are, lower even than the Shoulder of K2, down at a height maybe of 7,700 metres. Visibility is clear enough above them, but this terrible storm! Still, today is the only chance we have left of getting down. Without the visibility, it would be as good as hopeless to find that one passage left by the ice avalanche, between the seracs below the Shoulder.

It feels like having to learn to walk again as I take a few tottering steps into the storm …

Willi and Mrowka are outside, busy sorting out the ice-axes and ski-sticks. I take my ice-axe, and notice the slow, awkward movements of the other two: they are like robots. A moment later my axe seems suddenly to have vanished; full of panic, I search for it, and find it sticking in the snow. Fragments of words toss in the air, mixing with the icy gusts … I still feel dazed, in a dream … Then a clear thought: we have to reach Camp 3! We? Alan is finished, and who among us has strength enough to pull him? Willpower alone won't do it. I don't see anything of Hannes and Alfred; they must be in their tent. If they were still all right, they would be out here by now. I seem to recall Willi trying to get them going before, bellowing at the top of his voice … Now he is somewhere down below the edge, down the steep slope – does he think they will follow him, or is he just taking a look? The slope has a wind-scoured, rather hard surface, and is covered with drifted snow formations, imprinted by the force of the storm. It seems to be mostly slabs, all the way down and out as far as the lower end of the Shoulder. There is no deep snow, but in order to find the passage we will have to drop down where it levels off on to the steep side in the wind shadow. Will we be able to make trail there? That could be what Willi is checking out …

Really, it *is* just like learning to walk again. Stumbling, I lurch through the storm to the other tent. Yes, it must be that Willi is reconnoitring the critical section of the descent, where it goes down to the large crevasse on the left-hand side – or has he simply made a start in the hope that the others will follow his example? I don't know. Nobody *has* followed him, that much is sure.

Coming into the storm-shaken Korean tent, I find Hannes sitting by the entrance. He recognizes me, makes his inimitable wink, as if to say *'Servus!* We'll make it OK!' But I see his snow-white hand, which he is massaging in an endeavour to get the circulation going: the skin is absolutely white and bloodless, soft and wrinkled as if it has been soaking in water for days. Behind him, Alfred is slurping chunks of snow from a big pot. His face is dreadfully ravaged, his eyes bloodshot. Sometimes he stares, sometimes appears to be somewhere else – his condition reminds me of Alan's. I think he's confused, too. It does not look as if either Alfred or Hannes want to leave the protection of the tent. Mrowka and I now squash in with them, too, to get out of the wind. We've got no more water for Alan, I announce sadly, looking at the remains of the snow in the pot. In my tent, next to this, in which Julie is now lying, there's no water, of course. In any case, I feel shy about rummaging around in there. Now I see Willi puffing up the slope, obviously annoyed that nobody has followed him. I have moved outside in the meantime.

'*Aussa! Aussa!*' Willi yells at his companions. Out! Out! He pulls them from the tent. It is the only sure way to get them going. Dazed and staggering, Hannes and Alfred start the descent with him and Mrowka. I stay back here – with Alan and Julie.

What can I do? Benumbed, I go on looking for something for Alan, but there is nothing …

For a while I sit silently in the Korean tent, reflecting …

I remember Julie's small pocket-recorder: could she – could there be anything on it? I don't know a thing about her last hours. Almost nothing about her last two days. But there is nothing in the pockets of her down jacket which is lying in a corner. Anyway, it's unlikely she would have used it – the small camera must have been lost in the storm, too. I give up, dejected. I will never know. Timidly, I approach our tent. Willi tore open the roof with his ice-axe, when he put Julie in there – I know that from Mrowka.

I cannot see her face. The tent is half caved-in, but has not collapsed. I move the sleeping bag sealing the opening, and put the down jacket over her feet … see her mountain clothes, red and black. Julie … For the last time, I touch her – then I leave her alone. Somewhere inside the tent must be our two little bears, the mascots which coincidence brought together from a bus in Varese and a small village in southern England. They will stay with her. And I can still see Julie's proud smile in Base Camp after she had embroidered a new eye for one of the bears. The sleeping bag sealing the hole in the tent is completely dry – and remembering the dampness in Alan's tent, I wonder whether to give it to him. Yes – stuffing the down jacket in its place, I carry the bag over to Alan's tent. Every step I take is more reluctant … I have no water for him – nothing. The down sleeping bag is only a token because really I have nothing. I am just a helpless wanderer up here between my dead friend and another who will die. And I know that I have to go down.

Meanwhile, down on the flat part of the Shoulder, something terrible has happened. I registered it some moments ago, from this distance: Alfred and Hannes, after little more than a hundred metres, came to the end of their strength. Willi and Mrowka tried desperately to support them, helping up and holding first one, then the other – but they kept falling into the snow. It was simply hopeless, and they eventually had to give up the task.

Now I see Willi and Mrowka, close together, two stooping

silhouettes in the transparent grey of the fog on the lee-side of the
Shoulder, barely moving. They seem to be up to their waists in deep
snow. I hold the sleeping bag for Alan in my hands … He will want
water from me. And I have none …

'Dear Father, what shall I do?' If ever you are still near me, it will
be now! I know you are near me. At times, when I have found myself
in terrible situations and not known what to do, I have asked you.

Oh, Alan. Down into your tent, it's a dark hole: Do I see or just
imagine the bewildered eyes, hear the rambling voice above the
noise of the storm? Do I see the fingers reaching, moving, grasping
after something in the air …? 'Alan!' I yell into the dark hollow, 'I
have brought you a dry sleeping bag …'

No answer. Did he understand me? I push the sleeping bag down
towards him. Frightened, I notice that above me whirling clouds
spin across the summit face, multiplying, thickening, reaching
down towards me; those scudding clouds lower down, they are
creeping higher now – how much longer until they close together?
Till the inferno of clouds smothers the whole mountain again?

'Bua, du muasst abi.' Yes Father, I know I have to go down. Alan, I
have to go now. But I cannot take away your hope for water – if you
still understand me at all, that is. 'Alan, I will go and try to find
some water …'

In the grey of the depths I can hardly distinguish the shapes of Willi
and Mrowka. A thick felt of snowdust fills the air on the leeward
side of the shoulder, grey cotton wool swallowing everything –
them and the way down.

Go, Kurt, go! Clouds of snowdust … flashing sunlight … tablets of
snow bursting under my feet. I am grasping my way down the
slope.

Go more slowly! Don't trip!

Life is down there, that's what Mrowka said. Up here, now, is
only death.

And it's still a big question whether we can escape it. Perhaps.

I reach Hannes. He is sitting in the snow, with his back to me. A
few metres further on Alfred is lying face down on the furrowed
surface, completely still. He must be dead. Hannes moves his arms
weakly, rowing the air in slow motion, while ice crystals bombard
us unmercifully, and I can hardly keep my footing for the fierce
bursts of wind. Then I see his face. His eyes, blank, stare into space.
He does not see me. I shout his name, but he does not even move his

head. Only his arms keep rowing through the air. He cannot hear me. Perhaps he is in another world – is already dead. It is as if he were listening to something far away … He is no longer here, yet still I think, how much better it would be if he were back in his tent now – a better place to die than here, even if he does no longer feel the cold. 'Hannes!' I shout, 'if you can manage, somehow, go up to the tent!' But he does not move, does not even turn his head. Snowdust whips at the two figures on the wind-ploughed slope. Absurd sunshine – horror, impotence, resignation. Yet still, from somewhere, the will to live. The sun still shines. I cannot help here any more – I go on, passing along the snow edge … Somewhere here I have to go down to the left. Last steps in the light of the sun – already the grey is taking over. Here are the tracks of Willi and Mrowka – a small drop and snowslabs below. I climb down, spy their shapes ahead of me in the gloom, further down, half-immersed in a sea of powder snow and fog. They're clearly making progress, but only very slowly. There's the track again – almost a channel. Down there, Willi is ploughing through the snow like a tank. And Mrowka clings to him like a shadow. What a descent! If we survive this – then it will have been with the help of all the angels. Quickly I reach the others. Willi is the first to notice – he is clearly surprised to see me and asks suddenly, 'Do you have anything to eat? Have you brought a stove?' How could I have done? Nobody has either any more! I am astonished at the question and reply, 'No, of course not.' Willi says nothing and continues quietly breaking the trail, followed by Mrowka, slowly, step by step. It is fluffy, light snow, but it is a fathomless ocean. It would be impossible to climb upwards through it; even if the guys in Base Camp thought we might still be alive, they couldn't help us here. We're in the 'soup', and must rely on our own memory. The vague recollection of the ascent line must be reversed: the gentle incline, the seracs, the big crevasse with the bridge – those we have to find if we are to locate the only way through to the steep slope that follows, a slope that will be frightening now under many tons of fresh snow.

Vague outlines, grey on grey, increasing steepness – a descent under such conditions is madness, but the alternative is to die. We all know that. All safety rules are only fairy tales – we either break our necks or we don't … Cautiously, Willi pushes forward, infinitely slowly. Below us, faint and barely recognizable, the giant crevasse appears. It looks unreal in the empty greyness, as if we were floating above it. But down there, that must be the bridge we came over on the way up. Will the slope hold our weight? Or will we thunder down the mountain in a cloud of powder? Will anybody down there ever know what happened to us? I hold my breath, call to Willi: but we are agreed: there is no other possibility. This has to be the way to go.

While seconds stretch to eternity, Willi pushes slowly downhill, through the powder, step after step, pause after pause. He seems to have become part of the snowscape, and as if we had earned a miracle after all these terrible days the slope holds. We arrive at the bridge and get across the giant crevasse. For a few steps on the other side, we go slightly uphill, then the steepest slope of all follows, leading down into the void.

But now we have faith: the snow is deep, and it's indescribably tiresome to wallow through, but it holds. It doesn't slide off. We can make it. We have only to concentrate like the very devil not to fall into the bergschrund which yawns below.

It's done – we're over! Even though visibility is nil now, and we're floundering in snow up to the waist, we know from memory that we have to keep to the right … Mrowka relieves Willi for a short while in breaking trail, then I 'plough the ditch' for some time, until the outline of the serac wall, from which the avalanche detached itself, appears hazily to the right. Below it, the powder snow seems bottomless, it's an inhuman struggle and the output of energy results in a furious hunger. 'Hasn't anybody got a bite to eat?' I ask, but with little hope. 'Yes, there is a sweet,' says Mrowka, 'but I'm saving that for us tonight.' In vain I try to convince her that we could do with this last boost of 'fuel' now – splitting it between the three of us – because down in Camp 3 we should be able to find something anyway. But Mrowka is adamant.

The first bamboo sticks! Well, the last that Alan and I planted on the way up. We are therefore at about 7,700 metres. So, not even 350 metres still to go to Camp 3! The ploughing through the snow is over, the slope has now been cleared by the force of the storm or partly covered in the usual hard-packed snowdrift formations. I remember several dangerous patches from the way up: some sheer ice and blocks of insecure snow. There is still no visibility at all, and even though the temptation is great to descend facing downwards, I turn into the slope and climb down on all fours. Doing it this way, with ice-axe and crampons, is obviously safer, but inevitably slow.

Soon I am alone.

Another bamboo stick! Kurt, don't let the others hurry you …

don't change this technique – it is the only safe way to do down in our state. And as we are not belaying one another, you only need to make one false step and it's down into the abyss! That's why I told Willi and Mrowka some while ago not to wait for me, when they preferred to move faster, facing downhill.

We must have been on the go for about four or five hours now. I wonder what state Camp 3 is in?

A metre down, another metre, and one more – snow formations, furrows in the cloudy fog. A voice! Somebody is calling! Sounds as if they are waiting for me after all. A moment later I discover Willi and Mrowka near the blue ice cliff, below which Julie and I put our tunnel tent in a small gap during our first summit bid.

'Keep on going, descend to 3,' I call down. 'It's not that far now.' I'm taking it slowly. Just a few more bamboo sticks.

Camp 3! 7,350 metres. It's devastated. We cannot stay here. It must have been the force of the blizzard that wrecked this recently rebuilt camp. All I find is a squashed Korean tent under the snow, barely visible, and rip into it with my ice-axe! Anything to eat? I have to find something to eat – also our figures-of-eight, which Julie and I left here in the small bag. We'll need those to abseil down the fixed ropes. But nothing! I cannot find them! Disappointed, I rummage through the meagre contents of the tent. Willi and Mrowka do the same at the Austrian tent – a little further down and also destroyed by the ice avalanche. As Willi told me later, Mrowka found a gas cylinder for her stove (which she had brought down from Camp 4). The figures-of-eight don't seem to be anywhere! That is a severe blow – they save so much energy, give so much more security. What's this - orange sweets? No, effervescent pills! Something at least, the stuff fizzes in my mouth, mixed with slush … well, it's something. I put the rest in my pocket, will give some to Willi and Mrowka. And what about these red mittens? They're great, these Korean mittens. My own single mitten (for my left hand) is wet – I could exchange it for one of these. But I'll hang on to the leather glove on my right hand for coping with the karabiners on the fixed ropes, for changing over at the stances. I only need one, therefore – I'll leave the other here. (Today, I curse such blind-eyed logic – an example of the linear, step-by-step thinking which has taken over our brains since the high-altitude storm – that second mitten could have spared me nearly all the amputations on my right hand. Certainly I would have been slower on the fixed ropes, but it would

THE ENDLESS KNOT

have been enough to put it on from time to time instead of the leather glove. However, I was no longer capable of thinking that far ahead.*)

I give some of the fizzy stuff to Willi and Mrowka, still bemoaning the lost figures-of-eight. Willi hands me a grey screw-karabiner, which I accept, even though I have a blue one of my own already – it's always worth having a spare. So, sadly, not one of us has a figure-of-eight. Bad luck? Yes – to have one would have meant more than just making things easier …

1. K2 – Meteo: a silky grey veil has surrounded the summit (4 August 1979, from the top of Gasherbrum II). (2 & 3) This was the weather situation around K2 late in the morning and at noon on 4 August 1986, as the Yugoslavs saw it from 8,000 metres on Broad Peak.

4. The descent from the Abruzzi Ridge in a heavy storm along the fixed ropes below House's Chimney (view down a vertical wall with the fish-eye lens). (5) Kurt, tired and upset about another forced retreat.

* It was Kim Chang-Sun who left the two mittens in case one of us should need them on the descent. I am grateful to him. The tent which contained our figures-of-eight was probably destroyed and blown away by the storm.

5

WHERE IS MROWKA?

7,250 metres: the serac wall below Camp 3 is an imposing cliff of blue opalescent ice, interspersed with near-vertical white slabs, almost like marzipan in texture, made of compressed granular powder mixed with crystalline fragments. This is where the fixed ropes start for the descent from Camp 3. Almost all have been renewed by the Koreans over the last month; they promise a safe retreat down the Abruzzi Ridge, but only of course if you make no mistake, and provided you can locate the start of them when descending in a storm. Seen from above, the steep snowslope below Camp 3 ends abruptly at the edge of this drop; the wall itself, you only see from below.

Now, in our desperate flight from the Death Zone, having survived there so miraculously for so many days, all three of us – Willi, Mrowka and myself – were convinced that we had won. What could happen to us now? Descending the fixed ropes was as familiar to us as A B C. Naturally, the technique a mountaineer employs depends upon what he is used to, but everyone knows alternative methods of abseiling in the event of the loss of a vital piece of equipment. So, even without figure-of-eights, roping down was not a gamble – all of us knew the Abruzzi well, had often gone up and down it. No, by any normal judgement, we should be safe enough now! Even the weather did not look too alarming, and although we were all very tired, none of us was in a state of actual exhaustion. It was thirst and hunger that stressed us most. It is a complete mystery, therefore, why Mrowka did not make it to the foot of the mountain …

It is true that nobody had ever before survived as long at such a height as we had – we had been eight, in some cases nine, days at or above 8,000 metres, without artificial oxygen. None of us knew how seriously this had affected us, physically. Perhaps not only

6 & 7. Survived! K2 still wears the drifting veils of the storm. The Korean doctor Duke Whan Chung gives Kurt something to drink.

Mrowka but Willi and I as well were pushed so close to the limits of life when we were descending to Camp 2 that we were incapable even of registering the fact. Or did we feel something? In all of us, our blood had thickened like honey with the altitude, and probably we were each on the brink of an embolism. In that situation, the increase of oxygen as you get lower comes too late to have any effect – what you need is to drink, drink, drink … It is a race against time before a blood clot develops – was that the race that Mrowka lost?

Late afternoon, on 10 August, at the edge of the serac wall: here I dump the green and red rope we acquired from our Basque friends – that's half a kilo less – it won't be of any use to us now. For a moment Juanjo's tomb on Everest is in my thoughts, up on the ridge there, high above the neighbouring peaks – where Julie and I stood with Juanjo's companions, Mari and Josema (the two who gave us the rope). Julie is half-Basque herself … was, I mean. Again – something remains, something – of us, of her … Standing, waiting here, is horrible: the cold makes me shudder suddenly. Isn't Mrowka down the wall yet?

You have to be very careful not to descend too far here – or you could find yourself hanging over sheer ice, from where it would be almost impossible to get on to the traverse which comes after this. Moreover, there is one rope too many: when the Koreans were fixing it, it must have been blown out by a high wind to snag in a wide loop, about forty metres out among the overhanging seracs. I remember, on the way up, Julie and I wanted to pull it in as it was so obviously a danger, but we were unable to free it from the blue points of ice.

The blue and white fixed rope at my feet has not moved for a while. It is anchored just in front of me at the edge of the drop; it and several other ropes are all on one massive snow piton. Does that mean Mrowka is down? Can I go now? I can't stop shivering – from the fog, the cold, the dampness. (I had to leave half of my clothes frozen solid at Camp 4.) Down! I need to get moving!

Feeling a bit dizzy, I move to the edge, bend forward and take hold of the rope … Careful, Kurt! Get a grip – you can't afford any mistakes now, not while you're off the rope. The grey drop below me falls away for 2,000 metres, I know that …

Snap the karabiner into the sling at the piton, Kurt, the self-belay! Then take the other karabiner, put in a friction loop, and screw it shut tightly. God, that's awkward – my fingers are so numb in this icy leather glove ... As I start sliding down the rope, I peer into the murk below me: there's no sign of Mrowka. Probably I waited up there too long.

Hurry up, Kurt. Get a move on, while daylight lasts. Crampons scratch and bite into the ice as I abseil down ... Now I can see Mrowka: she's obliquely below me, pulling herself hand-over-hand along a transverse rope. Everywhere around is so bleak and gloomy – just fog, snow and ghostly shapes – I can't see Willi anywhere, whichever way I look. 'Willi gone!' I think, amazed. 'How come? He's the strongest of us. He must be running down to Camp 2! He can make some tea there – bet he's thirsty.' It's my own thirst making the assumptions! I hope to goodness nothing happens up here ... But what could happen – on fixed ropes we have swarmed up and down so many times? Right – that's the vertical wall of the seracs done. No, not completely. Kurt, don't forget the delicate section before the traverse. I lean into the blue ice, breathe and rest. Then I move the karabiner onto the next rope and pull myself towards the traverse – very hard work, this bit. Safely across, I draw several more deep breaths: it must be dreadful to make the mistake of going too low here when you are tired like this.

Mrowka seems to have disappeared again. She must be quite a way ahead. I hurry. It is easier now – you have only to loop the rope around your arm, snap in the karabiner, and off you go! There is the pink rope down the short vertical 'natural staircase' ... It was loose, I remember, flopping down into empty space, when Julie and I came up here the first time, probably due to ice or stonefall, or to the friction of the wind. Julie tied the rope to another line – and suddenly I have the feeling that she is near me, here, as if she wanted to see me safely across the traverse. There is one section without a rope, across snow ... take care on that, Kurt!

This is the smooth slab with the chimney – the fissure. Yes, thirty metres lower down there's an overhang to be coped with. The black and yellow rope is a good one – we used that before ... now there is a Korean rope running down beside it. There's a flat spot, just above here, where one night in 1984 we hacked away at the snow in a vain bid to clear enough space for our little bivouac tent – but it didn't work out, and in spite of the late hour, we had to go on down to 7,000 metres with Wanda.

My crampons scrape and scratch on the smooth rock on either side of the crack ... careful ...

Suddenly, I slip ...

Hold on, Kurt! Hold on!

Flung backwards against the edge of the crack, I come to a standstill. My right arm hurts, the one taking all my weight; my hand still has a tight grip on the rope … It was only a short fall, but one of my feet jammed inside the fissure, so that I was slammed around and into the edge. It takes some moments before I can move again. I hang there gasping, shocked at the unexpectedness of the incident. Then I pull myself up slowly. It was a good thing I had tightened the screw of the karabiner holding the friction loop – but I wish it had been a figure-of-eight. A figure-of-eight is unsurpassable – safety and speed together.

Julie and I left our spare one at the foot of House's Chimney in the duffel bag by the rock tower. Will that be gone, too, I wonder, like the others in Camp 3? Mrowka hasn't got a figure-of-eight either – she decided against bringing one because of the extra weight.

While I continue gliding carefully down past the black overhang, I discover Mrowka again, below me, and soon catch up with her. I watch and wait as she swops from one rope to the next, busy in some way with her sticht plate. Actually, it's quite easy here, not at all dangerous. 'Wouldn't you prefer to go down by karabiner now?' I cannot really understand why she is bothering with this slow technique, however well it works. 'No,' she says – and I don't press it beyond remarking that she'd get along much faster with a karabiner. This is obviously the way she wants to do it, and up here everyone has to make up his or her own mind about what is best. 'Do you mind if I go ahead?' I ask her. It is a comfortable spot with no problems about changing over. She has no objection. A little further down there is a narrow horizontal shoulder, one which we often used to rest on when we were coming up. There, she joins me as I clip the karabiners onto the next rope. 'Would you mind putting my ice-hammer into my rucksack for me?' she asks. Fiddle with buckles, now? With my hands in this state? It seems a bizarre wish on her part in our present situation, a complete waste of time: she won't need the hammer any more, it is just a useless weight. And we haven't got much daylight left …

'I'll let you have mine, if you want it, when we get down. Don't let's waste time! Just leave it!' I'm in a hurry to get going.

There's no feeling left in the fingers of my right hand at all; the leather glove got completely soaked coming down the fixed ropes. Why on earth didn't I take that second mitten when I had the

chance? But how could I have operated the karabiners with it? …
Logic, after a week in a storm at 8,000 metres, still exists, but it is
decidedly narrow.

I can still see Mrowka above me, abseiling down over the slabs
where there are several parallel ropes, some older ones with thick
knots, others reduced to fibres by the battering storms, and covered
in inches of frost. It's twilight now: dark clouds are approaching on
the horizon, and veils of grey mist drift here and there. It's almost
evening. This will be some descent in the dark!

A little later, I lean against the wall in the gloom, waiting for
Mrowka. Gusts strike the rocks and after a while I give up. It is
obvious that her technique is much slower, however safe, and I am
shaking with cold. I have to move! You can't lose the route here,
anyway the sequence of fixed ropes is uninterrupted.

Despite the stormy gusts, the snow holds off – luckily. At one
point, feeling the call of nature, I realize there is no way (with my
right hand stuck in this wet glove) of opening my over-trousers and
unzipping the blue down pants underneath – to say nothing of the
harness. So I pee down one side of the pants. It really doesn't
matter. The main thing is not to remove the glove – I'm terrified of
losing it. My fingers are already frostbitten, but perhaps something
can yet be saved …

It's getting dark now; that spells the end to any fast descent.

I'm too tired to hurry now anyway, I just have to be careful not to
make any mistake when changing over karabiners at the belay
stances. All my attention is focused on the rope, the rock I move
over, and the snow I plant my feet in. Even in the pitch-darkness, I
still know where I am – but I just have to take it slowly. I can't afford
a false step.

The most difficult section turns out to be the steel ladder; I have to
rest on nearly every rung …

But the whole time I have the sensation that there is an invisible
presence watching over me, a force around and within me, a
guardian being …

It has been with me for the last few days, up there in the tent. Is it
Julie?

Gradually, I slip into a state of numbness, no feeling any more, only
thoughts registering in slow motion … oh, I recognize this rope …
that pulpit … here is the beginning of the traverse … the knot in the
rope … now turn round … one step back onto the cliff – don't miss it

… the slab – that has a step, too … was there a storm? I think one did blow up for a while, earlier … now it has stopped … the air is rich and full of oxygen … it is a pleasure to breathe it …

It must be ten o'clock when I arrive at Camp 2 at 6,700 metres. At first there seems to be nobody there, all I can see is the dark silhouette of our Basque tent. Then, as I turn a rocky corner, there appears the shining green glow of a Korean tent, tucked against the wall on the highest seam of snow. A view of pure magic promising light, warmth, life – a giant green Korean lantern, shining into the pitch-dark night. Like a picture from a fairy tale.

I open the entrance, and what greets me is like a fairy tale come true: Willi is squatting there like a sorcerer swathed in wreathing vapours, stirring a big pot filled with an indefinable, brownish brew! Whatever it might be – and there are thick, swollen grains floating around in it – it has been ages since I have seen so much liquid! Without a word, he passes me the steaming pot, and I drink …

How it flows, so warmly, so wonderfully down my dry and tortured throat! Heavens, I'm thirsty! Willi's face is a flaming red; it is like a steam bath in here, the gas stove hisses …

'Where is Mrowka?' he asks suddenly.

'I think she'll be another hour,' I answer. Hard to say, now it's dark. It could be two …

When by midnight Mrowka has still not arrived, we start to worry. Is she bivouacking? I know she has her sleeping bag with her – in my blue rucksack. She also brought a stove down from Camp 4 and found a gas cylinder to fit it among the ruins of Camp 3 … Didn't she say something during the descent that she might stop over in Wanda's tent at 7,000 metres, just below the ladder? That's a bit off the route, but there is food there. If not …? We leave the light on, listen into the night, melt more snow … but Mrowka does not appear. Willi has frostbite on both hands – all his fingertips are affected. As for me, my right hand looks terrible – one finger has a big blister, one nail is missing and all the other fingers are damaged – only the thumb seems to be intact and that even hurts a little, which is a good sign. However, my left foot is completely without sensation and swollen. I massage it long and intensely, without result … the circulation must be quite blocked. It will have been the wet inner boot and the loss of one of my over-gaiters in the chaos of the assault camp that caused that. Depressed, I finally give up my futile attempts to bring it back to life, and turn my attention instead to my right foot. There I have more success; after a long, sustained massage, I recover all sensation. Of course, my right leg has always had the better circulation, ever since I broke the left one – twice (once while skiing and once on the marble steps of the post office). Willi's feet seem to have suffered no real damage – he wore plastic boots and his inners did not get wet.

We wait for Mrowka until almost noon, but she does not arrive. We're uneasy, full of foreboding. Today is 11 August: we have been on K2 for two weeks now, climbing up, down, being trapped in the tents … No one other than us has ever withstood so long a storm at 8,000 metres, a storm from which it was impossible to escape. Indeed, of the seven of us four died up there: can it be that the mountain has claimed another victim at the very last moment?

There only seem to be two possibilities: either Mrowka has reached the tent at 7,000 metres and is sleeping it off … or she has made some technical error on the fixed ropes and fallen. I keep thinking of that sticht plate and the small sling she was using: was it that? On the other hand, if she is sleeping in the tent, she could be up there two days.

Since neither of us has the strength to climb back and look, Willi decides to hurry on down to Base Camp as fast as he can and arrange for a rescue team. In the meantime I will continue down the Abruzzi at my own slow pace. In the end, Willi talks me into leaving my sleeping bag here as it is so icy and wet, offering me one of his from the camp below. After some hesitation I agree – even if I don't see much point in it. (I eventually carried his down, but never used it, and in the end had to borrow one from the Poles in Base Camp. No less than three versions of this story and the subsequent descent through the chimney were to appear later – all of them conflicting with each other.)

Willi sets off first. He wants to look through the Austrian tent at the foot of House's Chimney to see what is left there. He will wait there for me, he says. I struggle once more with my left foot, massaging it – but in vain. During the night I tried to dry the wet inner boot over the flame of the stove – it's well-scorched now. The large purple blister which had replaced the whole end of one finger has burst as a result of all these activities, but I feel no pain. Awkwardly – it's a strenuous job – I at last struggle into my boots and get going.

Some of the rungs of the metal caving ladder in House's Chimney have frozen into the ice at the back of the chimney, some are missing or damaged – I am forced into three pitches of demanding abseiling … When finally I reach Willi at the Austrian tent he hands me the sleeping bag and starts on his way again.

I am by myself on the spur.

Slowly climbing down the Jacob's Ladder of rocky steps, towers and snowfields, bringing me back to the increasingly more familiar lower levels, my thoughts keep returning to last night in Camp 2. I learned something then about Julie's death: she went to sleep and did not wake again.

And suddenly – I hear it still, above the sounds of the mountain, above the gusts of air blowing around our tent – suddenly Willi, in a faltering voice, emotion nearly robbing him of breath and with tears in his eyes, tells me, 'She just said … ' He stops, struggling for composure, and then – faster and faster, while I feel my heart contract at every word, it sounds so like an outcry – 'She just said, "Willi, get Kurt down safely" … ' He sobs.

So that is what she said … She knew then that the end was near … Emotion and waves of pain seize me: what else don't I know? Did she say anything else? '… That was all … the last. She didn't speak any more … just slept … ' mutters Willi.

I feel the darkness all around the tent, and the moving air. The night has suddenly found a voice … her voice.

So that is what she said.

I was only a few metres away, through the storm.

And still I did not know.

Why wasn't I allowed to be with her?

There is no answer.

Her last wish – that I should get down, for both of us.

Is that an answer?

It has to be. It is her answer to everything.

It is day. And I hear the voices of the night.

Julie …

PERPETUUM MOBILE

Whenever the pace was my own, things worked out fine. The result was never as good if someone else was urging me on. Mistakes, loss of control, burned reserves are all consequences of rushing.

The reason I am still alive today is because I have taken things at my own speed.

(from my diary)

I seem to be a perpetuum mobile *that has its own rhythm, a rhythm it can only find within itself, by day, at night, from sunrise to sunset, and again at night …*

I came from somewhere, and I'm going somewhere … even if the form changes. This place, and the path I travel, are part of Pelbe, *the endless knot.*

(from my diary)

11 August: afternoon. Still making my way down.

…The sun is shining. Fine weather. At last I have the figure-of-eight that I was so desperate for, retrieved it from our dumpsack at the rock tower below House's Chimney … along with the hammer ice-axe, which will be useful tonight. There's another 1,000 metres to go to get to the bottom of the mountain. At least abseiling is a piece of cake now I have the *descendeur* – I lean back as if in some fantastic aerial armchair, my descent gently controlled by the loop of rope running through and around the figure-of-eight, and all I have to do is let my feet walk down the rock. But I'll be needing all my reserves during the night ahead – I can't hope to be down to the final big slopes before then.

Night itself does not frighten me. I have often climbed at night – even the modern fast men who 'run' up eight-thousanders include the night in their planning. But I don't run – my speed depends on different principles: my natural rhythm, and also the particular circumstances on the mountain.

I can't get over the difference the *descendeur* makes! What a good thing that Julie and I left depots on the ridge like that. At the foot of the mountain, too, at Advanced Base Camp, there is everything I need for a retreat or stopover. I shall certainly rest there until midday tomorrow, before going on to Base Camp.*

Already I am feeling the revitalizing effect of being lower – there is so much more oxygen to breathe at 6,000 metres!

Willi could be in Base Camp by about now and getting a search party together to try and rescue Mrowka. But what about Mrowka? Sometimes, leaning back in my harness during an abseil, I peer up to see if I can detect any sign of her, but it would be a miracle if she were coming now. Did she, I wonder, reach Wanda's tent at the 7,000-metre camp? If so, most likely she'll be sleeping all today to make up for last night– she's safe enough there, there's food and she can cook with her stove and the cylinder she found. If she didn't make it … then something must have happened. And in that case, there's hardly any hope.

How ironic that the fine weather had to wait until now.

Camp 1. I look at it with bitter emotion: this is where Julie and I were sitting drinking tea with Hannes and Alfred before they went on to join Willi. Hanging inside the red dome tent should be the bag with our last film magazines, those showing Julie and me – with Hannes – holding the mugs of hot tea. Happy and optimistic we were then. Both of us knew that from there on the summit counted more for us than the film: we would definitely leave the camera behind. We had been given this one last chance; we should not let it go unused.

Everything is so different now. Tears well in my eyes as, with trembling hands, I undo the entrance to the silent tent …

---

* I did not know of course that there was nothing left at the foot of the Abruzzi Spur: a week after we were last seen ascending during our summit bid, everything had been cleared. We had been given up for dead.

My hand feels up under the dome. Yes, there it is! The bag with the movie camera and those last precious films is still hanging safe – the last testimony of our little team ... team that is no more.

They won't be left behind! While I stuff the bag into my rucksack, conviction rises in me like a vow: no, our spirit is not dead ... our ideas are still there ... so long as one of us remains alive, Julie, I will keep it going, the team, us ...

By the time I leave the camp, stepping down with the shadows of approaching evening to the last, steep section that still has to be descended, the ground seems to sink beneath my feet; around me, I see whirling ridges, veils of cloud, all caressed with the still, shining light of Tashigang's green fields ... through tears, I see the blurred outline of a mountain, dreamlike, beautiful. It was ours ...

Night ... Tired stars, half washed away. A steep slope against which I lean to catch breath ... the last 500 metres down. I no longer bother with the fixed ropes, which are hard to pick out and in places have disappeared under all the snow that has come down since we've been away. In any case, because of the melting of the ice sheets, they are often too far into the rocks where they are anchored to the side of the great bulk of the Abruzzi Spur, which sleeps like a dark dragon at my side. It would be too much of a torture to have to move on to the rocks to find them.

Alone, therefore, alone with the night, the heads of my two ice-axes clutched in my fists, I embrace the steep snowslope. Axes held high, in front of my face, the abyss below ... alone with my thoughts and with the passing time, I inch my way slowly, steadily, down the snow, swinging first one heavy leather boot behind me, and then the other, reaching down and kicking hard so that the power of the foot's own weight drives the front points of my crampons into the steep slope; and all the while keeping myself in balance with the axes. Feet secure, then move the hands, one at a time to lower holds, matching the rhythm of the feet, plunging the axes with all force into the invisible snow surface once more. Inch by inch, step by step, in the darkness I creep towards the Godwin-Austen glacier far below. It is still hours away. However desperate I am to reach the bottom, it is more than ever essential to be vigilant now. Here, alone, and with no protection on that open face, no error would be forgiven.

Tak, tak...tak, tak...tak, tak, the sound of my crampons penetrates the night, together with the rhythmic crunch of the snow under the picks of my axes. Every twenty steps or so I take a rest, leaning forward into the slope, forehead on forearms, lost to the darkness. I think of that water down there, the little stream between the stones, the water between the ice patches, its trickling murmur … I think of the few clumps of green – you could count them on the fingers of one hand – hidden among the rocks, like secret, magic gardens that you sense rather than see. How we both loved that place with its backdrop of wild ice towers and a view towards the third summit pyramid of Broad Peak. From a height of 5,300 metres, you could look along the sinuous course of the Godwin-Austen glacier all the way down to Base Camp (still two hours' walk away), that little 'village' with its milling activity. But here, the foot of the Abruzzi Spur, is a homely place. Why, it even boasts a homesteader: a little hamster-like creature with black button-eyes. This must be his summer residence.

Snowdust brushes past me. I breathe in the cold night air. Should I move on? The thumb of my right hand is sore from repeatedly thrusting my ice-axe into the hard surface, the other fingers are reduced to rigid, bone-hard claws with no feeling left in them at all. A few stars flicker in the sky. I could rest here indefinitely.

… that animal was living solely on titbits it could scrounge from expeditions and those few green leaves. One day we noticed how carefully it treated the secret garden; it never ate the leaves totally, just nibbled here and there a bit, so that they could continue growing … a clever animal …

But how does a hamster climb through an icefall? And why?

… Darkness all around me and dominating everything, the face, indistinct rock figures rising from the Abruzzi. I lean towards the snow, rest my head on my arm and hear the rush of glacier water far below, the sound carried up to me on a draught of air. I wish I could be down there.

Tak, tak…tak, tak…tak, tak. I go on. The sound of my own steps rings like a *perpetuum mobile* through the night. A steady heartbeat rhythm …

…When the Koreans came, tents sprang up like coloured mushrooms on the scree around our own small, dark-green dome (the same colour as the pointed leaftips). The little homesteader resented their intrusion at first and would not come out, but later he probably brought up all his family and friends as well, there was so much rice …

Tak, tak…tak, tak…tak, tak… yes that garden overlooking the ice towers was a very special place for Julie. We both loved it: it was our place. It makes me happy to think about it.

Tak, tak...tak, tak...tak, tak...

There will be something of her there? She will be down there? When I touch the water, she will be there ...

Tak, tak...tak, tak...tak, tak...

The snow is deeper now, but less steep. Like a huge python, the ridge at my side winds into the depths. I can only guess where it ends.

Why did you have to stay up there, Julie? It's something I'll never be able to understand. Tak, tak.

I wonder if you knew in your heart that it might happen? Why didn't *I* sense it? Both of us, of course, were aware that something like that was always on the cards ...

We wanted to be with our dream mountain once more, try one last time for the summit together before giving up, perhaps for good. It was so great being linked by the rope again.

Tak, tak...tak, tak...tak, tak...tak...

Now I am alone. All that's left is this longing for that place down there. Perhaps I'll find you down there. At the water ...

'I will be a little mouse and watch you,' you said to me in Tashigang once and smiled. It was the only time we ever mentioned the subject – what would happen if one of us were to be lost in the mountains? But the sun was shining over the roofs of the village, sunlight oozing from the green of the fields, we could feel its warmth on our skin and quickly spoke of something else. It was absurd to think of death. Unimaginable that only one of us might come back from the mountain. That would never happen.

Tak, tak...tak, tak...tak, tak.

But it has happened.

I am coming down from K2 alone.

We fulfilled our dream – and have given up everything else for it. We did not know...

There is the whirr of a stone in the air. Then all is still again. How long have I been climbing through this darkness? Two hours? Three?

Tak, tak...tak, tak......tak...tak......tak...

Why this tiredness? What's happening to me? Shivering, I stop. A strange sensation runs through my body, through my brain. An awareness of unlimited distance... I must sleep for a while. No! Get

it together, Kurt! If you sleep you'll fall! You have to get down –
now! It's not that far …

Tak, tak…tak……tak… but where are my usual steady movements? My confidence starts to crumble.

All of a sudden, it is finished. I can't go on any more… darkness
… it's all empty around me. Fear takes hold of me. Below me, the
deep: all of a sudden it seems bottomless. A never-ending abyss.
Stay calm, Kurt. Take a rest – and then go on. Ram in the two axes
firmly. Nothing will happen. Stay calm.

I sink my head on my arm…

I am part of the night.

Time passes, infinite time.

I travel measureless distances.

What is that moving there? It looks like people, lights… Lights!
People! A lighted tent? Or a hallucination? One moment ago there
was just darkness, I was alone in the vast night. It can't be people.
Go slow, Kurt. Don't be taken in. Look into that slope in front of you.

Tak, tak… now I've reached where the avalanche debris spills in
large lumps of packed ice across a boulder slope … I find a clear way
through, groping my way, still on all fours, crawling down, face to
the slope. I should turn round now, but I'm frightened I'll fall on
such uneven ground. I rest again. The people below me have
become a reality: they do exist. The lights are blinking with busy
movement. They have not yet noticed me. A sensation of relief
flows through me: I *have* made it. In a few minutes, I will be at that
place where the water is, will reach our Garden of Eden. Its little
landlord must be fast asleep, deep between his stones.

Who are they – these people? I am in a kind of trance, not
registering properly.

I keep climbing down, can feel with my feet the shallow depression at the edge of the snowfield. The dazzling beam of a lamp
suddenly penetrates the darkness, reaching up towards me. Have
they discovered me? I still feel that I belong to the night.

In that moment I look forward to meeting the people who are
coming…

Someone must have spotted me. I hear voices, calls, see lights
moving out across the boulders just below me, but I give no sign.

Mutely, I step down, unchanged, not knowing how to break the pattern of the perpetual motion of this night. Tak...tak...tak...-tak...... infinitely slowly.

I'm caught in a cone of light. There is a figure approaching. Now he is at my side. Slowly I turn and stand upright.

'You're safe at last!' the words are Jim's. Jim Curran's. He grabs my arm and supports me firmly as all around the night slowly vanishes, this night of which I have been part, and which now only grudgingly releases me.

More lights. More people gathering round.

You're safe at last. Why did Jim say that? Of course I'm safe, here at the place of our garden. I've made it, yes. But, she... Julie ... she is up there.

'I've lost Julie,' I tell Jim. There's nothing else to say.

It is midnight on 11 August. The 2,700-metre descent from the place of the fearful storm is over. Krystyna, Janusz, Jim... they lead me across the boulders to a tent, to their tent which they have just erected. Now I realize: the whole camp – Julie's and my tent included – has disappeared. It has been cleared; for days now we have all been given up for dead.

It was two weeks ago that we set off from here on our climb ...

There's one thing I've almost forgotten to tell: I groped my way down, as if I wanted to fulfil a promise, all the way to our garden by the murmuring water. I tripped, fell over in the splintering ice – and drank and drank and drank.

I am lying in a double sleeping bag, belonging to one of the Poles – soft, cosy and warm as only Polish bags can be. And 'Krysiu', white-blonde like my daughter Karen, feeds me hot tea. Oh, it's good to be looked after so caringly! A few minutes ago Janusz took off my boots for me, and Jim tells how he came to find me: '... There was this strange noise in the night, repeating itself over and over. Like a low, hesitant heartbeat – no, not quite like that – anyway, I couldn't make out what it was... and then I heard it again ... it sounded like metal, and yet somehow human ... living ...'

A heartbeat that propelled thoughts, and arms and legs and my ice-axe! An inextinguishable energy that came out of the night. A *perpetuum mobile*. I feel it a miracle to be still alive.

Doctors and scientists say that everything has an end, that

perpetual motion does not exist. Not inside you and not outside of you. But perhaps sometimes one participates in the wholeness of existence.

The next morning, completely unexpectedly, it was almost all over for me. With Jim, Krysiu and a high-altitude porter I was climbing down through the icefall; I was exhausted and moving gingerly because we were doing it without a rope as most people did in those weeks and because, since my frozen, swollen feet would no longer fit into my wet double boots which anyway weighed a ton, I had changed them for slippery moonboots. All of a sudden a handhold broke in the ice. I skidded, lost my balance, and it was only the quick action of Jim grabbing my arm that saved me from falling into a crevasse full of water, in which I would almost certainly have drowned.

A little later, hardly surprisingly, I was overcome with a terrible hunger and felt quite at the end of my strength until good Krysiu ran ahead and had a potful of hot soup sent up from Base Camp for me. Then, slowly, I went on again.

When, on the moraine about a mile from Base Camp, a group of mountaineers appeared with a stretcher, I made no fuss…

The search for Mrowka, by the rescue party alerted by Willi on his arrival in Base Camp the day before, met with no success. She could not be found anywhere at the foot of the mountain, nor was she, as I had hoped, sleeping in the small tent at about 7,000 metres. That was as high as the rescuers could reach. A year later a Japanese expedition discovered her body on the fixed ropes, somewhat above the ladder that starts near the tent. Her hand still held the rope and, as I understand it, she was upright, leaning into the wall. She had a thin cord around the rope, the significance of which no one could explain. Did she die of an embolism? Or had she simply fallen asleep? It will always be a mystery.

Mrowka was buried near Advanced Base Camp.

Of the other victims on the Shoulder, nothing has been found. The snowstorms have covered them.

*Whether or not you think it is possible to have any links with 'the beyond'
during life, it can certainly never be visualized, nor ever explained. Logical
people often dismiss it as so much moonshine, even though no logician has
yet come up with a satisfactory explanation for the enigma of life and death.
Nevertheless, even the driest of realists, the most sober of mathematicians, is
sometimes confronted with signs or experiences which belong in a different
world, which are inexplicable by normal standards. Yet they are still real —
and merely to put them down to coincidence sounds like a cheap cop-out on
the part of people who simply don't know.*

Similarly, what I am going to tell next can never be explained.

*A strange thing happened — I noticed — on my right foot, the one that was
the least frostbitten. There appeared more and more visible from day to day
in the nail of the big toe, as if inscribed there, a distinct number '11', blue at
first, then turning to black ... a frightening mark. It was so clear, that I
could not just put it down to a product of fantasy and began to brood upon
it. (I had more than enough time to think in the Innsbruck hospital.) Did it
mean I was destined to be the eleventh victim on K2? After Mohammed Ali,
the leader of the high-altitude porters, who was hit by stonefall on 4 August
near Camp 1, Julie, on 7 August, became the ninth victim of the terrible
mountain summer on K2; Alfred Imitzer was the tenth, dying during the
last desperate attempt to get down on 10 August, and he was followed by
Hannes Wieser, Alan Rouse and finally Mrowka on the fixed ropes. It was
11 August, just before midnight, when I won the fight for survival by
reaching the foot of the mountain after two days struggling down from
8,000 metres, most of which time I was completely on my own. It was 11
August, the end of that day, when on my last legs, I met the party coming up
to look for Mrowka (and to rescue me, too, if necessary).*

The 11th of August — was that to have been my last day? Or was I supposed to have died up there on the Shoulder as the eleventh victim?

However you looked at it, the black '11' was a sinister mark. I was under no doubt that I had escaped destiny.

CLOUDS FROM BOTH SIDES

Sometimes people say to me: You lost close friends up there, would you go back to climb in the Himalayas again?

They expect me to say 'No'. However, losing my friends was not all there was to it: I also lived with them up there. They found their Life up there …

I couldn't, not now, change the way I live. I have been going to the Himalayas for thirty years, I cannot imagine any sort of future that didn't involve going back there … I have to be with the big mountains – even if now only rarely do I get up to the summit.

August 1988: I'm sitting in a plane, on my way to Sinkiang. I am with Agostino, Gianni and the others. We will be exploring the mountain desert to the north of K2 – there, where the endless processions of green-blue ice towers march shoulder to shoulder down the lonely curving glaciers. Below the Gasherbrums, up behind Broad Peak … maybe even into that corner which Julie and I burned with impatience to see. We will be there, where the two of us roamed with shining K2 high above our heads.

Yes, I know – happiness and sorrow will go with me. And I shall still be searching.

Outside, not far from the window of the plane, enormous towers of cloud have appeared: I see them growing, watch the fluted outlines expand and change … we slide among them, through them; spectral threads of white cotton race by, weightless overhangs, meandering inlets, bays – into which we dive – giant, puffy shapes surround us, huge pillars and columns reaching up from the depths … beautiful cloud formations. Clouds, as Julie loved them.

I remember what she once said about the faces of clouds: 'there is one side, the beautiful face, which imagination allows you to see –

as a child I was always dreaming about those castles, seeing so many things in those silhouettes ...

'But they also have a dark face, which can destroy your dreams ...' and she explained to me why she intended to call her book *Clouds from Both Sides* ...

The many faces of the clouds ... white towers, building and rebuilding, endlessly re-creating themselves, changing their form; avalanches of vapour which extend into the sky with the same might and power as snowdust ... with the same power of fantasy that will always transport inquisitive souls who yearn to understand, to feel and touch ... what they see in the clouds. Because in that lies a sense of being.

But may clouds not hide storms? May they not rise, threatening, mighty, incomprehensible – like immense dark birds ... storm birds, that tear away everything, that destroy not only dreams? When they are over you, when you are in their power, there is no light and shadow any more. And you must fight for all that constitutes life, for all that is dear to you and your companion – and you fight for him, for those at home, for yourself – until one day the time comes when you sink back silently – as Julie did.

Yet stormbirds, too, have their end.

The darkness, the all-encompassing dreariness, lasted for a long time after the return from K2 – as if the storm, like a bad spell, had not fully worked itself out. There were gaps in memory ... full of fantasies; there were heroic poems ... and clichés. There were invented 'rescues' – when in fact nobody unable to climb down by himself could have survived. The most extreme opinions clashed together. But that time is over; it was a fight, but it was necessary – for the truth, for all those who will climb in future.

Luckily, I learned to know a different side, too: friendship, people who really helped me, and had to bear a lot, like Teresa, Karen, Hildegard, Tona. Like Ceci, Inge and Dennis, Terry ... it takes a long time to clamber out of an abyss like that.

Today I am flying between Julie's white clouds. And she is not sitting by my side and watching them. She is with them.

'Love is no possession; it is everywhere.' She wrote that once on a small piece of paper for me during a flight through clouds.

The voice ... there it is, I can hear it.

Today I am flying between white clouds ...

APPENDIX 1

K2 – EXPEDITION HISTORY (from the first reconnaissances to 1990)

Year	Expedition	Leader	Route (SE = Abruzzi Ridge)	Remarks
1272–4	Italian			Marco Polo's journey to China brought him into the vicinity of the Karakoram.
1835–8	British			G. T. Vigne visited Kashmir, Ladakh and Baltistan; in 1835 from Skardu he reached the snout of the Chogo Lungma glacier.
1856	German	Adolf Schlagintweit		Schlagintweit was probably the first non-local to get close to the Baltoro area and to reach one – the western – of the Mustagh passes (Panmah Pass).
1856	British	T. G. Montgomerie		In the course of mapping the Karakoram, Montgomerie was the first to employ the name 'K2'; from Haramukh (5,142m) in Kashmir (about 200km from K2) he numbered the Karakoram summits on a sketch in his survey-log: K1, K2, K3, etc. and remarked that K2 seemed to be the highest. During the next two years the surveyor G. Shelverton, from observations from Kashmir, computed the height of K2 and announced it as the second highest peak in the world. It was later fixed at 28,250ft (8,611m).
1861	British	H. H. Godwin-Austen		Godwin-Austen saw the summit pyramid of K2, 27 km distant, from a point 600m above Urdokas on the Baltoro glacier, and made what has become a celebrated sketch; previously he had been within 15km of Concordia. It was proposed that K2 be named after him. He made the first (1:500,000) map of the Karakoram.

1887	British	Francis Younghusband	Younghusband crossed the Karakoram mountains from China with a small group of porters; he discovered the Shaksgam Valley and passed close to K2 (he was the first European to see it from the north), crossing the Old Mustagh Pass to reach the Baltoro glacier.
1890	Italian	Roberto Lerco	He made the first reconnaissance of K2 (between May and October); also explorations around the Hunza Valley (see *Rivista Mensile* 1954); he appears to have climbed to 6,600m on the Abruzzi Ridge, but this is open to question.
1892	British	William Martin Conway	An expedition with scientific and mountaineering objectives, and the first to penetrate the full length of the Baltoro glacier. (Conway gave the enormous glacier junction its name Concordia, being reminded of the Place de la Concorde in Paris.) First ascent of Pioneer Peak (6,890m) on Baltoro Kangri – a world altitude record at the time; valuable topographical work (Baltoro map), six 'explorers' (climber/scientists), an ornithologist, four Gurkha soldiers.

K2 – the final 1,500 metres (from SE).

1902	International	Oscar Eckenstein	NE Ridge	Climbing attempt on North-East Ridge to 6,525m; six climbers – among them the notorious Aleister Crowley and the Austrian mountaineers Heinrich Pfannl and Victor Wessely.
1909	Italian	Luigi Amedeo di Savoia, Duke of the Abruzzi	SE	Exploration and attempt on K2's 'feasible' route, the Abruzzi Ridge or Spur to a height of 6,250m; twelve climbers.
1929	Italian	Prince Aimone di Savoia, Duke of Spoleto	(S; N)	Mountaineering attempt renounced in favour of important geographic and geological studies. Professor Ardito Desio took part as a geologist, exploring the Shaksgam Valley with three other members; on the Baltoro side his explorations included reaching the 'Possible Saddle' described by Conway, between the Baltoro and the Siachen glaciers (he named it after its discoverer).
1937	British	Eric Shipton	(N)	Exploration, scientific and topographical survey work, as well as climbs to the north of K2 in the region of several large glaciers and in the Shaksgam (E. Shipton, H. Tilman, J. Auden, M. Spender and seven Sherpas).
1938	American	Charles S. Houston	SE	First concerted attempt to climb the Abruzzi Ridge; seven high camps erected and an altitude of 7,925m attained (six climbers).
1939	American	Fritz Wiessner	SE	A push to 8,382m – without artificial oxygen. Nine high camps. During the final retreat, despite a rescue attempt four climbers, three Sherpas and the American, Dudley Wolfe, perished. (Members: six climbers.)
1953	American	Charles S. Houston	SE	Eight high camps erected and a height of 7,900m reached. A desperate bid to save the sick Art Gilkey failed and he was lost in an avalanche shortly after Pete Schoening astonishingly checked a mass fall. The Gilkey Memorial was erected below Base Camp. (Eight climbers.)
1953	Italian	Riccardo Cassin	SE	Reconnaissance expedition prior to 1954 attempt; Cassin and Desio went to the foot of the Abruzzi Ridge (September).
1954	Italian	Ardito Desio	SE	*First ascent of K2.* Nine high camps. Fixed ropes and oxygen apparatus employed. On 31 July at about 18.00 hours Lino Lacedelli and Achille Compagnoni

reached the summit, although their oxygen had run out a short while before. Eleven climbers; Mario Puchoz died of pneumonia.

Year	Nationality	Leader	Route	Notes
1960	German/ American	W. D. Hackett	SE	Bad weather made it impossible to surmount the 'Black Pyramid', a difficult and steep section of the Abruzzi Ridge (seven climbers).
1975	American	James Whittaker	NW	A new route, attempted from the Savoia Saddle; highest point reached – 6,700m. Diane Roberts became the first female mountaineer on K2 (ten members).
1976	Polish	Janusz Kurczab	NE	The Poles surmounted the difficult North-East Ridge; an attempt on the summit pyramid by Chrobak and Wroz reached 8,400m before insufficient oxygen reserves forced a retreat. This route had originally been attempted in 1902 (nineteen members).
1976	Japanese	Takayoshi Takatsuka	SE	Reconnaissance. On 7 August three climbers attained 7,160m on the Abruzzi Ridge. (Six members.)
1977	Japanese	Ichiro Yoshizawa	SE	*Second ascent of K2.* Mammoth expedition: fifty-two members, 1,500 porters. Six Japanese and a Pakistani reached the summit on 8 and 9 August. A 35mm expedition film was made. Oxygen used. At seventy-three years of age, I. Yoshizawa was the oldest person to reach the foot of K2.
1978	American	James Whittaker	NE/SE	*Third ascent of K2.* The Polish NE Ridge route was followed to a height of 7,700m, then an oblique traverse made to the normal route. Four climbers reached the summit on 6 and 7 September – with little or no use of oxygen. (Fourteen members, among them three women.)
1978	British	Chris Bonington	W	First attempt on West Ridge (to 6,700m) abandoned on the death of Nick Estcourt in an avalanche. (Eight members.)
1979	French	Bernard Mellet	SSW	South-South-West Ridge attempted by massive expedition with 30 tons of equipment. One of the steepest and most difficult ridges on the mountain: five summit thrusts were made. Succeeded in reaching 8,400m. (Fourteen climbers; death of one high-altitude porter.)

1979	International	Reinhold Messer	ML/SE	*Fourth ascent of K2.* Reinhold Messner and Michl Dacher gained the summit without using bottled oxygen on 12 July via the Abruzzi Ridge. Four high camps. An attempt on Reinhold Messner's projected 'Magic Line', the original objective of this expedition, was earlier abandoned. (Seven members; one porter killed falling into a crevasse.)
1980	British	Peter Boardman	W/SE	After an attempt on the West Ridge to 7,000m, 7,900m was reached on the Abruzzi. (Four climbers.)
1981	Japanese	Teruoh Matsuura	W	*Fifth ascent of K2* (and first via the West Ridge). On 7 August one Japanese and one Pakistani stood on the summit. Oxygen employed.
1981	French/ German	Yannick Seigneur	S	Attempt on a new route (on the South Face); 7,400m reached. (Four climbers.)
1982	Polish	Janusz Kurczab	NW	Attempt to force a new route without touching the Savoia Saddle; 8,200m finally gained on the Chinese side, where they were observed and ordered back! 3,500m of fixed rope employed (twenty-one climbers: fifteen Poles and six Mexicans).
1982	Japanese	Isaoh Shinkai	N	*Sixth ascent of K2*, and first from the Chinese side via North Ridge. Seven climbers reached summit on 14 and 15 August (a fatal fall during descent). No oxygen (fourteen climbers).
1982	Austrian	(Hanns Schell) Georg Bachler	SE	7,500m reached, and further attempts abandoned to help in the evacuation of dead Polish woman climber. Bachler was the effective leader since Schell remained in Austria! (Four members.)
1982	Polish	Wanda Rutkiewicz	SE	Polish women's expedition; death of Halina Krüger; they reached 7,100m (eleven women climbers, including one French, Christine de Colombel).
1983	Spanish	Antonio Trabado	W	A height of 8,200m reached via West Ridge and West Face (Juanjo San Sebastián and A. Trabado).
1983	International	Doug Scott	S	An attempt on a rib to the left of the Abruzzi reached 7,500m. (Three Britons, including R. Baxter-Jones, and one Frenchman, J. Afanassieff.)

1983	Spanish (Navarre)	Gregorio Ariz	SE	Mari Abrego and Roger Baxter-Jones – after their respective expeditions had given up – reached a height of 8,300m before bad weather turned them back. (Earlier the nine-person Navarre team had been to 7,700m.)
1983	Italian	Francesco Santon	N	*Seventh ascent of K2* (and second via the North Ridge). Summit reached by four members (three Italians, one Czech) on 31 July and 4 August, climbing without oxygen. Julie Tullis became the 'highest woman' on K2. (Twenty-three members in all.)
1984	International	Stefan Wörner	SE	7,500m reached.
1985	Swiss	Erhard Loretan	SE	Five climbers reached the summit on two separate days. No oxygen.
1985	French	Eric Escoffier	SE	Three climbers reached summit. Daniel Lacroix lost during the descent. No oxygen.
1985	Japanese	Kazuoh Tobita	SE	Three Japanese reached summit – probably without oxygen.
1985	International	Wojciech Kurtyka	SE	Attempt foundered at 7,000m. (With R. Schauer after climbing West Face of Gasherbrum IV.)
1986	Italian/ Basque	Renato Casarotto	SE/SSW	Mari Abrego and Josema Casimiro: summit reached by Abruzzi Ridge. Renato Casarotto died in a fall into a crevasse after attempting the SSW Ridge.
1986	French	Maurice Barrard	SE	Summit reached by all four members, Wanda Rutkiewicz and Liliane Barrard becoming the first women to climb K2. The Barrards, husband and wife, were lost during the descent.
1986	British	Alan Rouse/ John Barry	NW/SE	Attempted NW Ridge to 7,400m; Alan Rouse died after reaching summit via Abruzzi Ridge. (Eleven members.)
1986	American	John Smolich	SSW	After Smolich and Al Pennington killed by avalanche, attempt abandoned. (Eight climbers.)
1986	Italian/ International	Agostino Da Polenza	SSW/SE	Eight members reached summit by Abruzzi Ridge. Julie Tullis died during the descent. The attempt on the SSW Ridge was given up because of avalanche danger.

1986	International	Karl Herrligkoffer	S/SE	Two Swiss reached summit by Abruzzi Ridge; two Poles made first ascent of South Face (Kukuczka route); death of Piotrowski during descent. (Sixteen members in all.)
1986	Austrian	Alfred Imitzer	SE	Two climbers to the summit, two deaths during the descent (Imitzer and H. Wieser); seven climbers altogether.
1986	South Korean	Kim Byung-Joon	SE	Three climbers to summit, using oxygen. Death of sirdar in stonefall. (Nineteen members in all.)
1986	Polish	Janusz Majer	SSW/SE	First ascent of SSW Ridge; death of W. Wroz during descent. 'Mrowka' Dobroslawa Wolf died during descent after attempt on Abruzzi. (Eight members, including three women.)
1986	American	Lance Owens	N	Attempt on N Ridge to a height of 8,100m (eight climbers).
1986	Yugoslav	Viki Grošelj	S	Tomo Cesen soloed new route to left of Abruzzi Ridge, as far as the Shoulder, 7,800m.
1987	International	Doug Scott	S	Attempt on spur to the left of Abruzzi – 7,100m reached – after having reached 6,900m on normal route (six climbers).
1987	French	Martine Rolland	SE	Attempt to 7,000m (six members).
1987	Polish/Swiss	Wojciech Kurtyka	W	Attempt on West Face with Jean Troillet to 6,400m.
1987	Japanese	Haruyuki Endo	SE	Attempt to 7,400m.
1987	Japanese/ Pakistani	Kenshiro Otaki	SE	Attempt to 8,300m; one Japanese killed in a fall (fourteen members).
1987	Spanish (Basque)	Juanjo San Sebastián	S	Climbed the rib to the left of the Abruzzi as far as the Shoulder, then the normal route to 8,300m (seven climbers, plus a sirdar).
1987–8	Polish/ International	Andrzej Zawada	SE	Winter attempt on Abruzzi Ridge to 7,350m (twenty climbers).
1988	Yugoslav	Tomaz Jamnik	SSW	Attempt to 8,100m, then Abruzzi Ridge to 7,400m (fifteen members).
1988	American	Peter Athans	SE	Attempt to 7,400m (five members).

1988	New Zealand	Rob Hall	SE	Attempt to 7,400m (four members).
1988	Spanish (Catalan)	Jordi Magriñá	SE	Attempt to 8,100m (twelve members).
1988	French	Pierre Béghin	N	Attempt on North Spur to 8,000m (six members and a doctor).
1989	Polish/Swiss	Wojciech Kurtyka	NW	An attempt to open new route on NW Face couldn't get started on account of bad weather (with Jean Troillet and Erhard Loretan).
1989	Austrian	Eduard Koblmüller	E/SE	An attempt on the hitherto unclimbed East Face reached 7,200m. Death of one member. An attempt on the Abruzzi Ridge ended at 7,000m (seven members).
1989	Spanish (Basque)	Juanjo San Sebastián	SE	Attempt to 7,400m (eleven members).
1990	American	Doug Dalquist	SE	Reached 7,600m on the Abruzzi Ridge. At the end of July, they gave up further attempts due to excessive soft snow.
1990	International	C. A. Pinelli	SE	'Free K2' international cleaning expedition organized by Mountain Wilderness. No summit attempts were contemplated since they gave a specific commitment to the Pakistani authorities not to proceed beyond the Shoulder (nine members).
1990	Australian/ American	Steve Swenson	N	A small expedition of four attempted the North Spur. Three climbers reached the summit on 20 August at 8 pm.
1990	Japanese	Tomoji Ueki	N	Attempt of a new route (NW Face and N Spur). Two climbers reached the summit on 9 August from the Chinese side (twelve members and eight Chinese helpers).

APPENDIX 2

K2 – SUMMIT CLIMBERS (by Xavier Eguskitza)

No.	Name	Nationality	Date	Route	Expedition	Leader
1	Achille Compagnoni	Italian	31.7.54	Abruzzi Ridge	Italian	Ardito Desio
2	Lino Lacedelli	Italian	31.7.54	Abruzzi Ridge	Italian	Ardito Desio
3	Shoji Nakamura	Japanese	8.8.77	Abruzzi Ridge	Japanese	Ichiro Yoshizawa
4	Tsuneoh Shigehiro	Japanese	8.8.77	Abruzzi Ridge	Japanese	Ichiro Yoshizawa
5	Takeyoshi Takatsuka	Japanese	8.8.77	Abruzzi Ridge	Japanese	Ichiro Yoshizawa
6	Mitsuo Hiroshima	Japanese	9.8.77	Abruzzi Ridge	Japanese	Ichiro Yoshizawa
7	Masahide Onodera	Japanese	9.8.77	Abruzzi Ridge	Japanese	Ichiro Yoshizawa
8	Hideo Yamamoto	Japanese	9.8.77	Abruzzi Ridge	Japanese	Ichiro Yoshizawa
9	Ashraf Aman	Pakistani	9.8.77	Abruzzi Ridge	Japanese	Ichiro Yoshizawa
10	James Wickwire	American	6.9.78	NE Ridge/Abruzzi Ridge	American	James Whittaker
11	Louis Reichardt	American	6.9.78	NE Ridge/Abruzzi Ridge	American	James Whittaker
12	John Roskelley	American	7.9.78	NE Ridge/Abruzzi Ridge	American	James Whittaker
13	Rick Ridgeway	American	7.9.78	NE Ridge/Abruzzi Ridge	American	James Whittaker
14	Reinhold Messner	Italian	12.7.79	Abruzzi Ridge	European	Reinhold Messner
15	Michl Dacher	W. German	12.7.79	Abruzzi Ridge	European	Reinhold Messner
16	Eiho Ohtani	Japanese	7.8.81	West Ridge/SW side	Japanese	Teruoh Matsuura
17	Nazir Sabir	Pakistani	7.8.81	West Ridge/SW side	Japanese	Teruoh Matsuura
18	Naoé Sakashita	Japanese	14.8.82	North Ridge	Japanese	Isao Shinkai
19	Yukihiro Yanagisawa	Japanese	14.8.82	North Ridge	Japanese	Isao Shinkai
20	Hiroshi Yoshino	Japanese	14.8.82	North Ridge	Japanese	Isao Shinkai
21	Kazushige Takami	Japanese	15.8.82	North Ridge	Japanese	Isao Shinkai
22	Haruichi Kawamura	Japanese	15.8.82	North Ridge	Japanese	Isao Shinkai
23	Tatsuji Shigeno	Japanese	15.8.82	North Ridge	Japanese	Isao Shinkai
24	Hironobu Kamuro	Japanese	15.8.82	North Ridge	Japanese	Isao Shinkai
25	Agostino Da Polenza	Italian	31.7.83	North Ridge	Italian	Francesco Santon
26	Josef Rakoncaj	Czechoslovak	31.7.83	North Ridge	Italian	Francesco Santon

27	Sergio Martini	Italian	4.8.83	North Ridge	Italian	Francesco Santon
28	Fausto De Stefani	Italian	4.8.83	North Ridge	Italian	Francesco Santon
29	Marcel Ruedi	Swiss	19.6.85	Abruzzi Ridge	Swiss	Erhard Loretan
30	Norbert Joos	Swiss	19.6.85	Abruzzi Ridge	Swiss	Erhard Loretan
31	Erhard Loretan	Swiss	6.7.85	Abruzzi Ridge	Swiss	Erhard Loretan
32	Pierre Morand	Swiss	6.7.85	Abruzzi Ridge	Swiss	Erhard Loretan
33	Jean Troillet	Swiss	6.7.85	Abruzzi Ridge	Swiss	Erhard Loretan
34	Eric Escoffier	French	6.7.85	Abruzzi Ridge	French	—
35	Daniel Lacroix	French	7.7.85	Abruzzi Ridge	French	—
36	Stéphane Schaffter	Swiss	7.7.85	Abruzzi Ridge	French	—
37	Noboru Yamada	Japanese	24.7.85	Abruzzi Ridge	Japanese	Kazuoh Tobita
38	Kenji Yoshida	Japanese	24.7.85	Abruzzi Ridge	Japanese	Kazuoh Tobita
39	Kazunari Murakami	Japanese	24.7.85	Abruzzi Ridge	Japanese	Kazuoh Tobita
40	Wanda Rutkiewicz	Polish	23.6.86	Abruzzi Ridge	French	Maurice Barrard
41	Michel Parmentier	French	23.6.86	Abruzzi Ridge	French	Maurice Barrard
42	Maurice Barrard	French	23.6.86	Abruzzi Ridge	French	Maurice Barrard
43	Liliane Barrard	French	23.6.86	Abruzzi Ridge	French	Maurice Barrard
44	Mari Abrego	Spanish (Basque)	23.6.86	Abruzzi Ridge	Basque	(Renato Casarotto)
45	Josema Casimiro	Spanish (Basque)	23.6.86	Abruzzi Ridge	Basque	(Renato Casarotto)
46	Gianni Calcagno	Italian	5.7.86	Abruzzi Ridge	Italian	Agostino Da Polenza
47	Tullio Vidoni	Italian	5.7.86	Abruzzi Ridge	Italian	Agostino Da Polenza
48	Soro Dorotei	Italian	5.7.86	Abruzzi Ridge	Italian	Agostino Da Polenza
49	Martino Moretti	Italian	5.7.86	Abruzzi Ridge	Italian	Agostino Da Polenza
50	Josef Rakoncaj	Czechoslovak	5.7.86	Abruzzi Ridge	Italian	Agostino Da Polenza
51	Benoît Chamoux	French	5.7.86	Abruzzi Ridge	Italian	Agostino Da Polenza
52	Beda Fuster	Swiss	5.7.86	Abruzzi Ridge	International	Karl Herrligkoffer
53	Rolf Zemp	Swiss	5.7.86	Abruzzi Ridge	International	Karl Herrligkoffer
54	Jerzy Kukuczka	Polish	8.7.86	South Face	International	Karl Herrligkoffer
55	Tadeusz Piotrowski	Polish	8.7.86	South Face	International	Karl Herrligkoffer
56	Chang Bong-Wan	S. Korean	3.8.86	Abruzzi Ridge	S. Korean	Kim Byung-Joon
57	Kim Chang-Sun	S. Korean	3.8.86	Abruzzi Ridge	S. Korean	Kim Byung-Joon
58	Chang Byong-Ho	S. Korean	3.8.86	Abruzzi Ridge	S. Korean	Kim Byung-Joon
59	Wojciech Wroz	Polish	3.8.86	SSW Ridge	Polish	Janusz Majer
60	Przemyslaw Piasecki	Polish	3.8.86	SSW Ridge	Polish	Janusz Majer
61	Petr Bozik	Czechoslovak	3.8.86	SSW Ridge	Polish	Janusz Majer
62	Willi Bauer	Austrian	4.8.86	Abruzzi Ridge	Austrian	Alfred Imitzer
63	Alfred Imitzer	Austrian	4.8.86	Abruzzi Ridge	Austrian	Alfred Imitzer
64	Alan Rouse	British	4.8.86	Abruzzi Ridge	British	Alan Rouse
65	Kurt Diemberger	Austrian	4.8.86	Abruzzi Ridge	Italian	Agostino Da Polenza
66	Julie Tullis	British	4.8.86	Abruzzi Ridge	Italian	Agostino Da Polenza
67	Hideji Nazuka	Japanese	9.8.90	North Side	Japanese	Tomoji Ueki
68	Hirotaka Imamura	Japanese	9.8.90	North Side	Japanese	Tomoji Ueki
69	Steve Swenson	American	20.8.90	North Spur	American	Steve Swenson
70	Greg Child	Australian	20.8.90	North Spur	American	Steve Swenson
71	Greg Mortimer	Australian	20.8.90	North Spur	American	Steve Swenson

APPENDIX 3

THEY DIED ON K2

Name	Nationality	Date	Cause	Route
Dudley Wolfe	American	30.7.39	Probably high altitude sickness, exhaustion: in Camp 7 (7,550m).	Abruzzi Ridge
Pasang Kikuli	Sherpa	31.7.39	Disappeared between Camps 6 and 7.	Abruzzi Ridge
Pasang Kitar	Sherpa	31.7.39	Disappeared between Camps 6 and 7.	Abruzzi Ridge
Pintso	Sherpa	31.7.39	Disappeared between Camps 6 and 7.	Abruzzi Ridge
Art Gilkey	American	10.8.53	Avalanche near Camp 7 (7,450m).	Abruzzi Ridge
Mario Puchoz	Italian	21.6.54	Pneumonia at Camp 2 (5,900m).	Abruzzi Ridge
Nick Estcourt	British	12.6.78	Avalanche near Camp 2 (6,500m).	West Ridge
Ali, son of Kazim	Pakistani	9.6.79	Fall into crevasse.	Savoia glacier
Laskhar Khan	Pakistani	19.8.79	Heart attack between Camps 3 and 4.	SSW Ridge
Halina Krüger	Polish	30.7.82	Heart attack at Camp 2 (6,700m).	Abruzzi Ridge
Yukihiro Yanagisawa	Japanese	15.8.82	Fell during descent.	North Ridge
Daniel Lacroix	French	7.7.85	Lost during descent.	Abruzzi Ridge
John Smolich	American	21.6.86	Avalanche death at 6,000m.	SSW Ridge
Alan Pennington	American	21.6.86	Avalanche death at 6,000m.	SSW Ridge
Liliane Barrard	French	24.6.86	Fall during descent.	Abruzzi Ridge
Maurice Barrard	French	24.6.86	Lost during descent.	Abruzzi Ridge
Tadeusz Piotrowski	Polish	10.7.86	Fall during descent.	Abruzzi Ridge
Renato Casarotto	Italian	16.7.86	Fall into crevasse at 5,100m.	SSW Ridge
Wojciech Wroz	Polish	3.8.86	Fall during descent.	Abruzzi Ridge

Mohammed Ali	Pakistani	4.8.86	Stonefall below Camp 1.	Abruzzi Ridge
Julie Tullis	British	7.8.86	Complex of causes, after fall, in Camp 4 (8,000m).	Abruzzi Ridge
Alan Rouse	British	10.8.86	Probably high altitude sickness and exhaustion, in Camp 4 (8,000m).	Abruzzi Ridge
Alfred Imitzer	Austrian	10.8.86	Probably high altitude sickness and exhaustion, below Camp 4 (8,000m).	Abruzzi Ridge
Hannes Wieser	Austrian	10.8.86	Probably high altitude sickness and exhaustion, below Camp 4 (8,000m).	Abruzzi Ridge
Dobroslawa Wolf	Polish	10.8.86	Unknown (embolism?) between Camps 3 and 2.	Abruzzi Ridge
Akira Suzuki	Japanese	24.8.87	Fall from c.8,200m.	Abruzzi Ridge
Hans Bärnthaler	Austrian	28.7.89	Fell with collapsing cornice while photographing E Face from a nearby peak.	East Face

Note by Xavier Eguskitza: of the twenty-seven mountaineers who reached the summit of K2 during 1986, seven died on the descent (as well as six others). Since then three more have also died: Michel Parmentier and Petr Bozik on Everest in the autumn of 1988, and Jerzy Kukuczka on the South Face of Lhotse in October 1989.

1. The final days. The arrow on the summit slope shows the approximate line of our fall during the late descent on 4 August. B = the subsequent bivouac on the hanging glacier. C4 = the assault camp at the 8,000 metre level, where we were all imprisoned by the storm.

2. Julie, and (3) the clouds of the Karakoram (Gasherbrum II).

4. Veils of storm at sunset on K2, and (5) Kurt at the hospital in Innsbruck.

4

5

APPENDIX 4

THE MOST IMPORTANT PEAKS IN THE KARAKORAM OVER 7,200 METRES

K2 (Chogori)	8,616m*	Malubiting	7,458m
Gasherbrum I (Hidden Peak)	8,068m	Yazghil Dom	7,440m
Broad Peak (Falchan Kangri)	8,060m*	Sia Kangri (Queen Mary Peak)	7,422m
Gasherbrum II	8,035m	Haramosh	7,409m
Broad Peak – Middle Summit	8,016m	Ghent (Kondus Peak)	7,401m
Gasherbrum III	7,952m	Rimo	7,385m
Gasherbrum IV	7,929m*	Sherpi Kangri	7,380m
Distaghil Sar	7,885m	Chongtar	7,370m
Kunyang Kish	7,852m	Skil Brum	7,360m
Masherbrum	7,821m	Karun Koh	7,350m
Rakaposhi (Domani)	7,788m	Momhil Sar	7,343m
Batura I	7,785m	Yutmar Sar	7,330m
Kanjut Sar	7,760m	Bajohaghur Duam Asir	7,329m
Saltoro Kangri	7,742m	Gasherbrum V	7,321m
Trivor	7,728m	Baltoro Kangri (Golden Throne)	7,312m
Saser Kangri	7,692m	Urdok	7,300m
Chogolisa (Bride Peak)	7,654, 7,665m	Baintha Brakk (Ogre)	7,285m
Shispare	7,611m	Pasu Peak	7,284m
Broad Peak – North Summit	7,550m	K6 (East Hushe Group)	7,282m
Skyang Kangri (Staircase Peak)	7,544m	Mustagh Tower	7,273m
Yukshin Gardan Sar	7,530m	Diran	7,266m
Mamostong Kangri	7,516m	Crown	7,265m
Pumari Kish	7,492m	Apsarasas	7,245m
K12 (Chumik Group)	7,469m	Singhié Kangri	7,202m
Teram Kangri I	7,462m	Bularung Sar	7,200m

* New measurement (1987)

Compiled by Rudolf Jauk, Rosenheim

APPENDIX 5

CONVERSION TABLE – METRES TO FEET (from the American Alpine Journal)

metres	feet	metres	feet	metres	feet	metres	feet
3,300	10,827	4,700	15,420	6,100	20,013	7,500	24,607
3,400	11,155	4,800	15,748	6,200	20,342	7,600	24,935
3,500	11,483	4,900	16,076	6,300	20,670	7,700	25,263
3,600	11,811	5,000	16,404	6,400	20,998	7,800	25,591
3,700	12,139	5,100	16,733	6,500	21,326	7,900	25,919
3,800	12,467	5,200	17,061	6,600	21,654	8,000	26,247
3,900	12,795	5,300	17,389	6,700	21,982	8,100	26,575
4,000	13,124	5,400	17,717	6,800	22,310	8,200	26,903
4,100	13,452	5,500	18,045	6,900	22,638	8,300	27,231
4,200	13,780	5,600	18,373	7,000	22,966	8,400	27,560
4,300	14,108	5,700	18,701	7,100	23,294	8,500	27,888
4,400	14,436	5,800	19,029	7,200	23,622	8,600	28,216
4,500	14,764	5,900	19,357	7,300	23,951	8,700	28,544
4,600	15,092	6,000	19,685	7,400	24,279	8,800	28,872

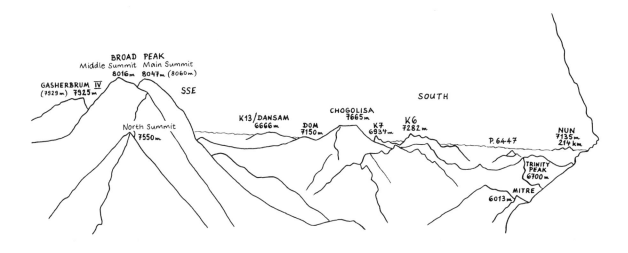

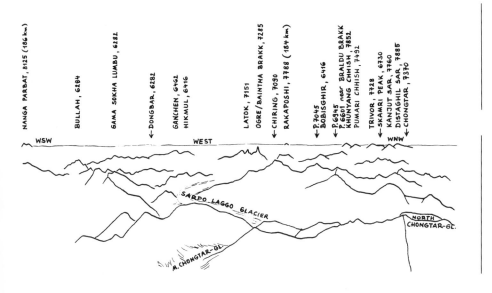

The view south from below the shoulder of K2, at 7,700 metres, towards Broad Peak and Chogolisa (see photo 9 between pages 120 and 121).

Panorama from the top of K2 to WSW, West and WNW, towards Nanga Parbat and the seven-thousanders of the Hispar Mustagh. (Drawing by Rudolf Jauk.)

BIBLIOGRAPHY

Abrego, Mari and Ariz, Gregorio: *En la cima, K2/Chogolisa*, Inlena S.A., Pamplona, 1987

Barry, John: *K2 – Savage Mountain, Savage Summer*, Oxford Illustrated Press, London, 1987

Berghold, Franz: *Bergmedizin heute*, Bruckmann, Munich, 1988

Berghold, Franz: *Sicheres Bergsteigen*, Bruckmann, Munich, 1988

Birtles, Geoff: *Alan Rouse – A Mountaineer's Life*, Unwin Hyman, London, 1987

Bonington, Chris: *Quest for Adventure*, Hodder & Stoughton, London, 1981, 1987

Buhl, Hermann: *Nanga Parbat Pilgrimage*, Hodder & Stoughton, London, 1956, 1981

Chamoux, Benoît: *Le vertige de l'infini*, Albin Michel, Paris, 1988

Curran, Jim: *K2, Triumph and Tragedy*, Hodder & Stoughton, London, 1987

De Filippi, Filippo: *Karakoram and Western Himalaya*, Constable, London, 1909

Desio, Ardito: *Ascent of K2, Second Highest Peak in the World*, Elek, London, 1955

Desio, Ardito: *Which is the highest mountain in the world?* (Report of Ev-K2-CNR-Expedition 1987: GPS – satellite measurement of K2 and Everest), Milan, 1988

Diemberger, Kurt: *Summits and Secrets*, Allen & Unwin, London, 1971; Hodder & Stoughton, London, 1983

Dyhrenfurth, G. O.: *To the Third Pole*, Werner Laurie, London, 1955

Dyhrenfurth, G. O.: *Der dritte Pol – die Achttausender und ihre Trabanten*, Nymphenburger Verlagshandlung, Munich, 1960

Fantin, Mario: *K2 – sogno vissuto*, Tamari, Bologna, 1958

Gillman, Peter: *In Balance*, Hodder & Stoughton, London, 1989

Houston, C. S. and Bates, R.: *K2, The Savage Mountain*, McGraw Hill, New York, 1954; Diadem, London, 1979

Kim, Byung-Joon: *Expedition Report K2 1986* (in Korean), Seoul, 1987

Lechenperg, Harald: *Himmel, Hölle, Himalaya*, Copress Verlag, Munich, 1958

Mason, Kenneth: *Abode of Snow*, Rupert Hart-Davis, London, 1955; Diadem, London, 1987

Mellet, Bernard: *K2 – la victoire suspendue*, Aventures extraordinaires, Paris, 1979

Messner, Reinhold and Gogna, Alessandro: *K2 – Mountain of Mountains*, Kaye & Ward, London, 1981

Messner, Reinhold: *All Fourteen Eight-thousanders*, Crowood, Marlborough, 1988

Reinisch, Gertrude and Bauer, Willi: *Licht und Schatten am K2*, Pinguin, Innsbruck, 1988

Santon, Francesco and Da Polenza, Agostino: *K2 – lo spigolo Nord*, Cooperativa editoriale l'Altra Riva, 1983

Santon, Francesco and Desio, Ardito: *Verso il cielo – K2. Appuntamento dal versante Cinese*, Cooperativa editoriale l'Altra Riva, 1983

Shipton, Eric: *Blank on the Map*, Hodder & Stoughton, London, 1938 and in the collection: *Eric Shipton, The Six Mountain Travel Books*, Diadem Books, London, 1985

Tullis, Julie: *Clouds from Both Sides*, Grafton Books, London, 1986; new edition 1987, with chapter on the K2 tragedy by Peter Gillman

Wiessner, Fritz: *K2 – Tragödien und Sieg am zweithöchsten Berg der Erde*

Wiget, Urs: *K2 1984*, Report of expedition doctor (duplicated manuscript – in German)

Wiget, Urs: *How to prepare for a trekking tour*, Congress of Int. Society of Mountain Medicine, Davos, 1988

PERIODICALS

Alpenverein Yearbooks 'Berg 85',
  'Berg 86' and 'Berg 88'
The Alpine Journal, 1987, vol. 92
The Alpine Journal, 1988–9, vol. 93
*Alpinismo, annuario del Club Alpino
  Accademico Italiano*, 1987, see:
  Tullio Vidoni, 'K2 – estate 1986';
  Roberto Osio, 'Mountain
  Wilderness'
The American Alpine Journal, 1987,
  vol. 29, contributions by Adams
  Carter, Charles S. Houston, Janusz
  Majer, Jerzy Kukuczka
The American Alpine Journal, 1988,
  vol. 30
Der Bergländer, Sektion Bergland
  DAV, July 88
Der Bergsteiger, 3/84, 4/84, 5/84:
  Franz Berghold: 'Höhenkrankheit
  I-III'
Climber, December 1986, Dennis
  Kemp/Kurt Diemberger, 'K2 – The
  Facts' (chronological account of
  tragedy)
Desnivel No. 39, 1988, D. Rodriguez,
  'Conversation with Kurt
  Diemberger'

High No. 47, 1986, November 1987
  and December 1987
Montagnes Magazine No. 97, 1987:
  article by J. M. Asselin
Mountain No. 106/1985 and Nos
  111, 112, 113/1986
Österreichische Alpenzeitung
  March/June 1961, 'Die
  Panoramen vom Broad Peak,
  8047m' by Eduard Sternbach
Österreichische Alpenzeitung
  March/April 1988,
  K. Diemberger's reply to Robert
  Renzler's analysis of the 1986 K2
  events, 'Versuch einer
  Analyse-Unglückssommer 86 am
  K2' (ÖAV-Mitteilungen 4/87)
Outside, March 1987, Greg Child and
  John Krakauer
Pyrenaica No. 144, 1986: article by
  Mari Abrego
Rivista della Montagna, April 1987,
  'On Renato Casarotto'; No. 96,
  April 1988; Roberto Mantovani,
  Conversation with Kurt
  Diemberger
Salzburger Nachrichten, 22–28 October
  1987, Günther Schneider on Kurt
  Diemberger

Sonntags-Blick, 16, 23 and 30
  September 1984, 'Der Berg blieb
  Sieger' by Stefan Wörner
Vertical No. 8, October/December
  1986, article by Michel Parmentier
Wisch No. 24–86/–6–, Adams Carter
  on the American attempt on north
  spur of K2

FURTHER SOURCE MATERIAL

Clemens Sievert: K2 interview tapes
  recorded in the Universitätsklinik,
  Innsbruck, August 1986
K2-Expedition, eye-witness account
  for the Austrian Embassy in
  Islamabad, 18 August 1986
Aufzeichnungen Film log 'Highest
  Filmteam', K. Diemberger/J.
  Tullis, Film commentaries and
  sound recordings
Information and contributions from
  Quota 8,000, particularly Agostino
  Da Polenza, Gianni Calcagno and
  Tullio Vidoni

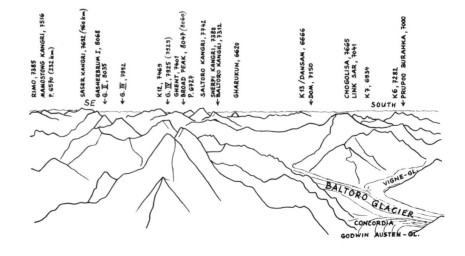

Panorama from the
top of K2 to SE and
South, from the
Gasherbrums to
Chogolisa and
Concordia. (Drawing
by Rudolf Jauk.)

PHOTO AND ILLUSTRATION CREDITS

If not specially mentioned, the photos in this book were taken by the author or come from his archives or the common 'Highest Film Team' archive of Kurt Diemberger and Julie Tullis (we photographed with Leicaflex R3 and R4, and at the highest altitudes we used various pocket cameras).

The author wants to thank the following photographers and artists for further illustrations:

Black and white photos:

Section II, number 2 (Karakoram mountains: Polish Kunyang Kish Expedition 1971, Bogdan Jankowski (Arch. Diemberger).

Section III, number 6 (Julie and Kurt with award): Terry Tullis.

Section IV, number 7 (on top of K2): Soro Dorotei.

Section IV, number 8 (the Bottleneck): Joska Rakoncaj.

Section V, number 2 (squashed teapot): picture from the documentary 'K2 – Traum und Schicksal', filmed by Kurt Diemberger and Julie Tullis and produced by BIBO-TV, Bad Homburg.

Section VI, number 5 (Kurt in hospital): Bryn Colton Assignments.

Colour photos:

Section III, number 9 (camp at 7,700 metres): Martino Moretti.

Section III, number 15 (Kurt and Julie with Renato Casarotto): Mari Abrego.

Section IV, number 4 (traverse below the ice balcony): Tullio Vidoni.

Section V, numbers 2 and 3 (meteorological pictures): Matevj Lenarcic.

Other illustrations:

Two watercolours (pages 211 and 234): Prof. Herbert Finster.

Three sketches of K2 (pages 39, 90, 286): Karen Diemberger (after designs by Dee Molenaar).

Sketch map of the Himalayan, Karakoram and Hindu Kush mountains (page 8): Karen Diemberger (after a design by G. Paton).

Sketch map of the main Karakoram ranges (page 15): Baron Eduard von Sternbach (after a map by Marcel Kurz).

Four designs of panoramic views from K2 (pages 111, 299 and 302): Rudolf Jauk.

INDEX